Effective Communication in the Travel Industry

Effective Communication in the Travel Industry

Robert T. Reilly, APR
Professor Emeritus
University of Nebraska/Omaha

DELMAR PUBLISHERS INC.
MERTON HOUSE TRAVEL AND TOURISM PUBLISHERS

NOTICE TO THE READER

Publisher does not warrant or guarantee any of the products described herein or perform any independent analysis in connection with any of the product information contained herein. Publisher does not assume, and expressly disclaims, any obligation to obtain and include information other than that provided to it by the manufacturer.

The reader is expressly warned to consider and adopt all safety precautions that might be indicated by the activities described herein and to avoid all potential hazards. By following the instructions contained herein, the reader willingly assumes all risks in connection with such instructions.

The publisher makes no representations or warranties of any kind, including but not limited to, the warranties of fitness for particular purpose or merchantability, nor are any such representations implied with respect to the material set forth herein, and the publisher takes no responsibility with respect to such material. The publisher shall not be liable for any special, consequential or exemplary damages resulting, in whole or in part, from the readers' use of, or reliance upon, this material.

Delmar Staff
Associate Editor: Cindy Haller
Senior Project Editor: Barbara A. Christie
Production Coordinator: Sandy Woods

COPYRIGHT © 1990
BY DELMAR PUBLISHERS INC.

10 9 8 7 6 5 4 3 2 1

Printed in the United States of America
Published simultaneously in Canada
by Nelson Canada
A Division of The Thomson Corporation

Library of Congress Cataloging in Publication Data

Reilly, Robert T.
    Effective communication in the travel industry / Robert T. Reilly.
        p.   cm. -- (The Travel management library)
    ISBN 0-8273-3125-8
    1. Travel agents. 2. Business communication.   I. Title.
    II. Series.
    G154.R45 1990
    338.4'791'0014--dc20
                                                            90-33109
                                                                CIP

OTHER BOOKS IN THE TRAVEL MANAGEMENT LIBRARY SERIES

GUIDE TO STARTING AND OPERATING A SUCCESSFUL TRAVEL AGENCY, THIRD EDITION

GROUP TRAVEL OPERATIONS MANUAL

HANDBOOK OF PROFESSIONAL TOUR MANAGEMENT

FOREIGN INDEPENDENT TOURS: PLANNING, PRICING, AND PROCESSING

EFFECTIVE COMMUNICATIONS IN THE TRAVEL INDUSTRY

THE DICTIONARY OF HOSPITALITY, TRAVEL & TOURISM

YOUR CAREER IN TRAVEL, TOURISM, AND HOSPITALITY, SECOND EDITION

TRAVEL AND TOURISM MARKETING TECHNIQUES, SECOND EDITION

COMPLETE GUIDE TO TRAVEL AGENCY AUTOMATION, SECOND EDITION

FINANCIAL MANAGEMENT FOR TRAVEL AGENCIES

TRAVEL AGENCY POLICIES AND PROCEDURES MANUAL

LEGAL ASPECTS OF TRAVEL AGENCY OPERATION, SECOND EDITION

TRAVEL AGENCY GUIDE TO BUSINESS TRAVEL

LEGAL FORMS FOR TRAVEL AGENTS

BUDGETING FOR PROFIT AND MANAGING BY GOALS

GUIDE TO TRAVEL AGENCY SECURITY

CONTENTS

PREFACE

In any field, communication is vital, but in the travel industry, it assumes a most significant role. Since travel is a service, the difference between success and failure often revolves around the ability to communicate on every level from management and sales to advertising and customer relations.

Because of this principle, this book was written — to attempt to provide an overview of the communication challenges within the industry. Both theory and practice are explored here, and both the written and spoken word are included. Even the power of body language is touched upon.

The author is grateful to Laurence Stevens who first suggested the idea, to those within the industry who supplied photos and illustrations, and to the quartet of anonymous readers whose helpful suggestions were, for the most part, incorporated into the final draft of this book.

ABOUT THE AUTHOR

This is the third book Bob Reilly has written for Delmar, joining *Travel and Tourism Marketing Techniques* (now in a second edition) and *Handbook of Professional Tour Management* (with a second edition due out soon).

Reilly's other ten books, fiction and nonfiction, cover a wide range of topics, from the Indian wars to a textbook in public relations. Many of his works have Irish themes, including *Come Along to Ireland,* which combines a tour through Ireland with glimpses of the country's history and culture, *Irish Saints,* and *Red Hugh, Prince of Donegal,* which was made into a Walt Disney film in 1966. Reilly's books have been translated into seven foreign languages. He has also published over 700 articles in a variety of national magazines, writes poetry, scripts films and TV shows, and has produced material for Fred Waring, Mike Douglas, Capitol Records, and others.

A native of Lowell, Massachusetts, the author now lives in Omaha, Nebraska, where, until 1987, he taught courses at the University of Nebraska, Omaha, in writing, advertising, public relations, and Irish literature.

Prior to his fifteen years of university teaching, Reilly spent over thirty years in the advertising/public relations fields, working on travel accounts in Boston and Omaha, serving as public relations director for Creighton University, and holding a partnership in a major advertising/public relations firm.

Bob and his wife, Jean, who retired in 1988 as a national sales executive with Travel & Transport, one of the nation's largest independent travel agencies, have led numerous tours, with Ireland and the British Isles ranking as their favorite territories. Reilly has also traveled widely in Europe, the South Pacific, and the United States — first as an infantryman in World War II, and later on film, tour management, and speaking assignments.

Reilly, who holds degrees in English from Suffolk University and Boston University, is also professionally accredited in public relations. He's been a consultant to the Ford Foundation and once lost a close race for Congress.

His honors include a number of foundation and research grants, plus: the Fonda-McGuire Best Actor Award from the Omaha Play-house, Hall of Fame Award from the American College Public Rela-tions Association, Professional of the Year Award from the Nebraska Chapter of the Public Relations Society of America, Midlands Jour-nalist of the Year, Boss of the Year, the Jameson Hibernian Award, the Henderson Medal, and the Kayser Chair at the University of Nebraska at Omaha.

Reilly, now a professor emeritus from UNO, is listed in: *Who's Who in Advertising; Who's Who in Public Relations; Who's Who in the Midwest; Contemporary Authors; The Dictionary of British and American Writers; Dictionary of International Biography; The Inter-national Writers and Authors Who's Who,* and *Writers and Photogra-phers Guide.*

THE NATURE OF COMMUNICATION

DEFINITION OF COMMUNICATION

Defining communication simply as "the transmitting of ideas and information" obscures the complicated nature of this act. To communicate effectively is very difficult, especially when the audience is diverse and distant. Even one-on-one relationships are marred by faulty communication, a complaint cited by employees, friends, even spouses. When the numbers involved in the communication expand, so do the challenges.

The first level of understanding in any area is diagnosis, so those in the travel industry must try to grasp the principles of good communication as well as the roadblocks which interfere with messages. A tour manager may have to discipline a tour member—the language used to do this must be carefully chosen. Commercial salespeople wrestle with the right words for a travel proposal. An inexperienced client may require additional repetition of details. Journalistic skills on the part of a newsletter editor enhance readership. Addressing a local Rotary Club on the European travel scene calls for specialized communication skills. There are hundreds of examples within the industry, from the drafting of a memo to the scripting of a slide show, but all start with one basic formula.

The formula involves a sender, a message, a means of communication, and a receiver. The sender, with a concept to transmit, chooses a channel to convey the appropriate language. The sender hopes that the receiver will interpret this language as the sender intends.

Let's assume, for example, that a travel agency manager wants to secure employee approval for a new group health plan. The manager—the sender, in this case—must decide what is to be said and how. Does the insurance company jargon have to be tailored for the agency audience? What questions might employees have?

Should a meeting be called, perhaps with the insurance representative on hand, or should the subject be covered in a long memorandum? Are visuals needed, especially if the presentation is done orally? The object is to inform, perhaps persuade the employees— the receivers. If the audience has been intelligently assessed, the material properly organized and conceived, and the presentation appropriately made, the receivers should understand what the sender intended. The ability of the employees to ask questions (more easily done in the live scenario) further enhances understanding.

COMMUNICATION MODELS

There are numerous communication *models*, diagrams that show how information is transmitted. Figure 1–1 shows two variations of communication models. Figure 1–1(a) shows two-way communication and Figure 1–1(b) demonstrates why rumors travel faster than the official line (there are fewer clearances). Another model might show the communication loop, where the sender transmits, the receiver receives, and then the receiver provides questions or feedback to the sender. Communication, in this instance, is continuous.

The sender is a vital part of the process. This individual must

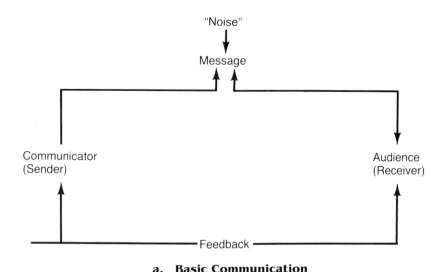

a. Basic Communication

Figure 1–1.   (a) Basic communication chart; (b) reactive communication chart

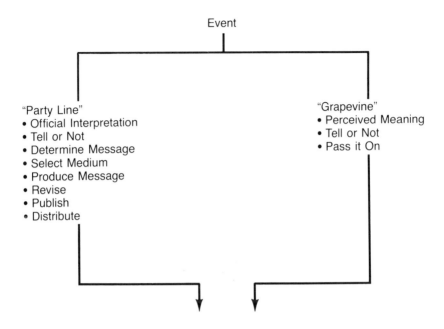

Event

"Party Line"
• Official Interpretation
• Tell or Not
• Determine Message
• Select Medium
• Produce Message
• Revise
• Publish
• Distribute

"Grapevine"
• Perceived Meaning
• Tell or Not
• Pass it On

b.   Reactive Communication

Figure 1–1.   Continued.

know what he/she wants to say and must be able to either put an effective message together or hire someone to accomplish this. The sender must also be committed to the communication method. This person must believe others have a right to know and must be able to bring topics to their attention in a complete and convincing way. Behaving in a secretive, authoritarian, or indifferent manner does not show commitment to communication. Poor communicators may be shy, overbearing, insensitive, suspicious, or inept.

The relationship between sender and receiver is also important. If there is a relationship characterized by trust and confidence, even by warmth and respect, the message is more likely to be accepted. A passenger who has had several bad experiences with a certain airline's tardy arrivals will not be a good receiver for a message about the same airline's on-time scheduling. A hotel porter who dislikes the assistant manager will not be receptive to suggestions about a change in the job routine.

The receiver has to be able to comprehend the message, to receive it relatively free of distractions, to find both the message and sender credible, to perceive some benefit in complying, and to act upon it.

Communication theory gets far more technical, but even these basics show that when merely two people are involved, the situation becomes complicated. To further confuse things, there are external factors that can affect the process. These are often called *communication roadblocks.*

COMMUNICATION ROADBLOCKS

Sometimes all of the factors that can interfere with communication are lumped under the heading of "noise." The causes are many and varied, and could include something as physical as noise, if it tended to obliterate a message. Many roadblocks, however, are more subtle.

Clutter

With all the advances in communication comes an accompanying congestion. Hundreds of messages are beamed at us daily; we can comprehend only a small portion of them. Letters, billboards, memos, telephone calls, computer printouts, bulletin boards, conversations, advertising—all of these compete for our attention. Consider the variety of conflicting data in one travel area alone—fares to foreign destinations. Prices, exceptions, schedules, brochures, posters, sales representatives, print and electronic ads, correspondence. The human mind can't absorb all of these details; only the computer makes retention possible. The more opportunities we have for securing information, the more difficult it is to sort out the individual message.

Lack of a Perceived Benefit

With this abundance of available information, we screen out messages based on their potential for benefiting us. That's exactly how we deal with fourth class mail or the Sunday newspaper inserts. That's why we spend more time reading some correspondence than others. There must be something in it for us, or we will merely scan the copy or tune out the oratory. If you're contemplating a cruise, you read all pertinent materials, but you ignore travel information on train excursions through Scotland. Good advertising copywriters realize they must speak in terms of the audience, not the manufacturer or supplier. The receiver asks: "What does this do for me?" If a communicator always keeps in mind the need to offer readers/listeners some reward for their effort, the communication will be far more successful. If you ask an employee to assume additional responsibilities, you must balance this request with more money, more vacation time, a promotion, or some other consideration. If a tour price is higher than the competition, it must include some feature that promises to make it worth the difference—like a higher grade of hotel. Without some obvious reason for accepting the communication, the receiver will ignore it.

Lack of Clarity

While there may be a lot of romance in the language of travel, there must be a corresponding accuracy and clarity. Not every writer or speaker is gifted creatively but, with practice, everyone should be able to convey a thought lucidly. If a traveler wants to know if a certain ferry runs on Sunday, that information should be clearly available. This is no time for fuzzy commentary about the sightseeing opportunities during the ferry crossing. Give the person the facts. Lots of messages are clouded, from memoranda and phone calls to very expensive campaigns. The sender must know what should be said, must anticipate questions or possible confusion, and must state things succinctly and precisely. Without such concern for the reader/listener, the message will fail.

Poor Definition of the Audience

Even the veteran public speaker sometimes prepares the wrong speech for the wrong audience. Celebrants at a collegiate pep rally, for example, would not appreciate a long intellectual discussion of educational theory by the president. A gathering of senior citizens is not the most appropriate place to pitch the joys of Club Med. If you have misjudged your audience, the communication will be inefficient, at best. The sender may assume an educational level beyond that of the actual audience or may presume an interest or knowledge that doesn't exist. The message should be tailored to the receivers. Know who they are and address their interests.

Confusion of Purpose

Every message should have a purpose. If the goal of an advertising campaign is to convince a certain public to switch airlines for a specific destination, then the sender must understand this aim and prepare the messages to accomplish it. If the scheduling of an open house for a new travel agency is directed at affluent singles, then the subsequent appeals should correspond to that end. Too many newsletters are issued simply because the firm has always done so. Too many letters and brochures are generic. If you don't really know why you are doing something, how can you possibly measure its ultimate success? This obviously dictates thoughtful planning for each communication.

Censorship

There are many kinds of censorship beyond the governmental control of news media. A chief executive may decide that the company publication will simply ignore some issue of interest to employees. An editor may eliminate a specific paragraph. There is even unavoidable censorship which comes about through lack of knowledge. If a travel consultant, for example, is unfamiliar with a tourist area being discussed and fails to mention some important details to the client—simply because the consultant is unaware of them—this is akin to censorship in terms of the availability of the data. Any elimination of information, whether natural or unnatural, is a kind of censorship. Therefore, if the required information is not given, the receiver cannot fully understand the message.

Improper Method of Communication

Instead of writing a letter to a person who complained about a rental car lease, the sender might have been more effective with a phone call. Advertising an expensive tour package on the radio might have been an error; some carefully chosen magazines and brochures might have worked better. Part of the secret of communication is to reward the expectations of an audience. They look in certain places to find certain information. You must know those favored media. In a small travel agency it would normally be wiser to communicate important material at a meeting of employees rather than trusting it to a note on the bulletin board. A letter mailed to an employee's home, so the spouse might share in it, could work more effectively than an announcement over the firm's public address system. Besides the contents of the message then, the sender must also give thought to the manner in which it is to be transmitted.

Lack of Skill

If the dancers are without talent, the audience will get a distorted view of ballet—or of soccer, if the athletes are stumbling amateurs. In the wrong hands, messages can also be failures. Everyone has been bored by long, rambling sermons, or confused by poorly written copy. The writer and the speaker must choose appropriate language, know what terms work, be able to arrange these thoughts in a logical and compelling fashion, and be able to present the data in an interesting, persuasive way. It's pretty difficult to obscure the fact that a firm's income fell 25 percent last year, but some communicators are so awkward and inexperienced they may manage to garble even this information. You must know the meaning of words, the differences in impact between words that mean almost the same thing, even the possibilities inherent in the choice of certain terms to conjure up related images. You must also know how to build a message, systematically, from an attractive opening to a compelling close.

Lack of Credibility

This roadblock may be the result of some shortcomings of the sender, based on a number of the flaws discussed previously, such as lack of skill or confusion of purpose. It could also relate to the past experiences of the receiver who doubts the reliability of the message. It might come about because there is a conflict between what is said and what is observed. A restaurant advertising fast service is contradicted by a crowded lobby; a hotel boasting of a friendly staff can be compromised by an irritable desk clerk. So the message must not only be interpreted, it must also be believed.

Adverse Timing

Many messages reach people when they are unable or unwilling to comply with them. An individual worrying about taxes due the IRS will not be overly attentive to an appeal for an expensive vacation. A sales call to a home during mealtime or while occupants are viewing a football game may be given a rude response. Timing also comes into play in terms of too many messages. Some institutions send out so many mailings, the recipients simply ignore them, failing to even open the envelope. Unfortunately, it is nearly impossible to predict the perfect time and the perfect number of repetitions for a mass audience, but research, testing, and common sense help avoid timing errors.

There are other roadblocks as well, Figure 1–2. A sender can be guilty of false assumptions about an audience or individual. Natural causes, like inclement weather or a strike, may interfere. Environmental circumstances like civil unrest in a proposed tour area, may intervene. Dozens of similar factors can influence the effectiveness of the communication. While the sender can't anticipate all of them, he or she should eliminate as many as possible in advance.

Figure 1–2.   While language remains a major roadblock to communication, curiosity impels all people to make an attempt to understand.

EFFECTS OF COMMUNICATION

As we'll see in the chapter on advertising, communication can have a variety of purposes. It can simply provide information, but it can also seek to persuade, to modify attitudes, to alter opinions, to reinforce beliefs, to move the receiver to action. Communication can serve to focus attention in a particular area or to broaden the perspective of the audience. It can be part of a larger whole, achieving results through variety and repetition. Communication can even have a "sleeper" effect, producing no immediately discernible results but creating a climate for later action. Readers may spend years looking at advertising for cruises before circumstances converge to cause them to sign up for such a voyage. It may also take a long time to convince readers and viewers about the advantages of using a travel agent or about the safety of air travel. Communication does work. Numerous tests check effectiveness and demonstrate that intelligently constructed messages do produce desired results. Even casual observation attests to this.

RATIONAL VERSUS EMOTIONAL APPEALS

Both rational and emotional appeals work in communication. In promoting its services to travel agents, for example, a tour company is likely to rely on rational appeals, citing commissions and repeat business. In its approach to potential travelers, the same tour company will concentrate more on an emotional appeal, although there could be a blend with rational arguments.

Looked at broadly, travel and its attendant services are sold more through emotional presentation. Cruises are depicted as romantic, relaxing, and accompanied by exotic shore excursions. Hotels promote their amenities, their comfort, their convenience. European destinations cite charm, history, cuisine, and cultural attractions. Restaurants may emphasize decor and atmosphere along with their menus. Some resorts project a sensual image; others feature bright lights and activity; still others focus on surf and sports.

While all of these are emotional reasons for making a choice, things like cost, comparative benefits, and even tax advantages could be part of the pitch. A travel consultant advising a prospective client will certainly sell the appealing intangibles of a trip but will also mention things like bargain prices, the relative value of the dollar, the preferable time of year, and other more practical considerations.

If the emotional route is more prevalent in selling to consumers, the rational context is more common in relationships with travel agents, with purchasing agents, and with corporate and governmental clientele. Proposals to handle commercial travel, or government travel are likely to focus on volume discounts or rebates and on guarantees of service. The business traveler, viewed corporately, will be interested in the best available fares, convenient and comfortable accommodations, easily accessible rental cars, and other practical items. However, emotional factors also come into play, even subconsciously.

The communicator weighs each situation and each audience and decides how much reason and how much emotion should go into each message. This is tricky, because the receiver doesn't always provide reliable cues on how much of each element should be in the blend. All of us, for example, like to pretend that our decisions are based far more on rational evidence than on sentiment. The wise sender keeps both sides of human nature in mind.

MOTIVATION, PERCEPTION, LEARNING, PERSUASION, AND PUBLIC OPINION

Motivation

Each person acts from a different set of motives. These are the causes of our actions and, sometimes, of our beliefs. The more a communicator knows about the motivation inherent in an audience or an individual, the more ably this sender will deliver a message. Tuning in on what makes people behave as they do is a key to communication.

Social scientists divide motives into *primary* and *secondary*, with the latter being "learned" motives and the former those that are essential to one's well-being or very existence. Hunger, thirst, and the avoidance of pain fall into the category of primary motives and do not figure greatly into communication about travel, except, for example, when some particular destination is viewed as dangerous. Secondary motives are more commonly part of travel messages. In fact, most of the regularly cited "learned" motives are sometimes subjects of such communications.

The desire for knowledge and understanding is a motivation for travel. So are the pursuits of health, pleasure, material comforts, and physical challenge. The existence of peer pressure creates travel opportunities and the climb toward success also sparks this interest. The secondary motive of security, on the other hand, may inhibit travel.

In his often-quoted book, *Motivation and Personality*, author Abraham Maslow compiled a hierarchy of values which determine behavior. These are based primarily on self-interest. A person will normally pursue a certain course of conduct when it seems comfortable and convenient to do so, and this same person will avoid behavior that may involve deprivation or pain. This isn't always the case. Some people do sacrifice themselves for what they perceive as a greater good. Even that, some would argue, is adhering to another set of values. A couple may delay a trip in order to care for an aging parent, or a supervisor may surrender a little authority and prestige in order to preserve office harmony. In most cases, however, self-interest dominates and successful messages assume this fact.

Perception

Perception refers to the way in which objective data is interpreted by individuals. A reduction in hotel rates may seem like a bargain to some observers while others may regard the move as an indication that the facility has somehow slipped, or was originally overpriced. Record attendance at a theme park may convince some individuals they must take in that attraction while others will be repelled by the thought of large crowds.

Most experts would agree that the major difficulties experienced in communication arise through faulty perceptions. For whatever reason, the receiver puts an erroneous—or an individual—interpretation on the message and may spread this opinion widely, causing numerous problems. As noted earlier, some misperceptions can be the result of communication roadblocks, but others stem from the background and attitudes of the receivers. They are conditioned in a certain way and make the message fit their experience.

One perception travel agents have dealt with for years is the public belief that there is always an add-on charge for their services. This misconception persists, regardless of experience and advertising. Mexico constantly fights the perception of their drinking water. Some travelers avoid Ireland because they think the periodic violence is characteristic of all thirty-two counties in that divided nation.

Not all perceptions are false, of course, and many accurate ones result in different actions simply because reponses are individualistic. The spirit of adventure lures one travel segment to an Amazon River voyage while another segment, attracted more by creature comforts, thinks only of the heat, insects, and other negatives of the cruise. The communicator, then, must speak to the right audience and must use the right language.

Learning

Our ability to derive guidelines from our experience is called *learning*, a condition of somewhat permanent behavioral change. We shun certain restaurants after a couple of negative encounters. We discover, through experience, that we prefer individual travel to organized tours. We take notice of the increasing number of women business travelers and modify accommodations to appeal to this audience. Communicators learn what approaches work and which do not, and they monitor these conclusions periodically to note subtle changes.

Learning separates us from lower forms of life. We can benefit from lessons of the past, repeating successes, averting failure. That's one argument for retaining good records and for employing experienced personnel.

Persuasion

Since salesmanship is a major factor in travel communication, the sender must be familiar with persuasive techniques. In some circles, persuasion is regarded as sinister and dishonest. Nonsense! We use persuasion all the time. After all, there are only three ways to get others to do what we would like. We either force them to do it, pay them to do it, or persuade them to do it. Obviously, in promoting travel, the latter course is the rule.

Two things are prominent in inhibiting persuasion. The first is making unsupported assumptions about those you seek to persuade. You want to be armed with as much research data as is available, including the comments of those experienced in this particular area. You want to determine motivations, consider perceptions, and design an appropriate message. Perceptions are vital clues in persuasion. You have to know how the target audience sees things before you can compose an effective appeal. While research is helpful here, it may not be perfect. In introducing its new Coke®, the Atlanta-based soft drink giant adequately tested taste preferences and learned that consumers preferred the new formula. What they failed to test, however, was the loyalty to the old favorite. Those contacted may have liked the new flavor, but this didn't say they were going to switch. Still, in most cases, a professional approach to fact finding will be beneficial.

In 1986, the perception among Americans was that travel to Europe was unsafe because of several instances of terrorism. These potential tourists stayed closer to home or made trips to other parts of the world. European countries spent a lot of effort and distributed millions of dollars worth of communication in order to bring people from the United States back to the Continent. Then they faced another perception — that the partial collapse of the dollar made many European nations incredibly expensive. This called for another set of messages, centered on value, pointing out bargains, offering myriad special events.

A second barrier to persuasion is the attempt to base communication on your own terms rather than those of the receiver. It's the self-interest argument again, the benefit syndrome. A client couldn't care less that you have added a second computerized reservation system. Only when you point out that this addition speeds up bookings and broadens offerings does this make sense to a consumer, who can then see in the equipment a personal benefit.

There are countless persuasive techniques that are applicable in selling clients, relating to suppliers, and dealing with employees. You try to find the right buttons to push. Most people react favorably to a bargain. Some are attracted by exclusivity. Employees may modify their behavior because of a perceived reward, a challenge, an appeal to their corporate loyalty, or even out of fear of dismissal. The deciding factor in a corporation's contract with a specific travel agency might be the speed and accuracy of monthly reports rather than a minor increase in the rebate formula.

Whatever works, works. In one-on-one sales situations, the travel consultant may have an opportunity to try a number of motivational techniques, while a mass-produced letter either tries to contain several different appeals or attempts to sort out the best prospects.

Public Opinion

In the mass media phase of communication, the sender wants to be aware of public opinion. Public opinion, of course, is made up of individual opinions which are brought to bear on any issue. Again, an action plus the perception of this action give us public opinion. When the terrorists bombed sites in Paris, London, and Athens, the American perception was that these cities couldn't contain the potential danger. So public opinion crystallized against travel. On the positive side, public opinion toward cruises has been enhanced by mass media presentations of the cruise as an exciting and romantic travel alternative.

Communication — persuasive communication — sets out to do one of three things in relation to public opinion:

❑ It seeks to alter, counteract, or neutralize unfavorable opinion.
❑ It seeks to convince uninformed or uncommitted opinion.
❑ It seeks to reinforce favorable opinion.

Some opinions are extremely difficult to change. If a hotel location is considered unsafe by business travelers, and if it is sited on the edge of a deteriorating neighborhood, it may be hard to turn this perception around. Perhaps the negative impact can be modified by testimonials of guests, by a reduction in room rates, by increased security, by expanded services. An irate passenger may not be completely assuaged by the offending airline but perhaps a presentation of facts may soften the complaint.

It's far easier to work with people whose minds are not made up. To them, the sender provides information and motivation to move them from relative ignorance to adequate knowledge, and from indifference to advocacy.

Finally, no group should be taken for granted. Aggressive travel agencies keep regular clientele informed and happy. These people are on a list for mailings, are invited to special events, and receive periodic phone calls. Professionals will explain that it's more cost-effective to convince the already committed to travel than it is to cultivate entirely new prospects.

While communication is important in shaping public opinion, significant events are even more critical. Airline disasters have more impact on the public than cleverly worded advertising campaigns for air travel, and news items about political unrest negate lovely brochures.

Public opinion is normally reactive, responding to events or communications rather than forming before such things happen. It usually takes a crisis to mobilize people to demand change, rather than having them anticipate problems and head them off.

As indicated earlier, public opinion, like individual attitudes, is primarily a product of self-interest. It's easier to organize opposition to a property tax increase in a neighborhood than it is to solicit support for decorating houses at Christmas. Once self-interest is involved, change in public opinion is more difficult. Self-interest may be sacrificed, however, in times of crisis or, at least among the educated, when a compelling argument can be made for altering this opinion. Peer pressure also plays a role in opinion change and so does the attitude toward the person or persons proposing change.

These and other clues to behavior are handy tools for the travel communicator who must, of course, seek to work within the dictates of public opinion whenever possible and, when public opinion runs against the sender's desires, to subtly instigate some change in opinion.

One final consideration. Every communicator finds it more efficient to deal with group leaders whenever feasible. You don't try to reach every employee in a corporation when pitching business travel; you work with executives, purchasing agents, and travel coordinators. Group travel appeals are made to organization officers. Even promotions for independent travel may be aimed at opinion leaders. If you can succeed at the top, you have a better chance to reach those below.

THE SOCIAL CLIMATE AFFECTS COMMUNICATION

In addition to understanding yourself and understanding others, you as a communicator must be cognizant of all the surrounding aspects of life that alter the message. We've already mentioned one of these — the combination of busy schedules and the abundance of communications. Only a fool would assume that today's citizen is committed to reading long pages of print. Instead, the conventional wisdom advocates shorter messages, more visuals, plus early and frequent references to benefits.

Other Trends Also Affect Travel

Industry Trends.   Some trends are within the industry itself: the popularity of certain resort areas, or the increase in cruise bookings; the effects of deregulation of the airlines; the shift to greater emphasis on business travel; even a minor trend like the growth of all-suite hotels, or hotels catering exclusively to businesswomen. Outside the industry, trends that embrace other aspects of our culture may spill over into travel.

Entitlement.   Once vacations were looked upon as bonuses, as luxuries. Today, they are generally considered a right. We work hard and we've earned this chance to relax. This concept affects the willingness to spend rather than save and also the scheduling of more than one vacation a year. This notion of grabbing all the gusto while you can may enable agents to "sell up" clients to a more attractive tour package.

Two-income Families.   When you combine the idea of entitlement with the relative affluence of a double income, this makes travel more affordable and more likely, especially for younger married people or those sharing expenses. Some trips that were once beyond the reach of couples may now be possibilities.

Delayed Families.   Married couples (and marriage, incidentally, is now back "in") may opt to postpone having children for a number of years, making them more mobile and with money for other things — like travel.

The Single Life-Style.   There are over sixty million single adults in this country and this group is the target of all sorts of special messages, from convenience food pitches to resort and cruise appeals. This trend obviously influences hotel accommodations, ship cabin size, tour development, and advertising.

An Aging America.   Some eleven percent of Americans are over sixty-five and the number is growing. We are also learning that this population segment is relatively well-off and has time to travel. Consequently, special attention is being paid to travel geared to this age bracket.

Youth Groups.   Travel during one's college years is growing as a practice and there are some shifts to small hotels and bed-and-breakfast stops instead of youth hostels. Trips to Europe are widely regarded as part of one's education.

Ethnic Sensitivity.   This trend manifests itself in a number of ways, chiefly in the segmentation of advertising to reach certain ethnic groups and also in the emphasis on the search for roots and return to one's origins.

Health Consciousness.   With the trend toward diet and exercise, many travel options feature a range of menu choices and outdoor activities. Walking tours of various countries have become popular. Health spas combine vacations with a return to a more robust constitution.

Higher Educational Levels.   The character of tours, the inclusion of certain tour features, even the copy in advertising is influenced by the fact that today's Americans are better educated than ever. The desire to travel is also enhanced by education and, indirectly, more education typically leads to higher salaries and this leads to more travel opportunities.

Feminism.   Communication about travel is colored by a consciousness regarding the role of women in today's society. This may eliminate some sexism in advertising, may convince hotels to provide a more secure environment for businesswomen, and may alter the kinds of appeals made to this market segment.

Terrorism.   We've seen the effects of terrorism on travel in recent years. This trend will continue to influence travel plans to certain tourism areas. Who would have imagined that political unrest would disrupt visits to idyllic Fiji in 1987?

Softening of Attitudes Toward Communism.   A change in our official stance toward countries like Russia and China, and their satellites, has opened the way toward travel to many of these nations. Similarly, tourists from those countries are also coming here in larger numbers.

Primacy of Independence.   The move toward independence in many arenas, from business to politics, also creates the need for more individualized travel and for relief from the image of crowded tourist scenes.

Communication Advances. Dozens of improvements and innovations in the way we communicate find their way into the travel industry. Television brings the world closer and whets the appetite for travel. Computers make the mechanical aspects of booking simpler. Automation creates problems internally and with clients. Adverse news spreads more quickly and widely. Marketing has become more scientific.

These are only a few of the trends affecting travel. Others may want to point to changing employee attitudes about salary and scheduling, or the practice of large agencies swallowing up smaller ones, or the opening up of governmental travel, or the impact of the declining dollar, or any number of other modifications. Not only must the able communicator consider extant trends when writing or speaking, but this sender should also try to anticipate future changes.

INTERPERSONAL, SMALL GROUP, AND MASS-AUDIENCE COMMUNICATION

Although this text concentrates more heavily on mass communication, one should remember that one-on-one dialogue and exchanges with a limited number of individuals are also characteristic of the travel business. A majority of sales are made to individuals, couples, or small groups. Agencies themselves are likely to be small businesses with a limited cadre of employees. Even the larger entities, like carriers, hotel chains, and tourism bureaus, are broken into smaller units, each with its own communication challenges.

Interpersonal Communication

Interpersonal communication relies on some generally accepted codes, like learning how to listen as well as speak, giving the other person equal time, sharing a bit of yourself in order to provoke a similar response, looking for common ground on controversial topics, and interacting without irritating. Various factors, such as the relationship between the individuals, influence the situation. If a client is suspicious of a travel consultant and wary of being talked into something, the situation is different from one in which the client is openly seeking information. Dialogue between a boss and an employee, or any individuals of differing status, is affected by

Figure 1–3. Even in one-on-one encounters, the communication can be complicated.

the roles each plays. There are also differences in the nature of the discussions. Some are persuasive, some defensive, some merely conversational. Even though only two people are involved, the exchange can be quite complicated, Figure 1–3. Whole college courses are built around the proper techniques of relating to others.

Small Group Communication

Small groups may exchange information, solve problems, or provide support, Figure 1–4. A hotel chain might include property managers in a round-table discussion of the following year's advertising campaign. A corporate sales executive could gather a firm's key personnel for a dialogue about potential travel services. There is a social benefit to group discussions, along with the production of more ideas and more solutions. These meetings may also be time-consuming and can be a source of conflict for some members. There are reluctant participants who say little, eager ones who talk too much, sensitive ones who react to criticism of their suggestions, and conformists who contribute little but agreement. A skilled chairperson manages these disparate personalities.

Figure 1–4. Most classrooms are examples of small group communication. Some teaching styles are basic, some reactive.

Mass-Audience Communication

In attempting to reach large, generally anonymous, audiences, communicators employ mass-media means, ranging from direct mail to electronic advertising. A travel agency newsletter fits this category, as does an airline schedule, a cruise brochure, an ad for a resort, or a statewide tourism campaign. While the message is personalized as much as possible, the aim is to reach a sizable number of potential consumers as efficiently as possible, Figure 1–5.

Each type of audience involves a different methodology, but each also shares some of the principles of good communication, from the concern for self-interest to the ability with language. Just as size must be factored into communication, so must the nature of the audience and the method chosen to reach these individuals. The succeeding chapters explore some of these options.

RESEARCH AND PLANNING

Research and planning should precede any communication. Factors like time and budget, along with the scope and importance of the

THE EXCITING FOREIGN DESTINATION WITHOUT THE EXCITING FOREIGN PROBLEMS.

Exotic, old world charm can really make an incentive trip or meeting. But it can also make it a headache. Fortunately, there's Holland, the thoroughly European country where Americans feel at home.

The scenery is ancient and the facilities are state of the art. From Amsterdam to Maastricht, our hospitality professionals know how to serve business with the combination of friendliness, efficiency and creativity that is uniquely Dutch.

So give your group the foreign experience of their dreams. And spare yourself the nightmares. And the best way to fly there is by KLM Royal Dutch Airlines.

Holland 🌷🌷
AN AMERICAN'S DREAM OF EUROPE

Netherlands Board of Tourism
355 Lexington Avenue
New York, NY 10017

Please send me more information about using Holland for my:
_____ Meetings _____ Incentive Trips

Name _____ Title _____

Company _____

Address _____ State/Zip _____

Telephone _____

BTN-4

The Reliable Airline **KLM**
Royal Dutch Airlines

Figure 1–5. American tourist concerns about traveling in foreign countries are countered in this print ad. (Courtesy of the Netherlands Board of Tourism)

message, will control the nature and extent of the research. You can't spend hours and money on a survey to determine if you should advertise in a local high school play program, but you would want to commit some resources to gathering data for a multimillion dollar government travel contract.

Research may be *formal* or *informal.* Formal research involves the use of a survey and generally calls for the employment of professional help. Informal research includes all other methods of collecting data, from use of the library to personal or focus group interviews.

Surveys can be extremely technical — and expensive. The goals must be clear; the questions carefully constructed to get honest answers, without misleading or promoting bias. The survey sample must be sufficiently large to guarantee reliability and probability, or sufficiently representative if a quota sample is chosen or a specific audience measured. The poll takers should be trained, and the responses should be professionally analyzed. There are lots of intermediate steps and intermediate concerns, all of which could affect the validity of the results. Done properly, this is the most thorough method of extracting information, but it is not necessary for every communication decision.

Sometimes all you need to do is look up information or statistics already available in published reports, directories, or books. Or you may talk with those who have relevant experience, or with your own salespeople. You frequently find help in the travel trade press, and even the general media may be useful, especially in areas like the sensing of national trends. Travel executives might sit down with a group of clients and solicit their opinions and suggestions. Correspondence could be thoughtfully analyzed.

However you accomplish the task, you should avail yourself, in advance, of any materials that will enhance the effectiveness of the communication. This data includes an intelligent profile of the intended audience, an awareness of trends, a familiarity with past or similar current campaigns, a knowledge of the competition, some grasp of timing, and conclusions about the motivational approach that will work best.

Cervantes' Don Quixote advised his companion to "think before thou speakest," a good recommendation in any age to any communicator. Research supports such thinking, or planning. Once the information is extant, the sender should formulate strategy to accomplish the mission. What is to be communicated, in what manner, and through what means? The speaker uses a text or an outline; the writer also devises some sort of blueprint and may organize several drafts. A plan, making use of all the considerations in this chapter, should be in place before the speaker rises or the fingers touch the keyboard.

CHAPTER HIGHLIGHTS

❏ Good communication is difficult. It involves a sender, receiver, message, and channel of communication. Securing feedback enhances the process.

❏ The sender must be skilled, open, and trustworthy, while the receiver should be able to comprehend and decipher the message, free of distractions, must perceive some personal benefit in it, and must be able to comply.

❏ Roadblocks to communication include clutter, lack of a perceived benefit, lack of clarity, poor audience definition, confusion of purpose, censorship, wrong choice of channel, lack of communication skill, lack of credibility, poor timing.

❏ Communication may be based on reason or emotion, may seek to inform or persuade, and is cognizant of behavioral factors — like motivation, perception, and learning — which influence it.

❏ Persuasion, which should be couched in terms appealing to the receiver, tries to win over, change, or reinforce different forms of public opinion.

❏ Current trends have their own impact on communication, and so does the size and character of the audience, which can range from a single contact to a group of thousands, even millions.

❏ Research and planning precede communication. Research may be formal, involving surveys, or informal, including all other means of gathering data. Using this research, the communicator organizes the material before producing and distributing a final draft.

■   ■   ■

❏ EXERCISES

1. There are many changes taking place today — cultural, political, and economic. List three trends not mentioned in this text that you think may have an impact on the travel industry.

2. Some print ads appeal to the reader's rational side — ads for investments, perhaps — while others are more emotionally oriented — offering fun, power, romance, and other benefits.

Bring to class two print ads you feel are based on rational appeals and two you feel are based on emotional appeals.

3. From your own experience, cite an example of a "roadblock" to communication, some instance where good communication was weakened or stopped by some communication flaw.

❏ CASE PROBLEMS

1. The travel agency you work for is considering arranging several special tour packages to the 1992 Winter Olympics in the Albertville, France area. Your boss asks you, one of the firm's senior employees, to check out the feasibility of these trips in terms of generating revenue. What sort of information would you like to have? Where do you think you might find these details? Be as specific as you can.

2. Every product, every service, every travel destination has its own selling points. The copywriter tries to discover features that are appealing, accurate, and, if possible, unique. Select a specific tourist spot in the United States — preferably one with which you are personally familiar — and list eight points you would make in persuading a prospective traveler to consider that destination.

Words Have Meaning

Mechanics have their tools. So do architects, artists, engineers, and plumbers. Those in the travel industry also share certain instruments, like specially tailored computer software, various printed guides, maps, and tour brochures, Figure 2–1.

All of these occupations employ another tool—language.

As communicators, we work with words, so it's necessary to know as much about these "tools" as we do about the more mechanical travel adjuncts. It's not enough to understand what words mean; we have to control them, to make them accomplish what we want accomplished. We can make them dance, sing, cry, persuade, convince, or amuse.

Most people don't feel this mastery. In fact, they balk at writing or speaking because they are unsure of their skills and afraid of making a mistake. Part of this fear stems from conditioning. Our parents and teachers corrected our grammar. Our term papers were returned with red marks all over them. Our first appearance before an audience was sheer terror.

Some people never get over these traumas. Others learn from mistakes, practice, read, and improve. The best way to deal with any fear is to confront it, understand it. Once you feel more comfortable with language, you'll be a far better communicator. Without this familiarity, you'll continue to be apprehensive about every letter and every personal contact.

WORDS HAVE HISTORY

Like individuals, words have a genealogy. Their ancestors contribute to their current meaning and effect and give them the little nuances a sharp communicator recognizes. The word *hotel*, for example, comes from the same root as *hospital* and both terms refer back to the Knights Hospitalers of the Middle Ages, monks who took care of pilgrims on their route to the Holy Land. The currently controver-

Figure 2–1. In the days when few people were literate, inns and other establishments used pictures to convey their names and, sometimes, their product lines.

sial word, *rebate,* comes from the Latin and Old French word meaning "to batter or beat down" and, by extension, to reduce. Since the first water craft were hollow logs, the Greek word for *hollow* finally becomes *ship.*

   This may be interesting, even diverting, but the reader might wonder why this is pertinent. Isn't it more the province of the English major and the scholar? Well, don't forget that part of conquering fear is understanding the enemy. In addition, when we choose one word over another, simply because it sounds better, the reason often has to do with the ancestry of that word.

   Grief is a stronger word than *sadness,* partly through length, partly through usage, but also because *grief* comes from *gravis* (heavy), the same root that produces *grave,* while *sadness* comes from the same line as *satisfy,* deteriorating into *sating,* or really overdoing it.

In describing restaurant fare, *tasty* is better than *palatable,* and *roomy* works better than *commodious* in describing a ship's cabin. The former terms are from Middle English and the latter from Latin.

Our English language is a mixture of other tongues—Indo-Germanic (thunder), Anglo-Saxon (reek), French (banquet), Latin (cook), Greek (democracy), American Indian (hominy), Spanish (ranch), plus terms borrowed from Gaelic, Russian, Japanese, and other languages. No wonder it's so tough to get a handle on what we write and say.

To further complicate things, we are inconsistent in pronouncing words we borrow. *Champlain* pretty much resembles the original French pronunciation, but *Detroit* does not. *Madrid* is accented on the first and last syllable in different locales. Beatrice Foods, which began in BeATrice, Nebraska, finally had to change its pronunciation to BEatrice in order to match the overwhelming number of speech errors.

We also play around with words, cutting some short, like *props* for *properties,* or lengthening them, creating *tourist* from *tour.* After we fashion *hamburger,* we design *cheeseburger,* and *motorcade* follows *cavalcade.* We make nouns like *eye* and *stomach* into verbs and verbs like *shave* and *hit* into nouns.

While our grammatical rules are fairly simple, our rules for pronunciation are all over the lot. Imagine you are a foreign student learning the English language and faced with the "ou" sound. It is pronounced as in m*ou*se, or w*ou*ld, or r*ou*gh, or furl*ou*gh, or c*ou*gh, or thr*ou*gh?

Perhaps this makes us a bit more tolerant of those travel agents or anchorpersons who stumble over foreign locales.

DENOTATION AND CONNOTATION

Denotation refers to a dictionary definition of a world. Even these may vary from author to author, but try to provide a scientific description based on current usage. *Travel,* for example, is defined as moving from one place to another or to participate in a commercial journey. *Connotation* refers to what a word implies, its overtones and suggestions. In this context, *travel* takes on a lot of meanings, conjuring up the ideas of pleasure, adventure, excitement.

Skillful speakers and writers are able to use language that creates such images, and travel writers are expected to be very good in this department. They try to put you on the scene by describing a beach so that you can feel the hot sand between your toes or by describing an exotic meal so that you virtually salivate.

IMPROVING YOUR VOCABULARY

Knowing a lot of words doesn't necessarily make you an effective writer. Some of the dullest writers may have the largest vocabularies. The trick is in making imaginative use of what you have.

Still, expanding your vocabulary does give you more options. You could do this by reading a few pages of a dictionary every day, or by faithfully doing crossword puzles. The problem with these techniques is that they are boring, sterile, and provide you with a lot of waste language. The best regimen is to read. Widely. Even in the realm of travel there are dozens of magazines and special newspaper sections which provide exemplars, and there are travel books written by masters of style like Hemingway, Steinbeck, Agee, and dozens of others. A few hours with them on a regular basis will help immensely, especially if you look up unfamiliar terms and if you analyze the success of certain words and phrases. Take a look at the matchless descriptions of the Southwest in Willa Cather's *Death Comes for the Archbishop* or the more contemporary landscape of Wyoming in Gretel Ehrlich's *The Solace of Open Spaces*. In the latter volume, when you see a flock of migrating geese "in great Vs as if that one letter were defecting from the alphabet," you wonder why no one thought to capture this in quite the same words before.

Reading can be informative, but it can also be inspirational. You can't steal from other authors, but you can pluck courage and ideas from them.

THE SPECIAL LANGUAGE OF TRAVEL

In some ways, travel writers have an easy task. The public is interested in what they have to say. It's not like trying to explain tax laws or a decline in the underground water table. People attend travel lectures, watch travel programs on television, read articles on travel. They want to share these experiences vicariously.

There are really two travel languages. The first is directed at potential consumers and combines the poetic and practical. Descriptive ability is paramount, but readers and listeners also want to

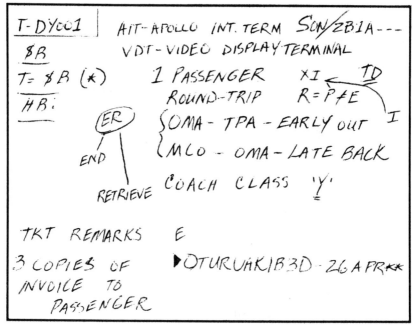

Figure 2–2.   The travel business uses its own form of shorthand.

know how much things cost and how long it takes to get there and what they should wear. The other travel language is internal, the jargon of the professionals working among themselves, Figure 2–2. There are acronymns for many items, like FIT for *Foreign Independent Tour* and GIT for *Group Inclusive Tour*. Agents and trade journals talks about *fam trips* to characterize familiarization tours and may borrow a foreign phrase, like the French *force majeure,* to connote an Act of God in a brochure's responsibility clause. Some terms are understandable to both audiences, like ETA (Estimated Time of Arrival), RT (Round Trip), and MAP (Modified American Plan).

Within the industry, the key considerations are accuracy and clarity of language. Externally, these two qualities are augmented by creativity and persuasiveness.

HEY, I HAVEN'T STUDIED GRAMMAR SINCE HIGH SCHOOL!

Most adults admit their grasp of grammar is shaky. That's understandable. Even those who use the language properly can't usually explain the rules that govern their speaking or writing. Besides, to a degree, grammar is in flux. Rules change because of usage, so everyone requires some help or updating.

Communicators used to say they relied on bright secretaries. Many still do. And now there are computer programs to check grammatical and spelling lapses. There are also numerous books that will refresh your memory. Everyone's favorite seems to be the classic *The Elements of Style,* a Macmillan paperback by Strunk & White. The tiny volume doesn't spend a lot of time on the more obscure rules but concentrates instead on the common mistakes in communication. Every major textbook publisher has a book on grammar (or style or rhetoric) and there are plasticized cards that capsulize the basics for the busy writer. Everyone should have at least one handbook on grammar as part of a personal library.

Usage

The most important factor in changes in grammar, spelling, pronunciation, and punctuation is the way those who speak and write the language use it in everyday parlance. Even though the initial alteration may be considered corrupt, continued usage breaks down the objections. Teachers used to warn students that "ain't ain't in the dictionary." Today it is. The rules for the use of *shall* and *will* and *should* and *would* have collapsed due to usage. Once the rule was that you asked a question in the same form you expected the answer. So, the grammatically correct query to a client would be, "Should you like an aisle seat?" because the response would be, "I should." But people don't speak that way anymore. So the agent asks, "Would you like an aisle seat?" The use of the verb *can* to express ability and the verb *may* to connote permission are also headed this way, but not without a struggle. "May I have one of these brochures?" is starting to sound too formal, even though correct.

Admittedly, we may often speak more colloquially and write more formally. Part of the reason for this is that writing seems more permanent, more subject to criticism. Another reason is that, in conversation, we may wish to sound more friendly, less austere or intellectual.

Communicators shouldn't take the fluidity of language or the pragmatic attitude toward style ("If it works, use it") as a license to do whatever seems right. If you say "Give it to him and I" just because you hear others make that mistake, you'll still be branded as inept by many who hear you. If you write "The Hungarian dancers was some of the best I've seen," your stock with the reader will decline. Unfortunately, perhaps, a communicator's intelligence is

judged by the written and spoken word. A perfectly logical suggestion sent by memo to a hostile receiver may be picked apart for
misspellings, even though the message deserves attention. You can't
allow these errors to interfere with the communication process.

To provide a comprehensive view of grammar would require the
remainder of this text. The best solution is to get your own book on
the subject. However, here are a few brief reminders:

Sentence.   Even though the sentence is the basic unit in most
languages, it's tough to define. Some refer to it as the expression of
one complete thought, while others categorize it as a group of words
containing a subject and predicate, and still others see it as a combination of two things we know that result in a new experience. All of
these fail to some degree. Isn't "Out!" a complete sentence, and "Up"
if you're heading for an elevator? "Great!" may suffice, depending on
the circumstances and "Be on time!" could assume the subject being
a group of normally tardy tour members.

The notion of combining two knowns to form a fresh idea can be
seen in sentences like "The hotel is booked" or "The ship has sailed."
We put the noun and verb together and create a new reality.

Sentences can be long or short, simple or compound (containing
additional clauses). Good journalistic style favors short sentences,
but varies them to retain interest.

Subject.   We usually think of the subject of a sentence as the
instigator of the action, although that's not always true. Subjects
may be nouns ("flight attendants"), noun clauses ("frantic flight
attendants"), a pronoun ("they"), a gerund ("Having lifted off . . ."),
or an infinitive ("To be airborne . . .").

Verb.   This usually, but not always, follows the noun and agrees
with it—meaning that if the subject is singular, so is the verb. A
predicate is a verb plus whatever else is related to it. Thus you have:
"He flies." "He flies erratically." "He flies as if he had taken only a
single lesson."

Object.   A *direct object* answers the question "what" or "whom."
"He boarded the *train*." An indirect object answers the question "to
whom or what" or "for whom or what," making it the receiver of an
action. "He gave *Frank* the tickets."

Word Order.   Normally you might have the subject first, then the
verb, and then the object. "Bill took a cruise." But this gets pretty
boring, so you reverse order sometimes to maintain interest.

Adjectives and Adverbs.   *Adjectives* modify nouns and usually
(but not always) come before them. "It was an active resort," or "The
youthful guests made the resort active."

Adverbs modify a verb, adverb, or adjective. "He *desperately*
wanted to take that trip." "He wanted to take the trip *most desperately.*"

Nouns may also modify another noun. Like "ski trip" or "love boat" or "travel agent." And prepositional and verb phrases can also modify.

Clauses.   A *main clause* normally contains a subject and predicate and is the heart of a sentence, while a *subordinate clause,* also with a subject and predicate, is merely a part of the sentence. "He missed his plane because he couldn't find his passport." The main clause is "He missed his plane," while the remainder of the sentence, after the "because" connector, is the subordinate clause.

When there is only the main clause, that's a *simple* sentence. The addition of a subordinate clause makes it a *complex* sentence. And when you have two or more subordinate clauses, it becomes a *compound-complex* sentence.

Enough grammatical *déjà vu!* We could talk about irregular verbs and verb tense and pronoun case, but it's probably more profitable to look at some of the common errors. These are generally flaws of the writer rather than the speaker, but could affect both.

Sentence Fragments.   In public speaking, this is no problem, and even in writing, we are coming to accept sentence fragments when they make sense. If you read a sentence that said, "Apparently without paying the bill," you'd realize this sentence just sits there and makes no sense as is. On the other hand, you'd accept a sentence fragment tied to a previous sentence, like: "The SST is comfortable. And fast." Doing a careful job of editing will save you from making this error, when it is an error.

Dangling Modifiers.   These clauses often begin with a gerund and don't really modify the subject that follows. "Having lived abroad for three years, Oakland seemed dull." Who lived abroad? Not Oakland! Read the sentence aloud and you won't make this mistake.

Wrong Connective.   When this happens, the communicator has just fallen asleep. You meant to say one thing and you said another. "She qualified for a fam trip, but she decided to travel."

Mixed Construction.   If the culprit would only read the sentence, the confusion would be avoided. Consider this: "I always wanted to visit Bermuda and when I did, a real pleasure."

Failure to Follow Parallel Structure.   This occurs when you assemble a list or draw a comparison and one of the items doesn't fit stylistically. "He went to Fiji to surf, scuba dive, enjoy the native food, and sometimes copra harvesting is done for visitors."

Split Infinitives.   This used to be a terrible sin, but we are more lenient today. Telling a hostess you want "to really compliment her on the dinner" may be less awkward than another arrangement. Usually, however, the split infinitive is more awkward. "We tried to gradually dock the ship."

Agreement of Subject and Verb.   If the subject is singular, the verb should be singular; if the subject is plural, the verb should be plural. Seems simple enough, but it gets complicated in some sentences. "Bill, Frank, and Ed *jog* every morning on shipboard," but "Either Bill, Frank, or Ed *jogs* every morning on shipboard." When you have a combined singular and plural subject, the verb usually agrees with the closest one. "Neither the crew members nor the captain was to blame." (If you get into a clumsy situation like that, it's better to rewrite the sentence.) When you have *collective nouns* in a sentence, it depends on whether the group is referred to as a whole or whether the individual members are meant. "The crew *has* held *its* first meeting of the cruise," but, "The crew *have* taken *their* tetanus shots."

Combined Subjects and Objects.   This is a common mistake, especially in speaking. The simplest way to avoid the error is to focus on one of the pronouns, then see how the sentence reads. "He and I relinquished our coach seats." You wouldn't say, "Him relinquished . . ." or "Me relinquished . . ."

Use of Vague Pronouns.   Just because you know what you mean doesn't guarantee the audience can follow. "The rainy weather made things unpleasant, but we went on with it." With what?

Stay in the Same Tense.   Writers sometimes forget where they are and they move from the present to the past like time travelers. If you say, "I boarded the bus in Baltimore" (past tense), don't say, "I get off in Cleveland" (present tense). Stick with the same tense unless there is some obvious shift in the situation.

All Those Little Flaws.   There are dozens of other common errors. *Good* and *bad* are adjectives, while *well* and *badly* are adverbs, so if you *feel badly,* there is something wrong with your sense of touch. *Lie* means to recline and takes no object, whereas *lay* means to place and may take an object. When used as relative pronouns, *who* refers to persons, *which* to things, and *that* to either persons or things. And there ain't hardly nobody who don't know about double negatives.

Although it's important to recognize your own shortcomings, it's equally important to realize that many others share these fears. Get yourself a good book on the subject and consult it when in doubt, but don't let concern cramp your style.

Punctuation

Consistency in punctuation is a virtue. Books and guides help here and enable you to stay up with changes—like less frequent use of hyphens and commas. Style, including punctuation, may also be governed to some degree by style books issued by wire services, publications, and companies.

The rules are numerous—over two dozen major rules each for the use of the comma and hyphen, for example. The student should review these in detail. Here, all space allows is a concentration on the principal errors.

It's or Its?   Remember that old rule that you use the apostrophe to indicate the omission of letters in a contraction? So, when "it is" becomes "it's" use the apostrophe—but not for the possessive. "Travel had lost *its* charm for Ralph."

But Don't You Use an Apostrophe in Possessives?   Sure, to change a noun to a possessive. Write "the agent's tickets" when you mean one person, and "the agents' tickets" when there are two or more agents involved.

What About the Comma?   This is a bit tricky. You use the comma in a variety of ways, primarily to set off words or phrases. "Captain Philbin, who is the commander of this vessel, studied in Vienna" or "First, we must pay attention to the stewardess" or "To make sure you get aboard the flight, plan to be at the airport an hour before departure." Subordinate clauses are set off this way, and so are coordinating conjunctions. When you list a series of things, you use the comma. "The menu featured rice, chicken, and fish." The comma is also used in setting apart a quotation, in dividing two identical words to prevent confusion, in names and titles, and in a dozen other ways.

And the Dash?   Modern writing may overuse this punctuation mark, but it's handy in separating thoughts or emphasizing related elements or in indicating missing letters. Script writers and speakers use it to denote pauses and the dash is a common way to separate dates, like 1989–1990.

Put It in Quotes.   You use quotation marks around direct quotes, like bits of dialogue, around names and titles, around a word you are "defining," or around a word you're emphasizing. Normally, punctuation marks go inside the final quotation marks, except for the colon and semicolon or when the question mark or exclamation point refer to an entire sentence and not just the quoted part. When you use a quote within a quote, use a single quotation mark, thus: "Then," recalled Larry, "he said, 'This plane is always late' and walked away."

The whole purpose of punctuation is to make things easier on the reader or the audience, or to give the prose some additional emphasis or character. These are hundreds of choices to be made each time you write, so a handy reference is essential. You may want to know, for example, when you use parentheses and when you use brackets. Or when the colon or semicolon is appropriate.

As mentioned earlier, the hyphen is a special problem. The rules tell us that we place the hyphen between compound verbs and compound adjectives, for example, "freeze-dry" and "double-breasted," but usage is diminishing the number of these. Compound numbers, titles, prefixes accompanying words that start with capital letters ("mid-America"), and many other combinations are aided by hyphens. When in doubt, check the dictionary.

Other Considerations

Besides the very few rules of grammar and punctuation we've merely glanced at, there are also questions about how you form plurals (not a very tidy exercise in English), and how and when you use Capital Letters, and how you write numbers.

The reference book should seem essential by now.

SPELLING

Even the best spellers stumble over certain words. "Practitioner" sounds like it should have two *c*'s in it. And why do you always look up "unnecessary"? Poor spelling reduces the communicator in the esteem of the receiver. When in doubt, look it up. Or check with someone. Or buy a computer program.

There are spelling rules, of course, like the manner in which you double a final consonant, and there are also those who insist that a strong preparation in Latin will save you. Both of these tips might help, but the quickest way to learn the correct spelling of words is by familiarity with them. You gain this through reading and through practice. Some systems suggest learning a new word every day by discovering it, defining it, using it in a sentence, and then practicing it on friends.

The more you know about language, the better able you are to sound out or work out correct spellings. But this method isn't foolproof. There are always exceptions. So—read more, challenge yourself, work at it.

PRONUNCIATION

Those who work in travel are a little like announcers for classical music stations; they are expected to pronounce difficult words properly. This means, in the case of the travel person, a knowledge of geography and a grasp of the way foreign destinations are pronounced. Good dictionaries include a Gazetteer as part of the index

Figure 2–3. Besides learning how to pronounce the names of foreign cities, it's sometimes good to also know how to pronounce the name in the native language.

and in this Gazetteer you'll find the phonetic pronunciation of hundreds of locales. When you come across a word in your work and you wonder about the pronunciation, look it up. If it isn't included in your dictionary, consult a more comprehensive one at the library. A basic familiarity with a few foreign languages doesn't hurt either, Figure 2–3. Even those pocket-sized paperbacks for travelers give you hints to pronunciation and you can check with more world-wise colleagues who have visited these spots.

Even asking natives isn't always satisfactory. Once I was heading for a week in Ireland's County Tipperary in a village called Puckane (also spelled *Puckaun*) and asked a stranger for directions to "Puck-AWN." This Irishman replied, "You mean 'Puck-ANN'."

Down the road I used that pronunciation for further assistance. This man said, "It's 'Puck-AIN'." Arriving in the village, I switched to the most recent version, only to be told it was "Puck-AWN" after all, just as it should have been.

When counselling an American traveler, you'd still say *PAR-ISS* and not *PAR-EE*, and *ROME* rather than *ROMA*, but *Cuernavaca* doesn't allow you any such latitude. It's KWER-NEH-VAHK-EH. If you mispronounce the names of foreign destinations, not every traveler will catch you—but those that do will lose faith in your advice.

Don't be intimidated, but read, listen—and practice.

CHAPTER HIGHLIGHTS

❏ Words are the tools of communicators and must be mastered. They have a history, affecting both denotation and connotation.

❏ Reading and analyzing what is read are the best ways to improve vocabulary. This is especially true of travel literature, since the vocabulary is singular.

❏ A desk copy of a book on grammar is a must for writers and so is a periodic review of the basics, keeping in mind that usage alters some older rules.

❏ Among the common grammatical errors are sentence fragments, dangling modifiers, wrong modifiers, mixed construction, faulty parallel structures, split infinitives, subject/verb agreement, vague pronouns, wrong tense, and others.

❏ Punctuation also changes, but many rules remain standard and should be reviewed.

❏ Mistakes in spelling or pronunciation detract from good communication and can be avoided by effort and practice. The correct information is usually available to prevent such errors.

■   ■   ■

❏ *EXERCISES*

1. To test yourself, write on a sheet of paper the words in this list that you believe are misspelled:

    separate   Chieftan   embarass
    occured   weird   recommend

irrelevant	benefited	sheriff
canceled	judgment	liason
inoculation	questionaire	feasible
credibility	allusion	accompaniment
override	prorate	conciurge

CHECK YOUR LIST AGAINST A DICTIONARY.

2. Punctuate this paragraph:
Mr Harold L Tyson corporate sales manager of Travel tours Inc wants to confirm the appointment for Tuesday March 1 the day you requested in your recent letter. Mr Tyson who remembers you from your days together with air india said I havent seen charlie in fourteen years not since he said see you in the states and took off for new york

3. Look up the proper pronunciation of these locales and bring your findings to class:

Oughterard, Ireland	Popo Agie River, Wyoming
Nadi, Fiji	Limoges, France
Worcester, England	Bologna, Italy
Seychelles	Oberammergau, Germany
Djibouti	Ciudad Real, Spain

BRING IN TWO ADDITIONAL NAMES YOU FIND DIFFI-CULT.

❑ CASE PROBLEMS

1. What courses in a typical liberal arts curriculum do you think would be valuable to a person entering the travel industry? Obviously, in such a broad field, all knowledge would have some benefit, but pick five courses you think would be especially helpful and list your reason(s) for each choice.

2. The manager of your travel agency is a fine salesperson and strong in financial areas. However, he has difficulty spelling and has large gaps in his use of grammar. His secretary, who is also unsure of grammatical usage, is afraid to change his work. The boss does have an ego, and a temper, and you recognize this as a delicate matter. However, you also realize that his correspondence reflects adversely on the agency and you want to change things. How might you proceed?

3

THE WRITTEN WORD

Writing for the travel industry takes a variety of forms. Some of this writing is purely functional, requiring accuracy and speed more than creativity—like the compiling of passenger lists or the writing of tickets. Computers accomplish many of these tasks once the individual has provided the basic data. Other writing assignments demand more skill. Letters, brochures, proposals, reports, advertising, itineraries, speeches, and other forms of written communication take talent and practice. No amount of training or experience will make a writer out of a person who has no aptitude for the task, but a person with minimum skills may become more proficient through education and practice.

That's the rationale for texts and courses on writing.

THE NATURE OF WRITING

Someone once said that writing is "telling tales to strangers." Keeping that in mind helps considerably. It frees the writer from assumptions, clarifies the relationship, emphasizes the need for careful and complete exposition. It also suggests that the written word must be interesting and must somehow benefit the reader. A person buying a house may carefully read a dull contract, but, except in these extreme cases, individuals will not wade through monotonous prose. Obviously, travel brochures that attempt to sell trips have to possess strong appeals, but the same is true of any correspondence that seeks to have impact.

One of the best single guides to writing effectively is to picture the reader engaged in reading. Too many writers produce messages for themselves rather than considering the audience. Envisioning the recipient reminds the writer that someone has to find the communication attractive, interesting, credible, convincing, and beneficial.

Figure 3—1. Even the simplest printing press revolutionized communication.

The writer shouldn't assume the reader knows too much about the subject. Don't write down to the reader, but don't leave out vital information. Better to include too much than not enough.

Another aid is curiosity, plus an instinct for the potential curiosity of others. A person who accepts his or her surroundings without any inquisitiveness will never be able to fathom the interests of others. Good sales writing, for example, anticipates the questions and concerns of the reader, either responding to them in advance or providing sources of answers.

Writing is thinking, planning, and execution. It requires a certain amount of inspiration, but even more dedication. The test of success is always the reaction of the intended audience.

In a moment, some tips for strengthening the written word, but, first, some of the common flaws that detract from effectiveness. Errors in grammar and punctuation hurt, and so do misspelled words, but those were covered in a previous chapter. It's possible to be correct and still fail to properly communicate.

Some Writing Lapses

Message Is Not Clear.   Communication can be garbled by many of the following errors. The way to avoid lack of clarity is to read the written material carefully and with the eye of the intended audience. If anything interferes with the reader's understanding, it should be explained, corrected, or deleted. This rule applies to short memos as well as to feature articles in the travel section of the newspaper. Regardless of how clever or humorous the writer's style may be, it fails if the content makes no sense.

Writing Is Pompous and Highbrow.   Some writers must declare in print how intelligent they are. They talk down to the reader, use words like "viaggiatory" to describe someone who travels frequently. Given the competition for attention, readers will quickly shun prose that keeps sending them to the dictionary. Readers also resent being told things they already know, like the fact that Paris is the capital of France. No one likes to be lectured, so the approach should imitate conversation, even if the written word is more formal and controlled.

Copy Is Dull.   Colorless prose is a tough flaw to correct. Many writers fail to realize they're dull. Some of them are simply unable to generate any sparks with their writing, while others have a deeper problem—they "think dull." Perhaps their experience is limited, or their vision narrow, but they just don't see things that others perceive. Some tourists could be caught up in the turmoil of a foreign coup and, when asked about it, all they can say is, "It was pretty scary." You need only watch television interviews a couple of times to appreciate how flat are the communication efforts of most people. And these are selected—and edited—interviews! Listeners tune out a dull speech and they skip through a dull letter, ad, article, or proposal.

Writer Uses Lots of Unnecessary Words.   Some people have a hard time getting started, an equally difficult time constructing a simple sentence, and an even tougher time stopping. You've read those memos that state:

> Realizing that this is a busy time of year for you and not wanting to create any extra burden on top of what you already have, I hesitate to approach you about this matter which has been on my mind for a considerable length of time. I'm talking, of course, about the proposed meeting of corporate sales staff members which will be held next Tuesday noon — a time which may not be convenient for you but which was decided upon last year and so it can't be changed. It would be good if you could fit this important meeting, which will be held at the Hotel Royal, into your already crowded schedule, and you know that I and the other company executives would deeply appreciate it.

All you really need to ask is:

> Can you make a noon meeting at the Hotel Royal next Tuesday?

The first example may appear exaggerated, but look through your own office files, if you work in an office, and you'll easily find similar ramblings.

Why use such expressions as "needless to say" or "defies description"? If a thing is "needless to say," why bother with it? And if something defies description, it should be allowed to sit peacefully until someone comes along who can handle it. Good writers always read over their copy to see what they can eliminate, even if the initial version isn't all that bad.

> "With skipping steps I walked along the shore" could easily read, "I skipped along the shore."

In this context, consider the word *that*. At least half the time it can be eliminated.

> "He told me that the airline tickets would be delivered Monday" is more concise if written "He told me the airline tickets would be delivered Monday." And it makes the same sense.

Some Sentences Are Disorganized.   Inept writers may bury the key thought in the middle of a long sentence, obscuring its meaning and importance. The main thought normally comes at the end of a sentence, sometimes at the beginning, almost never in the middle.

> And best of all, you'll enjoy the hotel's sauna, after a long day of sightseeing and shopping and making new friends in this interesting country.

The "sauna" is the key idea here and that phrase should conclude the sentence.

> And best of all, after a long day of sightseeing and shopping (and making new friends in this interesting country), you'll enjoy the hotel's sauna.

There are worse examples. Sentences may end up with so many dependent clauses and so much punctuation, you can't sort them out. Scholarly work often suffers from this malady.

You'll find advertising copywriters mentioning a "frozen supply of meatballs" when they mean a "supply of frozen meatballs."

"I may eat alone tonight" has even more impact when it reads: "Tonight I may eat alone."

"Deep sea fishing still excites me ten years later" would be far better if reversed, thus: "Ten years later, deep sea fishing still excites me."

Well, you get the idea.

Paragraphs Are Too Long.   We're lazy readers today. Even the sight of a paragraph that runs a full page turns us off. We're used to journalistic style. Short sentences, short paragraphs. You don't want the writing to be too curt, like Dick and Jane primers, but you take it easy on the reader. Like sentences, paragraphs should focus on one central idea or topic, and when the emphasis shifts, you should consider going to a new paragraph.

This helps both clarity and eyeballs.

Overwriting Makes Us Wince.   Well, perhaps everyone doesn't wince. Some readers claim to find beauty in otherwise purple prose. They enjoy exaggerated imagery and sentimentality. Most readers find such writing cloying and annoying.

> The deep azure blue of the Mediterranean caught my eyes with its majestic sweep of tranquil waters caught up in the panorama of history and the magic of a Hellenic world now, alas, absent from our view.

A bit much, the sensitive reader protests. This sin is compounded when the topic is too mundane to merit any grand adjectives.

A traveler who boasts about his completion of the Royal Mile in Edinburgh with the same pride normally reserved for conquerers of Everest is also overdoing it. And menu writers for some restaurants that aspire to greatness occasionally forget that their long-winded praise of an entree doesn't really disguise the fact that we are eating roast beef.

Writers should be sensitive and sensible, and must learn that understatement is often the more powerful tool.

Author Intrusion Detracts From Writing.   This is not always true. Some travel articles are written in the first person, but, even then, the author must refrain from giving his or her view on events, preferring an approach that allows the reader to experience things rather than be told what the writer believes. Clever little parenthetical interruptions also get boring after a bit. The writer should maintain a distance from the prose, allowing it to speak for itself.

It May Not Be As Funny As You Think.   Humor is difficult to write and even some excellent craftspeople have trouble with the comic muse. What seems laughable to you at some giddy moment may lose all of its flavor when locked into print. If the writer can handle humor, and if humor is appropriate and in good taste, then it may be effective. Unless it meets these standards, the writer should stifle the urge to elicit a few chuckles.

Qualifying Words Often Weaken the Sentence.   Describing a tourist attraction as "impressive" is stronger than calling it "pretty impressive" and a hotel that is considered "quite expensive" is less definitive than one that is simply "expensive."

Foreign Terms and Phrases Should Be Limited.   Writers should keep in mind that few Americans are conversant in foreign languages. They will be put off by sentences or paragraphs in another tongue. A word or two in an unfamiliar language, however, might be both educational and appealing, especially if the meaning is evident or is subtly explained.

Cliches, Jargon, and Euphemisms Impede Concentration.
Cliches were once acceptable but have been worn into sterility by overuse. Most cliches are a combination of noun and adjective which has lost its impact. Don't refer to a senior citizen as "eighty years young," don't make the Alps "snow-capped," and refrain from calling experienced travelers "seasoned veterans." Sometimes you'll read an article calling attention to cliches by asking, "How was it laden?" Answer: "Heavily." "And what sort of beach is it?" Answer: "Sun-drenched." It takes a little thought to recognize these and a little rewriting to eliminate them.

Jargon is also unconscious at times. Writers get so used to their own cant, they forget it has little meaning for the uninitiated. Rattling on about tariffs may be okay within the travel industry, but, to an outsider, it doesn't connote a fare or rate but suggests some form of duty on imported goods. Check your writing to see you haven't lapsed into a sort of code.

Euphemisms are employed when the writer either seeks to soften some phrase, or attempts to be cute, or tries to avoid repeating a word too often. Euphemisms have a place, but should be used sparingly. A locale that is in the middle of a rebellion is not experiencing "unrest" and an employee who is chronically late is not "failing to meet the posted schedule of working hours." Some euphemisms are deliberate lies, as when a miniscule ship's cabin is described in a brochure as "intimate," and a substandard meal is call "quaint native fare."

There are other flaws, like cluttering up a letter or article with extraneous matter, like promising something in copy that is never delivered, and like using a word improperly because you don't really know what it means. We'll meet some of these indiscretions in a more positive form in the next section.

TIPS TO IMPROVE WRITING SKILLS
Overcoming Psychological Roadblocks

Some of the roadblocks to writing are psychological, and these affect both the novelist and the memo writer. Overcoming these precedes the elimination of other, more concrete, flaws.

You Must Write When You Don't Feel Like It.   No one really feels like writing, once the process is underway. Anticipation may be pleasant and completion can be a relief, but everything in between is work. That's why writers procrastinate, find other less painful chores to accomplish, invent excuses. They delay the procedure as long as possible.

Professionals realize you have to go ahead and produce, even though it's rarely enjoyable.

You Must Write When You're Not Doing Your Best.   Sometimes the words just flow — with a little help from the author. Every sentence satisfies. On other occasions, nothing looks right, and the writer concludes that the muse is not operative, so he or she puts away the project. You must work through that temptation and continue the writing. It may not be as bad as you surmise, and, even if it is, at least you've provided an outline and you've learned what *not* to do. The point is, you can't surrender every time you're unhappy with your efforts.

You Shouldn't Exaggerate the Task.   Travel administrators may have a sales letter to write, or an article to produce for the company newsletter, or brochure copy to create. They talk about it, complain about it, invent reasons why it's just too much to expect of them. In the meantime, the project grows cold and the deadline creeps nearer. Even though experience tells them they can complete the assignment in three or four hours, they treat it as a week's work and just don't know how they will get at it. The only solution is to *do* it. Set the time aside and make yourself finish the job.

You Won't Find a Perfect Environment.   Allied to the previous excuse is the belief that everything must be perfect. You contend you can't write this itinerary with the phones ringing and people walking around and the thermostat too high. Besides, this is an unfamiliar typewriter and the chair is uncomfortable and there are no windows in this office. While it may be true that a more congenial environment is required for poetry, perhaps even a travel article, anyone should be able to produce a news release or office memo under just about any circumstances. You can't keep longing for a lighthouse or a mountain cabin, telling yourself that if you could inhabit these locales you'd really shine. You find the best spot you can at the time and you courageously tackle the writing.

You Have to Conquer Writer's Block.   Writer's block is not something that affects only literary geniuses; it can cripple the advertising copywriter or the company editor. Writers have devised all sorts of tricks to break free of this frightening state. Some of the most effective are:

❏ Write something, anything, even if you have to copy paragraphs from a cookbook, or draft a letter to a family member. Get the juices flowing.

❏ Read something, preferably something in the same field as your assignment. Perhaps this will stimulate you, or make you feel creatively competitive.

❏ Reintroduce yourself to the product or service or project. Take a fresh look at it. If you can use the service or visit the environment, that's even better. What you need is a new look at an old idea.

❏ Other writers recommend things like getting completely away from the project (if you have that luxury); cleaning up your work environment, just so you'll feel some sense of accomplishment; buying yourself something you need for your writing, but felt you couldn't afford; talking over the problem with another writer.

Every writer devises some technique to restart the engine. Whatever works, works.

Improving Style and Readability

Besides these broad and interior aspects of writing success, there are many concrete tips that improve style and readability. These include:

Show, Don't Tell.   This is especially true in feature writing, but has meaning for all forms of writing. It's the difference between allowing the reader to experience something and telling the reader about it. Instead of repeating in a brochure how much fun this cruise is going to be, it's far more effective to detail the events that will make it fun. Instead of launching a general complaint about sloppy work habits, it would be advantageous to cite the areas needing reform and let the reader draw the conclusions. Good travel writers place the reader in the scene, without explaining how she or he is expected to feel.

Use All of Your Senses.   Try writing copy for a restaurant. Few individuals have this talent. It requires the ability to conjure up images that trigger senses of smell and taste and sight. After you've used *delicious* and even *succulent*, where do you go? All of us share in sensory perception to some degree. Arousing these feelings is a potent form of writing, but it takes sensitivity and practice.

Work From a Plan or Outline.   Those who regularly employ word processors in their composition invariably praise the computer's ability to realign copy, add, subtract, alter. These are attractive options. Still, a suitable initial design will help reduce such changes. Anyone who plans a tour calculates things like mileage and cost. Often, a day-by-day routine is constructed. That's planning. Writing, too, requires this sort of preparation, allowing the writer to know where the work is going. Without such a plan, a lot of time is wasted in rewriting, or the finished item confuses the reader. More about planning follows in this chapter.

Concentrate on Nouns and Verbs.   Some who write about an emotional topic like travel assume they must fill their prose with adverbs and adjectives. Not true. The verb remains the strongest word in any sentence, and the right noun is next.

"The stucco houses plunged down the steep hillside" sounds far better than saying "the stucco houses were on a steep hillside." Verbs provide action, drama.

"A Wyoming winter laminates the earth with white," writes Gretel Ehrlich in *The Solace of Open Spaces*. "The pastures bend into me," she writes later.

Writers should avoid static verbs and seek for ones that are appropriate and, in that context, original.

Nouns, too, have potential. Concrete nouns are more effective than abstract nouns. It's better, for example, to refer to a "catalpa" than to merely indicate a "tree." In travel writing, in particular, such terms can be evocative. The same holds true for proper names. There's something magic about "Barcelona" or "Saint-Tropez" or "Kampala."

Write in the Active Voice.   The passive voice is awkward and dull. "An African safari was taken by Eleanor" has less impact that "Eleanor took a safari."

Prefer the Simple to the Complex.   A majority of great writing is simple writing, from Scripture to Hemingway (who was, by the way, a talented travel writer). Consider the level of your readers and write for them instead of writing to show off your own vocabulary. Long involved sentences are also taboo. Sentences should be short, but varied for effect.

Come to the Point.   If the message is simple, like a request for information, don't bury the appeal in a jungle of rhetoric. If the message is more complex, like an article or script or speech, provide the reader/listener with periodic benchmarks to show where the copy is going. It's like remembering to repeat the score in broadcasting a basketball game. The reader should have a feeling of progress.

Get Personality into Writing.   Even a brief memorandum should reflect the writer—well, at least the kinder, saner side of the writer.

While comedy may be difficult to inject into a message, the sense of good humor is not. Remember the communication principle that the attitude toward the sender affects reception. Warmth, concern, sincerity—these qualities can become part of the written word.

Learn How to Persuade.   Much writing in the travel industry is aimed at convincing or converting. This requires the writer to get the reader in the proper mood, to direct the presentation to the reader's interests, to be both honest and credible, to appeal to the reader's higher emotions, to make examples pertinent and potent, to cite recognizable authorities when appropriate, and to refrain from sounding too commercial. Persuasion starts with the first words, then the letter or brochure moves through arguments and benefits to arrive at conviction.

Develop a Style.   Easier said than done, but practice and experience help to create a manner of writing that is unique to the author. That's why readers can identify certain prose with the writer. Even letter writers put things in an individual way that stands out. Harvard alumni used to enjoy getting appeals for funds because the alumni director had such a great style. The personal technique can be vigorous, humorous, or direct, but it bears the stamp of the writer.

Cut with Sense and Courage.   Many communications are too wordy. These messages should be trimmed for clarity and impact. Every thought does not have to be spelled out. The writer must give the reader *some* credit. Eliminating the unnecessary language, as indicated earlier, is one solution. Even then, sentences and paragraphs can be trimmed, because filling in the unstated lines involves the reader more directly.

Writers sometimes get carried away with their own cleverness, or their own descriptive powers. On re-reading, they should realize that these attractive little passages impede the progress of the piece. We must murder our little darlings, the Irish say.

Rewrite.   It's an old adage that there is no good writing, only good rewriting. The person who publishes the pristine efforts that flow from the typewriter or appear on the terminal screen is either a genius or careless. Few fit the former category. In re-reading and rewriting, the communicator notices lapses, errors, unclear ideas, awkward construction, incomplete information, incorrect grammar or punctuation, and other problems. The writer may also see other, better, ways to word the message, or may discover paragraphs that could be condensed or eliminated. Everyone's writing improves with rewriting.

These are only some of the tips that aid in producing better communication. Some would add advice on developing a vocabulary, concentrating on organization, inserting color into the work, and even finding ways of not sounding exhausted at the conclusion of the communication.

Writers find their way and they find their voice, but they never accomplish this without reading, without practicing their craft, and without developing a self-critical attitude toward what they produce.

RESEARCH PRECEDES WRITING

Extensive training precedes a track meet; study comes before an exam; planning anticipates construction; and research must be in place before writing. Using the analogy of a trip once again, it's obvious that the person making the excursion (or preparing the way for another's tour) gathers all the available data on routes, hotels, restaurants, sightseeing, fees, transportation, local customs, tipping, weather, and so on. Before any itinerary is sketched out, the information is at hand.

Not every message deserves detailed research, but some research always helps. Even when inviting a client to lunch, it would be beneficial to know what day and location would be convenient, and even what cuisine could appeal. Brochures involve a lot of digging. So do proposals and government travel contracts and speeches. Even news releases take thought and analysis. Those writers who act on hunches and assumptions are doomed to repeat errors and to mistake the interest level of the audience.

Sometimes extensive research is not necessary, and sometimes it is too costly, or the time for study is too short. Even then, however, the good communicator does whatever is possible.

INFORMAL RESEARCH

Informal research covers all areas of fact gathering short of conducting a controlled survey. Precision is not normally as important as information in this form of research, although you want the details to be accurate and, when seeking opinion, to be as representative as possible.

The first source of information should be at the individual's fingertips, meaning desk volumes or access to a company library. The contents of this collection depend somewhat on the nature of the travel component, Figure 3–2. Cruise lines, for example, would want some special volumes on ships, ports, and other maritime topics, while the hotel industry might assemble books on accommodations, legal and safety regulations, and other specialized subjects.

Every professional, however, should have a good dictionary, a thesaurus, fact books, media directories, an atlas, an encyclopedia (perhaps the one-volume format), at least one text on grammatical usage, a book of quotations, a public-speaking manual, appropriate government manuals, perhaps a couple of books of humor, and other volumes that make specific sense. The individual's assignment and experience help with the selection.

Besides the books, those in the travel industry will want to collect trade journals and other publications that can be used for reference, including annual reports, and promotional brochures. Keeping a "swipe file" of potential copy and graphic ideas is also wise, and many travel firms carefully catalog their photos and stock photos.

There are a growing number of texts relating to the travel field, covering everything from buying a travel agency to planning a tour. There are also volumes about travel, plus hundreds of travel guides, city guides, and similar literature. In most situations, it makes for

Figure 3–2.   Among the many helpful books in the travel industry are the indispensable hotel and travel guides.

more efficient use of space to have these books in a central location, although key volumes—like the dictionary, thesaurus, and atlas— might be fixtures at every desk.

The Library

One of the greatest community resources is the public library, along with any university or professional libraries that may be nearby. Some cities have extensive holdings while smaller towns get by with a more limited selection. Most libraries, however, have an interlibrary loan arrangement, enabling the borrower to tap into larger collections. Computer-linked libraries also make finding books much simpler and faster.

The travel professional should be acquainted with the libraries that serve his or her area, paying close attention to the reference section. It helps to visit this facility when there is time to explore, instead of rushing in under pressure and trying to find the appropriate book.

Know the card catalog, the periodical racks, the reference works—and the staff. Be familiar with books and periodicals dealing with travel in its multiple aspects. Learn to use the expertise of librarians.

The professional should also know the location of university libraries and specialized collections in areas like law and medicine. Some cities have libraries specializing in subjects like genealogy, religion, foundation giving, and many other topics. Then there is the newspaper "morgue," where past and current materials on individuals and newsworthy subjects are filed.

In short, those in the travel industry should be aware of all local and regional resources.

Miscellaneous Materials

Like most professions, the travel industry has a number of national and international trade groups which may maintain files on pertinent travel themes. Information from these may be requested. Government agencies also constitute a source of such data.

Besides printed materials, tape and video cassettes exist in many areas, covering various locales as well as explaining some aspects of travel. A growing number of computer programs add to these aids, Figure 3–3.

It helps to keep handy a list of these sources, along with addresses and phone numbers. Being able to quickly assemble information from myriad sites is a definite plus.

Figure 3–3. Research precedes writing, and much of today's research is handled by computers.

Other Means of Gathering Data Informally

While the methods of collecting information are limited only by the imagination of the researcher, there are some common ways of capturing facts and opinions.

Obviously, talking to other people helps. Salespeople may be an excellent source, since they are closest to the ultimate client. Passengers can be queried regarding their experiences, much as hotel guests and restaurant patrons are currently surveyed. Internally, it's wise to sample employee opinion, preferably in an organized manner, like regular meetings. And some travel entities employ the technique of focus groups, inviting clients or potential clients, for example, to a freewheeling discussion centered on selected travel topics.

Those firms or industries that get considerable publicity may wish to analyze the content of such coverage. The airline industry, for example, has come in for considerable negative coverage by the media, ranging from complaints about service to more serious charges regarding safety. Anyone in the industry has to stay abreast of these stories since they affect the way airlines are perceived.

Even smaller travel units, which may not achieve any significant media coverage, can scrutinize their mail, determining what items are of concern to those who correspond. Since complaints outnumber praise in almost any situation, these letters have to be approached realistically, but they can be helpful.

Suggestion boxes, although an old device, still have value. If used, the suggestions should be collected, read, and, where feasible, acted upon. Employees and clients should not feel that their comments are ignored.

Company files provide information. Professional conferences may suggest new ways of handling situations. Subscribing to newsletters and other services can be worthwhile.

In the travel industry, there are unique ways to conduct informal research. Familiarization tours bring professionals closer to certain locales and properties, and there are representatives of tourism bureaus and tour companies and carriers who can be tapped. Even ambassadors and consuls may sometimes be the target of inquiries.

The list is endless. Information on travel abounds and, even though it's a complicated subject, the necessary data on virtually any issue is readily available. Consider, for example, the multiple methods of focusing on a resort area like Hawaii.

Libraries and bookstores have general volumes. Hawaiian tourist bureau representatives can provide printed matter and video tapes. Trade journals regularly feature the fiftieth state. Desk copies of fact books can provide details on items like population, major cities, annual rainfall, state flower, and similar data. Popular magazines contain articles that might be helpful, and government agencies publish pamphlets with relevant elements. You can chat with authorities over the telephone or talk in person to people who have lived in or visited Hawaii. Representatives of cruise lines and hotel properties may be contacted and there could be nearby museums with exhibits on this area. From these and other sources, the travel communicator gathers more than enough material to construct the intended message.

Every subject heading possesses its own peculiar sources. The job of the individual researcher is to plumb these sources in an efficient, thorough manner in order to provide a basis for planning and communicating.

FORMAL RESEARCH

Formal research centers on the survey as an instrument for gathering fact and opinion—especially the latter. Normally, surveys are conducted by professionals, although the sponsoring firm should provide input on the purpose, scope, and questions, along with some evaluation. This varies, of course, depending on the nature of the survey and the experience of those involved in the preparation.

Some travel companies may do their own limited surveys, circulating questionnaires among clients, patrons, guests, or passengers. Travel magazines often query readers on a range of topics. Larger firms may even do internal surveys among employees.

To adequately cover the subject of surveys, we'd need at least one long chapter, so the following paragraphs merely introduce the reader to some of the general principles.

Defining the Problem

Before anything else is done, those commissioning the survey should be certain they are agreed on the areas to be studied. Sometimes firms select one assumption and end up investigating the wrong thing. The place to begin any survey is with the answer to the question: What do we want to find out. If the purpose is to solicit reaction to a proposed new hotel location, then the questions should be phrased in order to determine such reaction—and the proper audience should be selected to furnish these opinions. If the goal is to discover why a majority of Americans have never taken a cruise, then the responses should fit this aim.

This means you should know how to phrase queries to produce the most honest and enlightening information, and you should also avoid cluttering up the questionnaire with questions that add nothing to the main topic.

Once you have identified the area to be surveyed, planners should sit back and discuss this option, just to see if they are on target, or if the topic could be defined more accurately. It's frustrating to invest in a survey and then learn you didn't get the data you needed to know.

Framing the Questionnaire

Writing the questions can be a matter for professionals, especially when seeking opinion rather than facts. It's one thing to ask if a person is planning on traveling to the Southwest this year, and quite another to inquire about the individual's image of the Southwest.

The key to asking the questions properly is, first, to understand what you are asking and why, and, second, to word the query in a way that is free of confusion and influence. You don't want to cause a respondent to misunderstand a question or to answer it in a way dictated by the wording. Unfamiliar language may account for confusion, or too complicated a question, or the lack of options for the respondent.

If you ask, "Do you like to eat out or would you rather stay home for dinner?" the respondent doesn't want to have to select one or the other because he or she likes to do both at different times. Asking "Do you read travel literature cursorily or with circumspection?" will turn off many individuals. Even common words may confuse if used in a vague context. "Was your last cruise a memorable experience?" Some words mean different things to different people. "Do you eat out often?" The word *often* is viewed differently by individuals. It could suggest once a week, or once a month, or some alternate interpretation.

Politicians are adept at phrasing questions to secure responses they want, but this tactic has no place in legitimate surveys. You don't ask if the respondent would prefer "a nice, cool, leisurely cruise with exceptional cuisine or a hot, stuffy bus ride with uncertain meals." Only an idiot (or an actor on a Wendy's commercial) would elect the bus ride. If you really want to determine preference, you eliminate the positive and negative words and ask the question as directly as possible.

Some questions admit only "Yes" or "No" responses, or a limited and specific response. Obviously, such questions are easier to tabulate. They're called *closed* questions. *Open* questions have many possible responses and are tougher to analyze. For this reason, open questions in a survey are asked before closed questions, since the latter narrow the replies.

A closed question would be: "Do you plan to visit New York this summer?" Only "yes," "no," or "don't know" apply here. Responses to open questions like, "Where would you like to vacation this summer?" admit of numerous possibilities.

In order to focus even closer on the intensity of an individual's feeling about a topic, surveyers may use a *semantic differential* technique, offering a range of choices. For example:

"Winter vacations are only for the wealthy."
Strongly agree _____ Slightly agree _____ Agree _____ Disagree _____
Slightly Disagree _____ Strongly Disagree _____ No Opinion _____

You want to make sure you have covered all potential options, including the "don't know" or "no opinion" categories.

Questionnaires shouldn't have too many questions, although a respondent will answer more if contacted in person or by mail than he or she will over the telephone.

Why would travel firms use surveys? To determine future plans of clients; to get reaction to new programs; to test assumptions about travel policy; to collect ideas about offerings; to help in the unit's own planning; and many other reasons. Airlines, cruise lines, hotels, travel agencies, and others in the industry need this data as much as any service industry.

Selecting the Sample

You have to know who you want to survey and how many of these individuals you will contact. If precision is paramount, at least 1500 randomly selected individuals should be queried. That's the number organizations like Harris and Roper and Gallup work with. It gives them a confidence level of ninety-seven percent — meaning that, if it were possible to survey everyone within the survey universe, the results would vary only three percent. Obviously, the more people you survey, the more accurate you'll be, but after 1500, the gain in accuracy is slight and doesn't rise proportionately.

Normally, a professional survey firm will use a system of random numbers applied to a census list or voting list or city directory, selecting enough locations to give them the end number of responses they need and then doing multiple surveys in that vicinity. If they wished to gather 1500 responses within a state, for example, they might select at random 150 sampling points across the state and do clusters of interviews of ten people in each of these geographical spots.

Only the larger travel entities would attempt anything like this. Most of those who seek data want only indications of trends or some insight on opinion. While they, too, want accuracy, coming within three percentage points may not be critical. A travel agency querying clients on which airline or hotel chain they prefer just wants guidance and not perfection. Still, every attempt should be made to make the results as valid as possible.

The more extensive surveys are based on the theory of probability, which revolves around respondents having an *equal chance* of being represented, even though they are not personally contacted. The old classroom example posits the notion of a sack of 1000 marbles, 500 red and 500 green. If a person extracts a shovelful of marbles from the sack and finds he has 400 marbles, *chances are* there will be 200 of each color. It would be straining probability to discover 399 red and only one green marble. The theory isn't perfect, but it's accurate enough to support planning and action and communication.

There are also different kinds of samples.

An *accidental* sample includes people who happen to be at a certain place at a certain time, like shoppers in a shopping mall. This sample can be misleading. The shoppers, for example, may be disproportionately female, or more affluent, or older. Or there could be a large number of teens there on weekends. This sort of sampling may be simpler and interesting, but it has the potential for a wide margin of error.

A *purposive* sample concentrates on individuals with known characteristics. Surveying a travel agency's clients or a ship's passengers, would be examples. As long as you stay within the boundaries of the sample when analyzing results, this technique is fine. However, you don't want to take the responses of this select group and apply them to a wider segment of the public.

Quota samples try to match in the survey sample the percentages found in the area sampled. If your city is fifty-four percent female, then fifty-four percent of those questioned should be female. Ditto for age statistics or religion or any other factor you care to isolate. Obviously, you can't feed in a whole series of variables but should concentrate on one or two elements, like sex or age or economic level. Most travel firms would use this technique seldom.

Those three types of sampling are grouped under the heading of *nonprobability* sampling, leaving *probability* sampling, which we've already described and which contacts people solely on the basis of where they happen to live rather than any other qualifying fact.

Choosing the Method

A majority of travel surveys are conducted by *mail*. This is a fairly effective method, can be randomized relatively easily, and also allows for more questions, longer answers, and an opportunity for the respondent to peruse exhibits. It can be expensive, when you consider the costs of printing and postage, plus the time taken to compile and evaluate the survey. Its chief weakness, however, is the inability to determine the source of the responses. Did you, for example, hear only from frequent travelers and not from those who haven't taken a long trip in years? Those who are most interested in an issue tend to reply, so the survey may be skewed in favor of their opinion.

Personal interviews also allow respondents to view exhibits (like lists of options, ads, and other items) and they also give the interviewer a chance to note personal habits, surroundings, and the level of intensity of the reply. But this is the most expensive means of gathering data and it also eliminates some people because pollsters are reluctant to venture into certain neighborhoods. It's also getting difficult to get people to let you into their houses for this purpose or even to persuade them to commit the time required to complete the answers. This technique also demands skilled professionals and should not be left to employees, friends, or students seeking part-time employment.

Nationally, most surveys are conducted over the *telephone*—as homeowners can readily attest. This is a quick way to get responses, is less expensive, and is the easiest way to randomize. You cannot ask too many questions, cannot show the respondent any exhibits, cannot note any personal nuances, cannot get too complicated, and cannot wander into areas that are too controversial. Poorer people, who may not have telephones, are underrepresented, as are those living in apartments, dormitories, and other similar facilities. Some states have a smaller percentage of telephones than others. There's also the annoyance factor which must be considered, and the nuisance of callbacks. Still, for a fast, cheaper way to collect information, this method works.

Some surveyers may utilize all three methods in the same survey, sending out a broad mailing (or asking magazine subscribers to reply), making a large number of phone calls, and interviewing a limited number of individuals personally.

The technique chosen will depend on the nature of the survey, the budget, and the time and personnel available.

Conducting the Survey

While anyone may compile informal research, formal research— surveys—should involve experts. Getting a group of friends or employees to call from their homes is fraught with problems. They may not call; may just call friends; may lead the responses; may fail to follow instructions for randomizing; may color the results.

It's far better to employ specialists who know how to interview. The travel firm may still help develop the questionnaire and evaluate replies, and can retain control over the survey, but the work should be entrusted to those who do this for a living. Again, if you are simply asking a few questions of your clients, patrons, or passengers—like what they thought of the service—there is no need to hire outsiders—unless you know nothing about framing questions.

Evaluating the Responses

When all the data has been collected, it still requires skill to determine what these facts mean. A large number of "no opinion" replies may indicate that the public is unaware or ill-informed on this subject. It may also mean they know, but are confused, or that they know but don't want to reveal their opinions. A decrease in stated intentions to fly might have to be weighed against an airline disaster that occurred as the surveys were being completed. Ditto for responses about certain tourist destinations that may have received negative press recently.

Replies in a semantic differential questionnaire may give a clue to intensity levels. Even though the negatives may outweigh the positives, if most of the negatives are moderate,.perhaps the difficulty may not be as great as it seems.

Responses also have to be measured against previous findings in the same subject area. Even though the figures may be encouraging at the moment, matching them against data collected previously may show a decline in interest or intent. More people may say they would take a bus tour than say they would not, but, if the pro-tour numbers are down from five years previously, that's not a healthy sign.

So those analyzing the information must make certain they derive the proper conclusions from the responses and, if they have doubts, they should realize they are dealing with uncertainties.

PLANNING

Research supports planning. Travel executives plan for the current year, for five years ahead, for ten years or longer. They need a blueprint, a guide toward their progress and activities. Even communicators require both research and planning, amassing their facts, then outlining the message. You must know what you want to say before you say it.

Travel owes its existence to planning. Airline routes have to be carefully scheduled; tours must be fashioned to meet travel needs and tourist expectations; cruise lines plot the best ways to expend their advertising dollars; and copywriters work against deadlines for producing ads, brochures, or company publications.

Besides facts, planning involves common sense and strict attention to details. It embraces the ability to learn from the past and present when scripting the future. Some experts have suggested that planning includes a searching look backwards, a deep look inside, a wide look around, and a long look ahead.

Looking at the past provides guidance from successes and failures, develops warning signs, supplies figures on things like attendance, personnel, budgets, and problems. If a hotel is planning a grand opening, it would want to examine any previous open houses, at its own facility, at other hotels in the chain, or at similar locations. If a public relations person decides to issue a new publication for employees, it would be wise to scan previous attempts and note how well they did.

Looking deep into any problem is a way to think about consequences. If you do publish this brochure about one local tourist attraction, will other attraction managers be upset? If you institute a profit-sharing system for veteran employees, will newcomers feel discriminated against? If you advertise adventure tours on the sports pages alone, will you get complaints from other segments of the newspaper readers? This exercise requires a little time and several good heads.

Virtually everything that can be done has been done. That's why looking around at the experience of others is worthwhile. Some organizations are willing to share their expertise and trade associations often provide case histories from their files. A letter or a phone call to someone who has lived through what you are about to do may save you considerable grief.

Planning really is looking ahead. Try to imagine where the current action will place you in future months or years. What are the chances for success? What are the pitfalls? How does this action blend into the trends you envision? Every futurist conclusion involves risk, but if you've done your research and carefully planned, the risk is minimized. Still, the ability to cast a ten-year glance at things is extremely beneficial.

For the communicator, planning often means outlining. Company magazines have to be "dummied up," taking stock of the content and the layout. The magazine staff for AAA works at least a year ahead in order to provide balance to their features and in order to assign the stories to appropriate travel writers. Brochures, too, are first compiled in rough form, to make certain all relevant facts are included, that the copy flows smoothly and logically, that appropriate visuals are added, and that, when necessary, some form of reply is made available. Even letter writers may draft several attempts before settling on the right wording.

Process of Planning

We've covered most of the essentials, but it may be sensible to review the steps of planning.

- ❏ First, you gather all possible and feasible data.
- ❏ Then you analyze this data and devise potential actions.
- ❏ Next you choose among the action options, considering budget in addition to other factors.
- ❏ You then examine the consequences of this choice.
- ❏ You make certain all appropriate parties understand and approve the option.
- ❏ You put the plan into some workable format, again carefully scrutinizing each element, and writing it up, completely and forcefully.
- ❏ You launch the program, including the communication of it.
- ❏ You continually monitor progress.
- ❏ If things go well, you may want to expand the successes, committing additional resources. If the plan is faltering, you may wish to shore it up or to return to the drawing board to repeat this entire process.

Methods of Planning

While various names are attached to the planning regimens devised by individuals and companies—titles like "Top-Down Planning," "Management by Objectives," and "Issues Management"—all are really means of reaching an agreed-upon goal. Some break the task into divisions (departments, perhaps) and have each unit prepare a plan based on the achievement of a stated objective. Other planning methods assign specific duties to task forces to research certain areas and provide counsel in these areas. Still other plans begin with the overall objective and widen the responsibility chart while narrowing the focus, moving, perhaps, from a goal of expanding readership to a specific of including more graphics in the publication.

Obviously, any printed piece involves planning, especially those that are issued regularly or those, like financial reports, that must meet certain deadlines. Editors work backwards from the date they wish the material to be in the hands of the readers.

If a tour company wanted to distribute a brochure on a certain date, their scheduling might look like this:

❑ Available to public (date)
❑ Brochures from printer, ready for mailing (date)
❑ Envelopes addressed (date)
❑ Read and approve proofs (date)
❑ Material to printers (date)
❑ Deadline for copy and photos (date)
❑ Deadline for rough layout (date)
❑ Begin copy and photography (date)
❑ Complete concept, rough, and copy platform (date)

These tasks would be completed in the reverse order shown.

A company publication would also work backwards from the date of distribution and would likely be tied to a yearly schedule as well. Many magazines plan their major articles a year or more ahead, assigning them to different writers and researchers and locating or commissioning photos and art. This sort of planning gives balance to a publication, plus variety and comprehensiveness.

Deadlines should be realistic. It's neither fair nor wise to hand copy to a printer within an unreasonable time frame. This is one way to run up costs and injure quality.

Even a news release requires planning. Decisions have to be made as to the timing of the release, the scope of the mailing list, and the time required to complete the mechanical details. If an airline has a new route to announce, the company may wish to time the release so that it occurs after employees have been notified or simultaneously with the employee notification. Planning might include a desire to have the story hit on a normally slow news day or in conjunction with an advertising campaign or to meet some other special need. Planning could also envision other uses for the release, like circulating the original or the printed item to key publics, like community leaders or field representatives or travel agencies.

Crisis Planning

Every travel firm should have standing plans for emergencies, and these would include plans for communication. If an airliner is hijacked, major airlines know what to do. Specific personnel gather to assess the situation; designated spokespersons interact with the media; other individuals communicate with government agencies and, occasionally, with the hijackers; still others are given the job of communicating with families of hostages.

This is only one form of emergency. Hotels have to consider everything from fires and food poisoning to strikes and structural accidents. Every large organization can experience financial emergencies ranging from impending bankruptcy to takeover attempts. Even a small business, like a travel agency, can have its own catastrophes, involving a tour, perhaps, or the behavior of one of the firm's principals.

Organizing for such negative events is done in quieter times and encompasses many areas. Legal considerations are important and so are financial dangers. Communication, too, is detailed. Who speaks for the firm? What things should this individual say, keeping in mind the legal and personal implications? How do you reach these individuals? Does everyone in the company know about making such contacts? Who is to be notified and in what order? What restrictions, if any, are to be made regarding media coverage?

Not every eventuality can be anticipated—but most can. Airlines know accidents are possible. Amusement parks realize visitors may be hurt. Hotels have to anticipate queries about the health status of kitchen employees. Every travel unit should be aware that lawsuits are common. It's comforting to know that some definitive guidelines exist to help steer you through these difficult times. Even with such aid, it's tough to operate; without such planning, even the smallest disaster can become major.

It's worth repeating that planning for communication is merely one phase, but it's generally one of the key ingredients.

CREATIVITY

Creativity is a somewhat rare commodity. It's also hard to define. It's usually seen as a talent for imagination, for inventiveness, for the development of original ideas. Someone originated the frequent flyer program. Someone else pioneered the suites-only hotels. Disneyland and Disney World are examples of genius. There are many less spectacular notions that are still effective in communication.

Clever ways of presenting a program. An unusual photograph. An open house event that is unique.

Communicators don't have to be original. They can function well if they have the requisite skills and exhibit a high degree of professionalism. But if they also possess imagination, their value is enhanced.

Planning can be routine and, even at this level, if thorough, it may be effective. If sparked by originality, however, it can be even more powerful. Calling New York "The Big Apple" helped take the emphasis off crime and crowds and put it on fun. Featuring a lovable character like Gavin MacLeod in the Princess Cruise ads not only recalls the romance of the "Love Boat" series but also adds an element of trust and credibility. Even a simple act, like presenting young travelers with miniature pilot's wings, came from someone's brainstorm.

Unfortunately, you can't force creativity. It arises naturally. But you can put yourself in a mode that supports creativity. A thorough familiarity with the product or service, especially as it exists when in operation, may provoke an idea or two, and the ideas of others, while they shouldn't be stolen, may give rise to creations of your own. Travel fairs and trade shows, for example, may supply ideas of how others sell their ideas and products.

Creativity should be encouraged. If a travel organization has someone who demonstrates potential, some allowances should be made for this individual. Maybe it's a more flexible work schedule, or a more compatible environment, or a different system of rewards.

Later chapters will explore creativity as it applies to subjects like advertising and feature writing.

DEVELOPING GOOD WRITING HABITS

As mentioned earlier, writing is hard work. It never really gets easier. That's why those assigned this task are tempted to procrastinate. You have to be able to psych yourself out, to play games with your mind, to convince yourself that you MUST get to work.

A regular routine helps. Some writers select a specific time of day to write; some like a special chair or room. No problem with these requests but, once they are honored, the writer should write. After all the excuses have been aired, the project still awaits.

Discipline is one of the most important elements in writing. It seems to be far more rare than talent or creativity. What the writer needs to do is conjure up a sense of urgency, a compulsion. Only this sort of drive will bring writing assignments in on deadline, time after time.

EVALUATING AND TESTING COPY

Periodically, writers should check their work for effectiveness. Editors may survey readers, or submit publications to experts for appraisal. They can discuss their efforts with staff members, with other editors. They can read back issues, or the work of others. It's not wise to continue to crank out copy without occasionally assessing results. You want to know that you are reaching your intended audience and that these individuals understand the message.

Readership surveys can be simple or complex. Some just ask what readers like or dislike and solicit feature suggestions. Others probe into how much time is spent with the publication and whether there is any "pass-along" readership. Even the retention level of readers may be examined.

There are a number of special "readability" tests designed to check the comfort level of prose for readers at varied educational stages. "The Cloze Procedure" subtracts words from the copy and then determines if it can still be understood. "The Dale-Chall Formula" matches copy against its own list of easily comprehended words, and "The Flesch Formula" also employs a definitive roster of accessible language.

"The Gunning Formula," one of the easiest to use, allows the writer or editor to select a passage of approximately 100 words from the magazine, brochure, or report. The number of words may exceed 100 because the sample passage should contain complete sentences. The number of sentences in this passage is then counted and this number divided into the total word count to derive an average sentence length.

Next, words containing three or more syllables are counted, excluding common compound words, some verb forms, and proper names.

These two figures—the average sentence length and the number of three-syllable words—are added together and the result multiplied by 0.4 to provide the approximate number of years of education a person would need in order to easily read the passage.

Suppose, for example, that the passage selected contains 106 words and that there are 6 sentences therein. There are also a total of 19 words of 3 or more syllables. Divide 6 into 106 to get the average sentence length—17.5 words. Add 17.5 to 19 (the number of words of 3 or more syllables) and this gives you 36.5. Multiply this result by 0.4 and you get 14.6. This means that this passage may be easily comprehended by a person with a couple of years of college—a person in his or her fourteenth year of education.

This doesn't mean that someone with less education may not understand it, nor does it mean that the college sophomore or junior may not find this too simple. It's just a guide. What should alert the writer/editor is a finding that the copy is written at the level of a graduate student when the readers are typically high school graduates, or that the copy is written at a grade school level for readers who are far beyond this sort of prose.

CHAPTER HIGHLIGHTS

❏ Effective writing is "telling tales to strangers."
❏ Writing lapses include unclear messages, a pompous attitude, dull ways of looking at things, word clutter, lack of organization, overwriting, author intrusion, faulty attempts at humor, jargon, cliches, and other flaws.
❏ Writers must overcome psychological barriers, like writing when uninspired, or when not doing one's best work, or when not in the perfect environment. They must learn to show, rather than tell, to use all the senses, to outline, to be familiar with grammatical rules, to develop a style, to cut when necessary, and to rewrite.
❏ Research, formal and informal, precedes writing, with informal data gathering more prevalent in the travel industry.
❏ Formal research—the art of surveying—requires professional skills and should not be attempted at the amateur level, although the travel firm may want to be involved in the planning and evaluation.
❏ Planning also precedes writing and all planning invariably includes planning for communication. Every printed piece requires a certain amount of writing and production planning.
❏ Creativity, though not a widespread talent, is a plus for the writer.
❏ Writing should be evaluated periodically, using some formal or informal survey method, or employing one of the readability formulas.

■   ■   ■

❑ *EXERCISES*

1. Select an appropriate-length passage from some travel magazine, brochure, or book, and apply the Gunning Formula test to it.
2. Select an article from a travel publication and critique it using the list of flaws contained in this chapter.
3. Select a travel area—either a geographical area or some facet of the industry, like cruises or state tourism—and create a bibliography for this topic, using the resources of your local and school library.

❑ *CASE PROBLEMS*

1. Assume you were hired as an intern by a medium-size travel agency in your area. Among the jobs they give you is an assignment to survey students at your college or university in terms of their potential as travelers. The agency would like to know whether they should bother advertising in the school newspaper and, if they do advertise, what they should talk about. Where could you go for informal research help? What would you be looking for? If you decided to survey the student body, how would you go about it? List three questions that you might ask them.

2. In recent years, there have been any number of airline emergencies—terrorist hijackings, mid-air explosions, pilot error, hostile takeover by financial speculators, strikes by personnel, and so on. Based on what you have read of these emergencies, and what you have seen on television, how well do you think the communication has been handled in these instances? What sort of planning do you feel would make things smoother in terms of communication internally and externally? Discuss in class the problems created for those charged with communication and what they might have done in advance to plan for these.

SOME COMMON WRITING ASSIGNMENTS

Not every writer can handle every assignment, but a good professional writer should be able to dip into different forms of expression with a fair amount of success. Copywriters, for example, could be expected to tackle a brochure, print ad, even a poem or jingle lyrics. These writers, of course, are the more talented types. Not everyone can transfer skills. Some fine novelists might never be able to write a successful mail-order appeal and, even within advertising agencies, some writers who do well with print find it tough to switch to radio scripts. Few experts are adept at fashioning copy for outdoor advertising.

Travel firms that can afford outside help should avail themselves of this advantage, but many companies haven't the volume or the budget to attempt this. Even within companies that employ advertising and public relations assistance, many routine tasks require internal writing skills.

LETTER WRITING

Travel employees may never write a slide script, or even a speech, but all must write letters. A majority of them balk at this elementary task. They hate to write letters or feel insecure about it.

For purposes of public relations, individuals should welcome the chance to write letters—should, in fact, seek out opportunities.

There is one overriding secret to writing an effective letter and that's to *picture the recipient and the mood this person is likely to be in when your letter is opened.* Too many people write in a vacuum, concerning themselves with what they intend to say rather than what the receiver should hear—or wants to hear. Every good communicator envisions the audience. When writing to another individual, the task is simpler. Composing a letter for a mass audience is more difficult, but a little common sense helps here. You should know, for example, that the recipient gets a lot of unsolicited mail and that much of it gets a cursory reading at best. What can you do to break into this person's consciousness? You should know, too, that on most occasions, your message isn't a must, so you have to spark and maintain interest. Be sensible, be reasonable, and imagine your reader with your letter, Figure 4–1.

Did ye nae hear those pipes skirling?

They are signalling the second requests for deposits or commitments for the 1989 (May 28–June 11) tour through Scotland and England. After this we'll have to accept people only on a space-available basis.

Some 31 adventurers are already signed up, but we can handle a few more. Still, we have to tie things down pretty quickly in order to settle on accomodations and transportation.
I realize the holiday season isn't the best time to solicit deposits — or even to get people thinking about spring — but the long lead time is necessary in order to organize things.

Remember, your deposit is refundable right up until the time we request full payment — sometime in March. Remember, too, that even if your Christmas generosity finds you temporarily embarrassed financially, we'd still like to hear from you if you plan to join us.

We have reading lists and other tips prepared for tour members and will make them one of several mailings to tour members. We'll also get together at least once.

Call me (572-9094) if you have any questions — and I hope you'll be able to join us on this unusual trip.

Bob Reilly

- -

MAIL TO: Travel & Transport, 9777 "M" St., Omaha, NE 68127   ATTN: Audrey

Please hold a spot for me on the upcoming Scotland/England Tour

NAME _____   ADDRESS _____

CITY _____ STATE _____ ZIP _____ PHONE _____

☐ $200 per person deposit enclosed
☐ I'll make my deposit shortly, but I want to stay on the list.

Figure 4–1. A letter doesn't have to be fancy or expensively produced, and even the chore of collecting deposits can be done with a light touch.

Letters also take a little *planning*. Think about what you want to convey, what you need to accomplish. This may require a few drafts, plus some careful reading, including the review of others. Then comes rewriting. Assuming you have a purpose you can define, have you managed to fulfill this, or have you wandered all around, obscuring the intent? This stage allows you to outline (if the letter warrants this), to polish phrases, and to keep preparing drafts until you're satisfied with the result.

The Salutation

When you know the individual, there's little problem, although you may be stuck with spelling or a title, Figure 4–2. That's why having a City Directory is valuable, along with an accessible filing system. Besides these, there are other directories covering everything from the clergy to political leaders. As a final resort, call the recipient's office and get the details straight. Even if it's a long-distance call, it's worth it. In circumstances that make it difficult for the writer to inquire, a secretary might accomplish this.

Figure 4–2. In tasks like letter writing, word processing makes personalizing much easier. (Courtesy Travel Careers Institute)

I'm writing a letter to Mr. Telemon, and I just wanted to be sure I
spelled his name correctly and that I have his proper title . . .

Salutations tend to be very formal, although they needn't be,
and many writers have experimented successfully with variations.
It's worth checking, or even a phone call, to avoid writing, "Dear Sir
or Madam, As the Case May Be," which sounds—and is—archaic.
With our increased sense of gender, we may also stumble over the
"Dear Sirs" salutation. If the letter is important enough, check it
out.

What about salutations on mass-produced letters?

Here's your chance to be both creative and intelligent. If there is
a common denominator addressee, fine. Say "Dear Client" or "Dear
Frequent Flyer." These can get awkward, too. Many writers forgo
the formal salutation and substitute a narrative hook, something to
get the reader into the letter. They serve the letter the way a headline or illustration serves a print advertisement.

"Worried about overeating on your cruise?"
    or
"It costs no more to use a travel agent. Remember that!"
    or
"Haven't you used up all your excuses?"

The body of the letter then picks up on this salutation, and
extends the idea.

Body of the Letter

Many letters are longer than they need to be. Writers can't get
started and don't know how to finish. Pull out a few letters from any
business file and they could be cut fore and aft without losing
anything. Business letters shouldn't appear curt and they shouldn't
omit vital details, but they should give the reader a sense of
progress and the conviction that the writing is organized and
efficient.

Business letters should sound like a person talking and not like
a legal document. They should be conversational in tone. That
doesn't mean wordy or chatty, it means friendly and personal. Keep
them as short as possible but as long as they need to be. Cover
everything that needs to be included, but don't waste time and space
with unnecessary language.

A letter setting up a luncheon date need merely fix time and
place and, perhaps, set a general agenda—unless the locale is hard
to find. There is generally no need to exceed a paragraph for this.

On the other hand, a letter pitching a proposed tour may require several pages, even if accompanied by a brochure. No problem here. People who are interested in this subject will read it carefully.

The Close

It's wise to stick to conventional closes, like "Sincerely" or "Sincerely Yours." There are acceptable variations and substitutions, but readers may react against phrases like "Affectionately Yours" or "With Deepest Gratitude" or any of the many cute substitutes.

Some General Tips About Letter Writing

Be Wary of Slang or Humor.   There's a difference between being warm, even lighthearted, and trying to be a comic. If you're good at humor, it may work. Most people aren't as good as they think they are, and a busy reader, faced with this copy, may become angry. Know your audience, and know your own limitations. Slang should also be used sparingly and only for effect. This type of speech is easily dated and may presume a relationship you don't have with the reader.

Don't Get Too Familiar.   While Europeans may look on us as open and unaffected, that doesn't mean our one-on-one contacts by letter should have a breezy "howdy" style. Don't use first names of recipients unless you know them or unless they sign their correspondence to you that way. It's still a good idea, even in this democratic age, to let the senior correspondent (in age or position) make the first move toward the first-name basis. Even then you may opt for a more formal address. Even if your Senator signs his first name to a letter, your reply (unless you are friends) would be safer addressed to Senator _____ and not "Dear Jim."

Be Careful About What You Write.   There is not only a legal concern here, there are all sorts of other negative results of writing things you wished you hadn't. Letters stay around in files. Perhaps one is pulled out when you are being considered for promotion or when a client is deciding on an agency to use. There's a permanence to correspondence and the writer should not commit to paper anything he or she doesn't want to be viewed by others. Libel is not the sole lapse. Letters can also promise things that can't be delivered, include remarks that are tasteless or offensive, or raise issues that needn't be raised.

Don't Mail a Letter You Wrote When Angry.   Perhaps you may post it later, but it's a good idea to reflect on things written in a white heat. Perhaps the hotel in Cairo failed to provide a sufficient number of rooms for your tour group. Maybe the airline delayed a flight that threw you off schedule. These events are annoying, and the culprits may deserve castigation, but prudence dictates that you behave in a dignified manner, expressing displeasure but without boiling over. You could be wrong—and your idiocy is there in writing.

Don't Fret Over Crank Letters. Sooner or later everyone receives a nasty letter, usually anonymous. Some people let these bother them, speculating on the sender, letting the message get to them. Better to see if there is anything worth considering—or changing—in the missive and then toss it away. With all the things that can go wrong in the travel business, the individual is foolish to allow a single complaint to fester and irritate.

Since these letters are cowardly and hurtful, it figures that those who don't like to get them should refrain from writing them.

Avoid Fraud. You know the sort of letter that assures you that you've been selected among your neighbors to get a special deal on a tour? Or the one that tells you the writer has been up all night trying to compose this message? These are obvious fakes. Don't exaggerate, don't lie. Good writers know how to make things attractive without resorting to falsehood. Lying is a dangerous practice, one that inevitably catches up with the individual. Brochure copy should not talk about "the finest hotels available" if these are two-star facilities. Walking tours, if strenuous, must be characterized as such. Cramped cabins shouldn't be advertised as spacious.

Remember All the Rules for Good Writing. Some people are good conversationalists but stiffen up when they come to write a letter, forgetting this is also communication. Everything one knows about writing should also go into letters. Grammar, spelling, punctuation, and style remain important.

Letter Forms

There are numerous forms of letters and each industry and profession has its own correspondence challenges. Some writing responsibilities are common—regrets, thanks, congratulations—while others demand a special acquaintance with the topic. *The basic principles still apply—be yourself, be conversational, be sincere, be prudent.* Everyone approaches the letter in a singular way, but some suggestions may help.

Sales Letter for New Business. Like resumes, most sales letters don't try to do the whole job themselves; they seek to get an interview. However, this in itself is a talent.

Although some introduction may be necessary, plus some explanation of services, the focus should be on potential benefits to the letter's recipient. What reasons have you included for securing an appointment or prompting a client's call or visit? The sales letter tells who you are, what you can do, and why the reader should do business with you. Maybe you're writing to a corporate client and promoting your efficient service, qualified personnel, and state-of-the-art equipment, while the client is more interested in the existence of quantity discounts. If you're pitching incentive tours, you have to make clear why the corporate client should deal with your firm. Hotels soliciting convention business learn to center their appeals on items key to convention planners, like convenience, costs, types of facilities, and other amenities. Minimize the number of "I" and "we" references and think "you."

Sympathy Letters.   These are tough to write, mainly because the writer is afraid of making some dumb error. Be genuine. Say what's in your heart. If you can think of some meaningful incident involving you and the deceased, include it. Write sincerely and naturally. And keep it short. Long letters of sympathy inevitably turn maudlin.

Letters of Complaint.   As someone once wrote, you get two kinds of complaint letters—those you send and those you receive. You feel your efforts are models of restraint but that those who complain to you have overreacted. Letters of complaint shouldn't be written unless there's a real chance they'll do some good. You might even suggest a possible solution in the complaint letter itself. Merely venting anger isn't a sufficient reason for writing. These letters should be fair, balancing good points with bad, and they should be specific, detailing the purported error or wrong. If the complaint is complicated, then sufficient details should be supplied to support the allegations. If the complaint is minor, don't blow it into a major issue.

Rather than agonizing over myriad drafts of a complaint letter, it often makes more sense to pick up the telephone and deal with the individual and the issue directly.

Answering a complaint should be done quickly and thoroughly. If there is substance to the complaint, apologize and state what is being done to correct the situation. If the complaint is groundless, remain polite and spell out what your investigation unearthed. In neither instance is sarcasm, rudeness, or indifference called for. You may have to bite your tongue, but keep the venom out of any response.

Thanks and Congratulations.   A supply of simple cards with these messages will save you a lot of stationery. Get the ones with the inside blank so you can personalize the thought. People with public relations sense are always looking for excuses to send these notes. Promptness also counts. Get a thank-you note out as close to the event as possible. When the society's president returns to his/her hometown, it's great to find a note waiting from the hotel manager. And vice versa. Noticing a positive item in the newspaper about one of your travel agency clients should call for a little congratulatory message. No great prose is required in these instances; it really is the thought that counts.

The problem is that people in the travel business are generally fully occupied and attending to the niceties of life may be shunted aside. A pity. Someone within the firm should be given the task of recognizing opportunities for thanks and congratulations and alerting the proper people to send the cards.

Letters to Clients and Customers.   Travel agencies, hotels, cruise lines, and other travel businesses keep lists of those who have used their services or facilities. Most also send them periodic mailings. Perhaps these letters announce some new offering, or perhaps they just keep the association fresh. Some firms send out "haven't-seen-you-in-a-while" letters while others mail special "customer only" deals. This is an important constituency and shouldn't be ignored. It's always easier to get repeat business than it is to start with a cold list.

Letters to the Media.   News releases, which form the normal means of relating with the media, will be discussed in Chapter 5. However, there are occasions when a travel firm may want to inquire about the possibility of coverage of an event, or may wish to disagree with something they witnessed on television news, or may want to alert local reporters to a local angle for a national story. Again, you want to be aware of media needs and deadlines, and to speak in terms of news interest rather than your own publicity interests. Think like an editor in presenting your point of view or appeal. If it's a critique, be specific. If a request for coverage, show why this item has news value.

Occasionally, a travel firm may want to interest a publication in a feature idea. The letter should outline the theme and, if the travel person intends to write it, present this person's credentials. The one thing you want to avoid in dealing with the media is any suggestion of puffery or any lapse from professionalism.

Miscellaneous Letters.   People in this industry have to reply to students wanting information and to adults seeking brochures. They need to stay in touch with business leaders and, at some levels, with elected officials. A letter may be required to accompany a survey of regular clients or to support a supplier request. There are requests, apologies, and explanations. Each is different, but the considerations offered earlier in this chapter still apply.

MEMOS

Recent studies claim that forty percent of business memos are unnecessary and unread. They are often issued by chronic memo writers. These folks just like to crank out memos, partly to display authority, partly to cover themselves, and partly to give the appearance of activity. A number of these memo writers also write "mean," offending those who receive their handiwork. They may not even realize what they are doing.

There should be a reason for writing a memo, and even the weak excuse of getting something in writing is better than no reason at all. If the message can be communicated more effectively in another way—like at a personal meeting—then the memo can be bypassed. Whatever the purpose of the memo, the writer should check to see that this purpose is realized.

Memos should be succinct, friendly, and professional. They shouldn't try to cover too many points, but they should also be careful not to leave loose ends. Like letters, they should be organized and rewritten, especially if they are to be distributed widely.

Everyone who needs to see the memo should be included in the mailing and, if these names appear on the memo, there should be a pecking order, listing recipients in order of importance. Some thought should be given to this list so that key people are not accidentally eliminated. Many will see this slight as deliberate.

Final warning. Unfriendly eyes may see the memo. Staff people not on the list may get a peek and spread rumors. Therefore, keep the content businesslike and refrain from personal asides that can get you into trouble.

PROPOSALS

It's the rare person in the travel industry—or in any vocation—that doesn't have to make a proposal for more money, more space, a new program, or for some similar goal. There are even a number of specialists in certain aspects of proposal writing, especially those dealing with federal or foundation grants. These experts supposedly know how to write appeals that have a high rate of success. This tactic is called *"grantsmanship"*.

But there are other appeals besides those for money.

Hotel managers may propose expansion to the president of their chain. Local and state tourism managers propose budgets and activities to governmental bodies. Airlines propose new routes and travel agencies propose policies to boards. Even individual employees may suggest procedures or programs to management. Each of these proposals goes through a number of steps.

Know Purpose and Gather Facts

As with other endeavors, writing proposals dictates that the *composer know why the appeal is being made*. Some goals are vague or general. They must be clear. What is the real reason for this proposal? Can it be put into a single sentence?

Once the aim is properly identified, then the supporting data must be gathered. Techniques discussed in the previous chapter may be used. The principal arguments are going to feed on such information, so it should be complete and appropriate. Available statistics, results of surveys, historical antecedents, projections—all are part of this research.

Consider the Negative Reactions

If you begin by asking yourself why authorities should respond positively to this proposal, you'll probably divine most of the likely objections. How are you going to respond? What persuasive techniques can be employed? This latter consideration may involve more than the writing. It could encompass plans relating to distribution, timing, and even the support of other personnel. Think the whole presentation through—realistically.

Emphasize Main Points

Especially if the proposal is lengthy, the writer should be certain that the essential elements are clear to the reader. Sometimes the appeal gets so complicated and confused, it's hard to dig out the gist of the proposal. Underlining might help, but the best advice is to have the copy so directed that the substantive items stand out. This is especially helpful when those reading the proposal have several appeals to consider. Even a quick scanning should tell them what you're about.

Anticipate Questions

Like the expert direct sales copywriter, the proposal writer tries to figure out in advance what things a reader might ask while going through the document. Since the writer is not usually on hand to reply to these queries, it's well to include the answers in the body of the proposal. These could take a Q. and A. form at the end of the appeal or they could be worked into the narrative.

Review the Situation at the Outset

After the title page, if there is one (containing the title of the project and cost, if appropriate), the proposal should sketch in the background. A request for a new airline route, for example, might embody a little history of the airline and what it has accomplished thus far, along with its need and ability to expand. Also included might be a review of the proposed destination city and its current status. If the proposal is to a corporate client by a travel agency, this is the place to outline a bit of company history along with general commentary on business travel and what can be accomplished in this area.

Much of the statistical and research data may be incorporated here, and many of the generic questions can be answered. This sets the stage for the meat of the approach.

Cover Problem or Opportunity

Specifics of the proposal are called for here. In the illustrations mentioned, like the new airline destination or new corporate client, this section would examine the current condition, showing how the destination could be served by a new carrier or how the corporation could benefit from the agency's service. If the problem is more complicated, there could be one part for the problem, followed by the solution.

Include Budget or Other Considerations

What will your services cost? How will you amortize costs of expansion? What will the budget be for the addition of the new tour package? Is the proposed coach route cost-efficient? Every project has some cost or personnel involvement. Spell these out.

Summarize and Add a Little Sell

The proposal must be pulled together, synopsized, and a final pitch made for the project.

Attach Exhibits

Perhaps charts, maps, graphs, illustrations, tables, survey forms, or other information needs to be added as a sort of index. Reference to these entries may be made within the body of the proposal. Care should be made to insure that these additions are not mere window-dressing but add to the understanding of the proposal.

Check Guidelines

Companies may have guidelines for internal/external communications and these must be reviewed when preparing a proposal. Government agencies expect that their guidelines be followed. Proposals to provide travel service to federal agencies—an activity permitted by recent legislation—require adherence to specific instructions and are very comprehensive. The airline application for new service routes mentioned earlier would have to fit within federal directives. Whatever the rules happen to be, the people preparing the appeal should see that they are met.

Even though there may be a formula for organizing proposals, that shouldn't eliminate the necessity to display creativity and persuasiveness in the writing.

REPORTS

Reports are common in the travel industry. Tour managers file reports at the conclusion of a trip; travel agents summarize fam trip experiences; corporate clients expect reports on their travel; major travel and hospitality firms publish quarterly and annual reports; the government expects reports from some suppliers; local tourism bureaus report regularly to elected officials; individual employees may file annual reports on their progress. While the key factor in all of these reports is a realistic cataloging of all that occurred, the ability to present information attractively is a plus. It is also an advantage to be able to highlight salient features for easier reading.

Research and organization precede any report; so does planning. The result should be logical and comprehensive, with key items underlined and illustrations included, if appropriate.

Besides reports on events that happened, there are also reports that serve as planning instruments for future occurrences. A tourism bureau planning to host a hundred travel writers for a weekend will develop some sort of report to sell their superiors on the event. This document will also serve to guide planners and direct local personnel. A motorcoach company investigating the feasibility of adding a route will welcome a report covering all aspects of the potential move.

The biggest complaints about reports are that they are hard to read and incomplete. Both of these criticisms should be corrected in a careful rewrite. Allow time for this scrutiny and revision.

Often, management will provide guidelines or an outline for reports. Tour managers, for example, are expected to include in their coverage any major problems encountered, their analysis of hotel and restaurant experiences, a critique of the tour operator, comments on adherence to the itinerary with any reasons for alterations, remarks about events scheduled, a few details of day-to-day travel, plus a rundown on expenses. Some managers may expect even more.

ITINERARIES

Not every person in travel gets involved in pulling together an itinerary. Much of this is mechanical anyway, based on experience, on the recommendations of tour operators, or on the specifics of existing tour packages. Consideration must be given to the time of year, to what accommodations are available, and to other items. Computers can pull up some of this data; phone calls and correspondence complete the picture. If you are then going to sell the tour to prospects, the itinerary must be assembled and this is where some writing skills are advantageous.

The prime requisite is that the itinerary be accurate and complete. The person writing the copy must make certain there are no errors, no promises that go unfulfilled, no exaggerations. Before committing details to paper, the writer should be certain the specifics are both feasible and certain. Go over the route on a map, even if you've been there before. Make certain you haven't packed too much into one day—especially if the previous day is also a full one. Have you allowed the group sufficient time to see what you've scheduled and still have time to eat dinner and get to a play?

Remember that the itinerary may be compared to other tours that appear similar. Are the differences clear? Do prospects know what they are getting for their money? Many people read only the tour price and the number of days. They may neglect to note that there is a difference in the quality of hotels, in the number of meals, in the cost of attractions. Some itineraries suggest entertainment but leave the ticket price to the traveler, whereas other trips are all-inclusive and contain these ticket costs.

Planners normally start with the dates and with a map. There are usually many ways to get from one place to another. You can go clockwise or counterclockwise, directly or indirectly. What do you want to see, and at what pace? It's a good idea to do a number of drafts, playing around with a variety of travel sequences, keeping in mind things like bank holidays, store closings, availability of special attractions, and even the problem of Sunday church attendance. Once you have something that looks workable, check it with the domestic or overseas tour operator. Some compromise may be in order.

When all details are set, it's time to formalize the itinerary. Keep in mind that some tour members read this as if it were a legal document. They expect to experience everything on there. So it's smart to include some sort of disclaimer about the right to alter the itinerary if circumstances demand. There is no sense in driving out to the Cliffs of Moher in Ireland if it's foggy; you might as well be staring at your living room wall. And, if there is student unrest in Seoul, you may want to substitute for both accommodations and the planned city tour.

A number of format options are available, but the outline shouldn't be too tight. Don't include departure and arrival times for the daily coach schedule unless these times are critical. You want some flexibility. Leaving a little white space around the copy for each day is a good idea. This gives tour members a chance to write in notes, or their room numbers, or times of meals and departure. The tour manager also has space to add things like phone numbers of local contacts or reminders of things to be accomplished that day—like calling ahead to the next hotel.

Since the itinerary is also a selling tool, the copy should have the capacity to persuade—even within a very brief space. Instead of writing "Visit Culloden Battlefield," substitute "Walk through historic Culloden Battlefield, where the Scots suffered their final defeat." Don't merely say "Overnight in Nice;" characterize the hotel and the setting in a few words.

True, the itinerary is designed to give readers an idea of their daily activities, and there isn't room for long essays. However, just a few words can change a bit of information to an image. "Swiss buffet" is better than "Dinner," and "leisurely luncheon cruise" is an improvement over "luncheon cruise."

Besides the day-by-day events and the facts clarifying costs and responsibilities, some itineraries also contain additional material. Photos, for example, or information on the tour escort, or a summary of what the tour price covers, or even some specific tips for travelers.

It's worth repeating that the key elements are comprehensiveness and accuracy, but that anything that adds to the tour member's anticipation is a plus.

BROCHURES

Tour brochures are often expansions of the itinerary. They read like a continued short story, beginning with some general comments about the tour, the destination, and the tour operator, Figure 4–3. Some brochures run to dozens of pages; others are confined to a two-fold leaflet suitable for mailing in a #10 envelope. The larger offerings may include a number of tours.

Brochures communicate through word *and* picture, so the visual aspect must also be considered. While the copy forms the meat of the printed piece, the design provides the impetus for a prospect to pick the item off a travel agency rack, or to write for it when prompted by a travel ad. So, knowing something about layout helps. You not only have to think about what you want—and need—to say, you also have to envision the appropriate package for this message. Just reviewing available literature in a travel agency is a rewarding exercise. You'll see how different people solve the same problem, through variant styles and varying messages.

There has to be a logical continuity to the brochure. A Pan Am brochure, for example, might focus on holidays in Europe and run to more than 130 pages. Because of its size, it will feature an opening index to the list of tours, followed by an introduction, then a definition of types of tours, then a spread on the sights of Europe. A map follows, then four pages on Pan Am's brand of travel. Next come several pages describing and listing the hotel options and, finally, a collection of travel tips. Over 100 pages outlining and highlighting 70-plus tours and city stays comprise the bulk of the brochure. The closing pages summarize the conditions of the journey.

Individual tours are covered more succinctly, with an introduction, perhaps a word about the tour director, the itinerary, the cost, and the responsibilities of both tour operator and tour member.

Virtually every hotel issues some sort of brochure. These may or may not include rates, since charges can change. What will be contained in the short booklet will be a brief word on the facility and a typical room, plus a rundown on the other amenities, like restaurant and pool. Location is also featured, plus, perhaps, some of the attractions within walking distance. Essential information, like address

Tour No. IT2E11-1376

Day-by-Day Itinerary

Sunday, May 9—OMAHA - NEW YORK

Depart from Omaha this morning via UNITED AIRLINES, connection with the evening AER LINGUS flight to SHANNON. You'll hear your first brogue and get your initial taste of Irish hospitality aboard this scenic flight.

Monday, May 10—SHANNON

Arrive in Shannon this morning where you are met and transferred to the FITZPATRICK'S SHANNON SHAMROCK INN with the balance of the day at leisure.

This evening—a special Irish banquet to welcome you to this enchanting land.

Tuesday, May 11—SHANNON

Exciting tour of Ireland's most musical country. Visit the spectacular Cliffs of Moher, the resort town of Lisdoonvarna—then slip into County Galway to see William Butler Yeats' hideaway castle, Thor Ballylee, and the classic ruins of Coole Park. An evening trip along the lovely shores of Lough Derg and stop in the famed Merriman Tavern.

Wednesday, May 12—KILLARNEY

South to Ireland's most famous locale, the Lakes of Killarney. Stop at Adare, through to Rathkeale, Newcastle West, Castleisland and Tralee to Dingle. Tour Dingle with lunch in Dingle Town. Stops at

Dunquin, at Tomasin's pub and scenic areas. Evening is at leisure, with overnight at the KILLARNEY TORC HOTEL.

Thursday, May 13—RING OF KERRY

You will thoroughly enjoy this swing around the Dingle Peninsula, one of Ireland's most scenic and historic spots. Lunch at the Derrynane Hotel. Balance of day free for shopping, jaunting car rides and activities on your own. Special evening of folk lore. Overnight at the KILLARNEY TORC HOTEL.

Friday, May 14—BLARNEY

Leave Killarney and drive over beautiful country. Pass Daniel O'Connell's birthplace and residence. Lovely Glengarriff, favorite vacation spot for De-Gaulle, to mystic Gougane Barra, source of the River Lee and seat of Saint Finbarr's monastic settlement, fresh salmon lunch at Johnny Cree-don's country hotel in Inchigeela, then to Blarney for a castle tour and a chance to kiss the fabled stone. Overnight at the HOTEL BLARNEY.

Saturday, May 15—WATERFORD

Depart for Cork City, for sightseeing and shopping. Leaving Cork, follow the coast to Waterford, with a stop enroute, if possible, at the Waterford Crystal Factory. An evening of traditional Irish Music. Overnight at the WATERFORD ARDREE HOTEL.

Sunday, May 16—GALWAY

Time for church this morning before departure from Waterford via Carrick-on-Suir, to Cashel for a tour of the Rock, historic site dating back to the Sixth Century. Travel along the lake coast road via Poch-ane to Portumna, then to Galway with its lyrical bay. Dinner and overnight at the GREAT SOUTH-ERN HOTEL.

Monday, May 17—CONNEMARA - GALWAY

Today—a tour of rugged Connemara, with its lakes and hills. Stops at Kylemore Abbey and Clifden. Stops will be made at Celtic Crystal and Conne-mara Marble factories enroute. Overnight in Gal-way with a special program arranged for you.

Tuesday, May 18—GALWAY

This is a free day. We suggest a day-long trip to the Aran Islands . . . or shopping, or perhaps a long walk around the Bay. See the Gladdagh, Spanish Arches, or the islands made famous by John Millington Synge. You may choose to relax and simply enjoy a day without activity for rest. Overnight in Galway.

Wednesday, May 19—ROSSES POINT

Leave Galway this morning for Tuam and Knock, with a stop for a visit in Knock. On to Sligo, a tour around Lough Gill before continuing your trip to Rosses Point.

An evening on Yeats this evening in one of Ireland's loveliest settings. Overnight at the YEATS COUNTRY HOTEL.

Thursday, May 20—SLIGO - DONEGAL

A morning stop at Drumcliffe, then to Bundoran, Ballyshannon, with a possible stop at the Beleek Factory if available, Donegal town and on to Killy-begs. Circle Mullaghmore with Lord Mountbatten's modern castle, dinner at the hotel, with an evening visit to ELLEN'S PUB for traditional Irish Music.

Overnight at the YEATS COUNTRY HOTEL.

Friday, May 21—DUBLIN

Leave Sligo, via Carrick-on-Shannon to Cavan, Kells, with a stop at Navan. Continue to Dublin with overnight at the ROYAL DUBLIN HOTEL. Dinner at the hotel with an evening at the ABBEY THEATRE.

Saturday, May 22—DUBLIN

This morning a comprehensive tour of the city of Dublin. The afternoon is free for shopping or tour-ing on your own. Lunch and dinner are both on your own today. The evening is free. Overnight at the ROYAL DUBLIN HOTEL.

Sunday, May 23—DUBLIN

Time for church services this morning. An after-noon drive to Glendalough, Avoca with a stop at Avondale. Return to Dublin along the scenic coastal route.

Tonight will be the gala CABARET evening—an ex-perience to treasure.

Monday, May 24—DUBLIN - NEW YORK - HOME

Depart for the airport for a morning flight to Shannon and thence to New York and on to Omaha.

Figure 4–3. Brochure copy should do more than just spell out the itinerary.

and phone number, is given. Interior photos and a location map are common.

Nations, states, and cities publish their own brochures, all aimed at getting you to spend some time in their locale.

"Golfing, sea angling, river fishing, riding, hunting, tennis, swimming and hiking—all are available in the immediate locality" reads a brochure for Hunter's Hotel in Ireland, a small country inn that "has been run by the same family for five generations."

Quality Inn's Capitol Hill Hotel makes the most of its convenient location, using a fisheye lens cover including the hotel and the familiar Capitol dome.

Washington's most convenient location. Adjoining the Capitol grounds, just steps from the centers of politics, history, and culture.

The eight-page, off-size brochure is mostly pictures and captions, with a few back-page facts.

Tourism brochures are generally more elaborate, especially those for states or nations. "Welcome to Switzerland" the headline reads when you turn inside from the Alpine panorama on the cover. The initial copy theme centers on the pressures of today and the need for relaxing holidays, particularly one to Switzerland.

Here in the heart of Europe it is almost possible to spy the palm trees in southern Switzerland from the top of the highest peaks covered with ice and snow, truly Europe in miniature.

Tour Alaska spreads its big story over nearly 100 photo-filled pages. Rail travel and cruises share the pages and, again, the unique differences are spotlighted.

While other tour operators stop at Denali National Park only long enough for lunch, all Tour Alaska vacations include an overnight stay—and a wildlife search.

Greyhound's "On the Road to America!" brochure discusses professional drivers, customized coaches, comfort, and reliability. They also remind readers of their theme.

By leaving the driving to us, you can enjoy everything you see along the way, worry free.

One of the smaller cruise lines serving Alaska is Catamaran CruiseLines, which reminds readers its more diminutive ships can go places the larger liners can't navigate. "Intimate-sized," they call their ships which accommodate little more than three score passengers, and the copy sings.

You'll never forget the beauty of this breathtaking wilderness—lush rain forests, soaring granite cliffs rising up from the water's edge, sky-high waterfalls, wild streams and rivers spilling into the sea, and the magical, romantic mist enveloping it all . . . Few other cruises include Misty Fjords—none explore it more completely.

Even the most literary brochures are heavy with facts. You need to know schedules and costs and ports of call and an indication of what the tour includes or what type of rooms are available. Some brochures, like airline schedules and hotel directories, are primarily informational, although they usually contain introductory copy and some advertising.

"I'd like to invite you to discover all the exciting changes we're making at Howard Johnson," one brochure begins, introducing the reader to more than 150 pages of capsule information and location maps for hotel units. American West Airlines manages to insert a quartet of ads into its schedule of arrivals and departures.

Brochure copy is terse, like that found in an ad, and it has to move the reader along and also provide both pertinent details and references for further contacts.

MISCELLANEOUS

There are many other writing assignments in the travel business, besides those mentioned here and the ones to be covered in later chapters. There are mechanical chores, like writing tickets or attaching notes to bills. There are schedules and bulletin board notices and daily logs and contest rules and job descriptions and resumes and a hundred other special writing tasks. Even the most pedestrian of these can benefit from imagination, organization, and accuracy.

CHAPTER HIGHLIGHTS

❑   Every individual must learn to write a good letter, and the secret to doing this is to visualize the person receiving the letter. Writers may experiment with the salutation, but should use a standard close.
❑   Letter writers should avoid slang, jargon, forced humor, fraudulent statements, and should also avoid writing angry letters that come back to haunt the sender.
❑   Memos should reach all those concerned, and in the proper order, and should be tightly written and carefully worded.

❏ Proposals begin with research and planning, anticipate questions and objections, and follow either predetermined guidelines or a logical sequence from background to budget.

❏ Reports also require research, planning, and organization, and should be complete and accessible to the busy reader.

❏ Even a mechanical writing task like an itinerary can contain some "sell."

❏ Brochures are written in a terse style, blending exposition with hard details, and moving the reader from page to page.

❏ Every writing project benefits from imagination, organization, and accuracy.

■   ■   ■

❏ EXERCISES

1. Select any hotel in your area and assume you are the manager. Write a proposal to the local Rotary Club inviting them to use your facilities for their weekly luncheon meetings.

2. Collect a brochure for a hotel, tourist location, cruise, or attraction. Critique its effectiveness and bring both brochure and critique to class.

3. Bring to class a direct-mail letter you feel is particularly effective. It can be on any subject.

❏ CASE PROBLEMS

1. As public relations director for an airline that prohibits smoking on all its domestic flights, regardless of length, you have just been handed a letter from an irate passenger who objects to the policy and uses abusive language in complaining about discrimination against smokers. Answer the complaint.

2. You are the manager of a fifteen-person travel agency. Morale has been good. People have generally been good about keeping regular working hours and have even been willing to work beyond closing without complaint. Lately, however, four or five employees have been tardy in coming to work, have extended the lunch hour, and have been periodically absent, especially on Mondays. You have a good relationship with these people and you know they are not overpaid, so you are reluctant to come down too harshly on them. However, this isn't fair to other employees and it also leaves you short-staffed at times. Write a memo to all employees about this.

ADVERTISING AND PUBLIC RELATIONS WRITING

Much of the communication in the travel industry is on an interpersonal level. The travel agent visits with the prospective traveler. The hotel desk clerk interacts with the guest. Some of the contact may be with small groups, like the passengers at the captain's table on a cruise ship or those taking a city tour on a bus.

While more personnel and more hours may be spent in those interpersonal pursuits, most money in the travel industry is expended on mass-media communication. When we need to reach large numbers, we rely on forms of the mass media—primarily advertising, public relations, and other promotional activities. If possible, these communication tasks are best left to the experts, but many of the smaller travel agencies or tour companies may find it necessary to tackle such chores on their own.

While there are many facets to mass communication, this text focuses primarily on the basic principles and the required skills. Another book in the Delmar travel series (*Travel and Tourism Marketing Techniques*) goes into more detail on advertising and public relations.

MARKETING

You may get arguments about the proper organizational placement of public relations, but marketing frequently claims jurisdiction over both advertising and public relations.

Marketing involves all phases of moving a product or service from seller to buyer. Some economists refer to the "Four *P*'s of Marketing," including product, price, place, and promotion, while others add to this list the elements of distribution and personal selling.

Considering the "Four *P*'s," we have to be aware that the product or service must fulfill a need, must have some distinguishing features, and must possess credibility or some relative sense of quality. The price must be competitive and within reason for the item and for the target audience. "Place" refers to location and to the convenience of that location—a prime consideration in siting a travel agency, for example. These three factors affect the fourth P or promotion, since advertising and public relations must be conscious of the differences inherent in their service.

Take one example. A tour to France that is priced higher than other similar tours being advertised has to convince a mass audience that there is sufficient value in the first tour to make the cost variation palatable. The initial tour might feature better hotels, or include more meals, or promise superior tour management. So advertising will reflect these differences. If a tour happens to be the cheapest, promotion probably highlights the price without including too many details.

Convenience of location may be headlined, too, or a firm name may be pushed, and these aims affect advertising. Then, too, many ads are merely trying to get you into contact with a personal sales representative.

Every aspect of marketing is important, but this text is concerned with promotion.

ADVERTISING

Advertising is a controlled, paid form of mass-media communication aimed at influencing purchase of goods and services. This differentiates it from public relations which is less controlled and which doesn't buy space or time for its messages. There are exceptions to this neat distinction, however, and some areas—like public relations advertising—which bridge both promotional approaches. The point is that the advertiser is able to decide what shall appear in the advertisement, exercise some control over placement, and avoid any media editing.

Advertising is not merely being clever; it's reaching the right audience with the most appropriate message. First you must determine what should be said and only then do you divine attractive ways to present the message. Too many advertising copywriters sit down and dash off snappy phrases without reflecting on their effectiveness for this particular product or service.

Appeals in advertising may focus on any number of different personality traits. Even in the limited area of travel, think of the different approaches used, Figures 5–1 and 5–2. Some prospects respond to the spirit of adventure; some are influenced by status;

some travel primarily on business and look for schedules and lowest fares; some look for companionship; some want a warmer or cooler climate. Ads aimed at travel agents discuss commissions and return business. Each ad presumably has a purpose and the theme of the campaign matches that purpose. Cruise lines, for example, may highlight experience, equipment, price, entertainment, ports of call, food, or other facets of their service. Airlines may advertise their comfortable seats, cuisine, or reliability. "If you miss a train in Britain, there are always 15,000 more," reads a BritRail Travel ad, making the most of the country's comprehensive train schedules. Car rental companies most frequently feature price, but can also stress make and model of car or speed of service. Hotels talk about location, comfort and luxury, staff, bargain weekends, or other items. Restaurants can concentrate on name recognition, menu, entertainment, convenience, or decor.

Testimonials are the basis of a 1988 Royal Caribbean campaign, with snippets of letters from satisfied travelers making up the illustrations. For potential passengers Royal Caribbean headlines a print ad: "We're the last people to blow our own horn," and, for travel agents, a similar testimonial piece says, "We get more dissatisfied passengers than any other cruise line," a double-take come-on to let

The Registry Resort, Scottsdale.

NEAR THE PAINTED DESERT OF ARIZONA, A MASTERPIECE AWAITS.

You're invited to experience a masterpiece in the desert of Arizona so beautiful that the sun shines on it over 300 days each year–The Registry Resort, Scottsdale. A setting rich in the West's most cherished natural wonders–The Grand Canyon and The Painted Desert. Where the Wild West has a more comfortable side, too. With award-winning dining, 21 tennis courts, two championship golf courses, 3 pools, health club, nightly entertainment and, of course, horseback riding. Add The Registry's impeccable style and service, and your vacation will be nothing less than perfect.

The REGISTRY Resort

A member of
The Leading Hotels of the World
7171 NO. SCOTTSDALE ROAD
SCOTTSDALE, ARIZONA 85253

1-800-247-9810
1-602-991-3800

THE MOST BEAUTIFUL RESORT IN ARIZONA.

Figure 5–1.   This print ad uses 2 Mondrian layout (see Chapter 7) and colorful copy to appeal to the upscale client. (Courtesy The Registry Resort)

Figure 5–2.   Price is the feature in this campaign. (Courtesy of The Kemwel Group, Inc.)

you know about all the folks who have switched allegiance to this Norwegian carrier. The psychological factor at work here is the message that all these people are willing to confess they had a great cruise, so perhaps you might, too. Credibility and conviction are the aims of the campaign. Sure, the headlines are catchy—and important, but they are only part of the main goal.

Before a word is communicated, the copywriter must have some research data in hand to justify the intended approach and must have given some thought to the way the campaign can accomplish its mission. If the target audience for a tropical resort is the young successful woman, then the choice of message and media will both be influences on the writing style, the theme, and the illustrations. For the male business traveler, a hotel advertiser will couch its appeal in totally different terms.

So, there are any number of tangible and intangible factors that have to be weighed before the form and content of the communication is determined.

FORMS OF ADVERTISING

Advertising can be classified in many ways. As just noted, intellectual and emotional appeals could be listed and ads collected under a variety of headings, from messages directed to motivations of thrift to those aimed at satisfying the intellectually curious. Ads could also be assembled under headings of intent, with entries meant to identify a brand name, cause you to change vendors, reinforce a decision, even get you to buy stock in a certain firm.

Advertising is also distinguished by audiences. National advertising, for example, seeks out a national audience and may not specify a place to buy a product or service. Beer and cigarettes are advertised this way. So are cruise ships and airlines and tours. These become local when XYZ travel agency asks the consumer to book a cruise through their location or when a tour is sold out of another travel agency. There is advertising that is industrial in character, like a concrete supplier advertising in a contractors' journal, and advertising that is professional, as when a pharmaceutical firm places copy in a medical magazine.

In the travel industry, the two principal forms of advertising are trade and retail. Trade advertising normally involves the selling of goods and services to middlemen who will then sell these to the ultimate consumer, Figure 5–3. Hertz reaches travel agents through their trade publications and attempts to interest the agents in recommending their vehicles to the traveler. Ditto for tours and hotels and airlines and other travel entities. As with any effective communication, these trade ads are worded to emphasize the benefits to the reader—in this case, the travel agent. Things like customer satisfaction, repeat business, and commissions are mentioned.

Retail advertising relates directly to the consumer and is the type of advertising most travelers see. These are the ads in the Sunday travel section that list tours or airline schedules and similar offerings. Even here, there could be other forms of advertising, like institutional ads which merely sell you on using a travel agent or national ads as defined earlier.

MEDIA

Advertising may be typed by the media in which it appears. Keep in mind that each mass medium has its own plus and minus factors, its own assets and liabilities, and no one medium satisfies all requirements.

In general, print media (primarily newspapers, magazines, brochures, and direct mail) dominate in the travel industry. Outdoor advertising is common for airlines, hotels, and tourist destinations, while radio is used intermittently by all travel units. Televi-

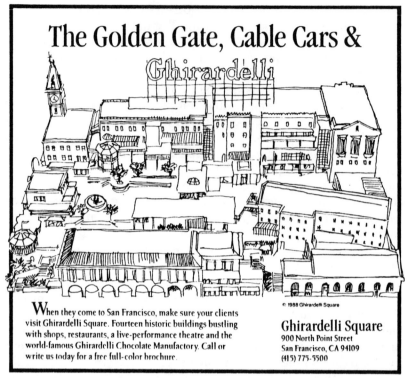

The Golden Gate, Cable Cars &

When they come to San Francisco, make sure your clients visit Ghirardelli Square. Fourteen historic buildings bustling with shops, restaurants, a live-performance theatre and the world-famous Ghirardelli Chocolate Manufactory. Call or write us today for a free full-color brochure.

© 1988 Ghirardelli Square

Ghirardelli Square
900 North Point Street
San Francisco, CA 94109
(415) 775-5500

Figure 5–3.   In smaller space print ads, artwork often reproduces better than photography, as in this lighthearted rendition. (Courtesy of Ghirardelli Square)

sion, which is more expensive, is more common for national than for local advertisers.

Let's look at some of the options.

Newspapers

Virtually every member of the travel industry uses newspapers—the nation's largest advertising medium. Travel prospects are conditioned to look in the travel section (usually a Sunday feature) for information on this topic. Readership of newspapers is high, cuts across all economic levels, allows for the clipping of coupons, and provides a ready means of referral. Newspapers stay around a while, get passed on, are published frequently, can be selected geographically by the national advertiser, have a relatively low cost for advertising, permit the advertiser to change copy fairly easily, and make it easy for co-op advertising—where a supplier or national advertiser may share the cost of an ad with a local agency.

However, newspapers are not the best means of showing a product or service in color and, when used nationwide, can present production problems with different measurement requirements. A chief drawback is that the wide range of readers makes for a lot of waste circulation. Many people who are not prospects will still be exposed to your ad, and you're paying for this useless coverage.

Magazines

There are specialized travel magazines as well as other general-circulation publications that regularly carry travel advertising. Magazines do well with color and also provide some opportunity to target certain audiences. You'll note that many magazines directed at professionals and their families carry travel ads. Magazine readers are generally more affluent than newspaper readers or television viewers and ads in magazines also benefit from more prestigious surroundings, Figure 5–4 (pages 96–98).

On the negative side, production and placement costs may be high; you have to plan several months in advance in order to make deadlines; and, if you use several magazines, you may be reaching the same reader more than once (which is not all bad). Magazines have the further disadvantage of not being able to dominate a local market.

Radio

In recent years, thanks to changes in format and portability, radio has made a comeback. It's an accessible medium, intimate, somewhat selective as to audience, relatively inexpensive, flexible, and it has the potential to dominate a market. There are, however, time restrictions as to length of message, no visual appeal, and no means of referring back to the message.

For travel advertising, radio, with its unique property of conjuring up images with sound, could be used more than it is.

Television

For pure advertising power, television commercials seem to have it all. TV combines sound and picture, uses color well, is popular, can demonstrate a product or service in use, has huge audiences, possesses impact, and is a strong means of identification. A thirty-second spot on Hawaii can show you the beaches, the tourists learning the hula, the luau, the surf. You can hear the music, the tides, the wind in the palms.

But television commercials are expensive to produce and air, and they are limited to certain standard time segments. You can't always schedule spots where you want them because those availabilities are already sold. There is waste coverage and no easy way to respond or refer back to messages. Sponsors even worry about viewers ignoring their efforts.

GUIDER (ghee-day) *v.* to guide, to direct.
1: Primary function of lithe, likeable, congenial hosts (a.k.a. "G.O.s") who lead congenial guests (a.k.a. "G.M.s") in organized activities of physical or more intellectual nature (see JOUER).
2: The above-mentioned G.O.s also possess the expertise to offer instruction in such disciplines as windsurfing, scuba diving and horseback riding. (Note: our congenial hosts are available at all villages and in both genders.) **CLUB MED**
The antidote for civilization.

Figure 5–4.   Ads rarely stand alone; they are part of a larger campaign. Here and on pages 97 and 98 are a few ads from a successful print series. (Courtesy of Club Med; photography by Gilles Bensimon)

JOUER (zhoo-ay) *v.* to play. **1:** Primary reason for world-weary, fun-famished individuals to visit (and revisit) the world of Club Med. **2:** Term covers near-endless list of activities beginning with **a:** night tennis on lighted courts **b:** coed volleyball on pink-sand beaches **c:** snorkeling and spotting striped yellowtails beneath the Caribbean **d:** meditating to Brahms or Ravel at dusk and **e:** discoing until dawn. **3:** Includes option to do all or none of the above. **CLUB MED** The antidote for civilization.

Figure 5–4.   Continued.

Out-of-Home Media

The outdoor poster is the most familiar form of this medium which also includes transit posters, taxi signs, bench signs, and other variations. With the outdoor poster you can get location selectivity, large size, repetitive impact, decent color, and, all things considered, a reasonable price.

Billboards have a somewhat negative image, however, and, because content must be absorbed rapidly, they are also limited in

S'ÉCHAPPER (say-chah-pay) v. to
escape, to flee. **1:** The inalienable right of free-
dom-loving guests to enjoy an activity-less,
group-less beach accompanied only by **a:** a
swimsuit **b:** sunglasses **c:** sunscreen **d:** a good
book and **e:** nothing more than brief visits from
inquisitive starfish. **2:** Option may be exercised
daily as an alternative to more group-intensive
pursuits (see JOUER, AIMER). **CLUB MED**
The antidote for civilization.™

Figure 5–4. Continued.

terms of the message. There is waste circulation, problems with
weather, traffic, and location, and a lack of flexibility.

You still notice many outdoor boards near airports, announcing
fares or destinations. Hotels invest highways with them, providing
directions and name recognition. Smaller signs may be found in
airports for hotels, restaurants, attractions, and car rental.

Most experts claim the chief value of such signs is name recognition, Figure 5–5.

Direct Mail

Next to newspapers, direct mail makes up the next largest advertising budget item for most segments of the travel industry. This $15-billion-a-year medium is a specialized field and does the best job of reaching specified target audiences with a more personalized message and without as much competition for attention. Direct mail has production flexibility, scheduling flexibility, provides the best method of response, and is the easiest medium to track in terms of eventual sales.

Besides its "junk mail" image, there is also the relatively high cost, the mailing regulations and restrictions, and the fact that it's hard to find real experts to prepare the packages.

Direct mail is the means of responding with brochures and information to those who write after viewing an ad in another medium. It may also promote its own sales by contacting former passengers, clients, or even a cold list of potential prospects. Compiling and keeping current these lists is another direct-mail headache.

Miscellaneous

These media do not exhaust the possibilities for communicating through advertising. Novelties like ballpoint pens and nail files carry ads. So do airplane banners, directories, displays in travel agencies, play programs, T-shirts, marquees, even some video cassettes.

Whatever is used should be appropriate to the item being advertised and should fit within the confines of the campaign. Most advertisers use a blend of various media, mixing them in some logical balance.

THE ADVERTISING AGENCY

Airlines, cruise lines, hotel chains, major tourist attractions, major tour operators, large travel agencies—all of these companies employ advertising agencies to give a professional look to their ad campaigns. Smaller travel firms and agencies may try to do this on their own.

Travel agencies are often too small to attract ad agencies, especially since their expenditures are likely to be in noncommissionable newspaper space. Like travel agencies, advertising agencies also work on commission, usually fifteen percent, which is paid by the media. Since newspapers grant travel agencies the local rate,

Figure 5–5. Although we're more accustomed to print ads and commercials on radio and television, there are endless other varieties, including point of purchase signs and decals.

there is no room here for ad agencies to make any money. So, if they are employed, the travel agency must find other ways to compensate them.

When the travel account is large enough to generate commission revenue, the advertising agency gets the bulk of its income from the media, meaning that the travel firm pays no more for this service than they would if they placed the ads themselves. There may well be additional production charges or add-on fees for work on brochures and other promotional tools. Overall, however, using the services of an advertising agency makes sense.

Why?

The advertising agency provides creative input, market strategy, media knowledge, production skills, and a means of simplifying advertising billing and checking. The travel firm not only has extra hands to help, but these hands are presumably expert in their specialized field.

When such a relationship exists, the burden of developing a campaign falls on the advertising agency, but the travel entity must still supply guidance, budget, and supervision. The travel client spells out what is to be accomplished and the advertising agency figures out the most effective way to communicate this message to the appropriate publics.

Without this skilled help, the smaller travel firm must rely on assistance from the media, plus its own resources. Books may be of value, and it also makes sense to review the ads of others. Having a person in the firm who has a flair for advertising copy or layout is another plus.

WRITING THE PRINT AD

Copywriters should remember that, before they set down a single word of ad copy, they should have completed whatever research was necessary, including some concept of the target audience and the publication to be used. From these analyses, the writer extracts a theme, or copy platform. Perhaps a list of main points is compiled as a sort of outline. Only then should the copywriter start experimenting with drafts for the print ad.

Advertising writing is, above all, a practical exercise. Something has to happen as a result of reading the ad. A purchase, perhaps, or a visit to a locale, or a request for a brochure, or even a subtle planting of a notion about a trip.

This form of writing also has its own style. Sentences are generally short, perhaps incomplete. The language is punchy, colorful. The ad must be written so that the reader is immediately pulled into the copy, and it must close with some reference to action—unless the goal is merely institutional awareness. While the copy may embrace a variety of formats, from poetry to curt captions, it should be believable, honest, consistent, and conversational.

The AIDCA Formula

To help writers remember the elements that should be present in the writing of advertising copy, there's been an acronym used for several decades. It's called the AIDCA formula, where

A	stands for Attention
I	for Interest
D	for Desire
C	for Credibility
A	for Action

First, you have to attract the busy prospect; then you have to develop and retain interest; next you instill an inclination to purchase; then you respond to potential doubts; and, finally, you provide some means of acting on the ad proposition. This latter item may be a phone number, address, coupon, or just a suggestion about seeing your local travel agent. This formula embodies a logical set of steps, just as a successful salesperson might develop a presentation.

The Four Elements of a Print Advertisement

Normally, a print ad contains a headline, illustration, body copy, and signature.

There are exceptions. Illustrations are not always part of an ad. Some use only a headline and photo and no other copy, while still others omit a headline. Even the signature could be part of the illustration, although this is rare.

Headlines. The purpose of the headline is to attract attention and, just as in life, there are many ways to do this, from arousing curiosity to raising a smile. Some headlines report news; some challenge or command; some make promises or offer advice. There are headlines directed to a certain group, like backpackers or senior citizens, while others use a number of word games (puns, parodies, slang, and so on) to stop the casual reader.

Here are some examples:

"Announcing the Royal Princess Debut in Europe." (NEWS) Princess Cruises

"America's No. 1 Foreign Destination." (CURIOSITY) Canadian Tourist Bureau

"Being American helps us see Europe from a special point of view." (PLAY ON WORDS) American Airlines

"Soaring inflation can be beautiful." Illustration by the Des Moines, Iowa Convention and Visitors Bureau shows a hot air balloon. (DOUBLE MEANING)

"What is a Best Western?" (QUESTION) A campaign by Best Western that provides different answers for different target audiences. In *Modern Maturity,* for example, a magazine for senior citizens, the answer reads: "Dependable lodging on a retirement budget."

"The living you've been working for." (JARGON) Air New Zealand

"Sun Line cruises the Greek Islands, where the dollar is stronger than Hercules." (LITERARY ALLUSION) Sun Line Cruises

"We sell adventure!" (CHALLENGE) Younkers Travel Service

"We promise!" (PROMISE) Budget Rent A Car ad shows employees with hands raised, as if being sworn in.

"Don't send your clients to the wrong Hawaii." (DOUBLE-TAKE) American Hawaii Cruises

"Stop the Car!" commands the Crete, Illinois tourism staff, asking you to visit their shops and attractions. (COMMAND)

There are dozens of other catchy ways to grab the reader. That should make writers realize how dull headlines are that read: "Discover _____," or "The Perfect Hideaway," or "Explore _____." However, some old words are still fine for ads—like "FREE" and "NEW" and "GUARANTEED." Like the rest of the ad, the headline should also be tied to the main theme and it should lead into the copy and not be something clever but irrelevant.

The Print Copy. The pace of advertising writing is generally rapid, although some pieces selling a laid-back tropical paradise may be more languorous. Sentences tend to be short, incomplete, and may start with conjunctions. The prose should be colorful and descriptive—and convincing. Like the sales pitch mentioned earlier, it carries the reader from the headline to the action phase.

"Experienced cruisers know what makes a cruise perfect," reads a Sitmar Cruises print ad. "And so does Sitmar. We've designed our ships to meet the demands of cruisers who know exactly what they want. We've planned our itineraries to satisfy their dreams. And handpicked our crews to provide that *unforgettable* (TM) combination of warmth and professionalism experienced cruisers have come to know as *Sitmar Class.*"

Smaller ads, like this one for the Americana Hotel in Kansas City, Missouri, are even more terse:

"CENTRAL TO EVERYTHING THAT IS KANSAS CITY. Just minutes from Worlds of Fun, Royals Baseball, Crown Center, Plaza, and more. Two blocks from I-35 & I-70. Restaurant, Lounge, Outdoor Pool, Gift Shop." (The low price is the feature of this ad and address and phone numbers are included).

An advertising piece for Kauai, in the Hawaiian Islands, is more poetic:

". . . passengers disembark to explore the hauntingly beautiful Fern Grotto. Your North Shore trip will be liberally sprinkled with a host of perfect beaches, sugar and pineapple fields, and a variety of unusual churches. But the highlight will be the incredible beauty of Hanalei

Valley and Hanalei Bay. Their magic will linger in your memory for decades to come . . . you'll also visit Kalalau Lookout for a view of the awe-inspiring Na Pali Coast valley whose emerald cliffs plunge 4,000 feet to the crashing surf below."

The trick is to conjure up images without becoming trite or without losing credibility. Proper names—like Hanalei Bay—aid the exotic flavor, and choice of adjectives like "hauntingly" and verbs like "sprinkled" and "linger" bring the sentences alive.

Each type of travel and hospitality field presents its own problems and opportunities. Copywriters charged with creating restaurant ads soon learn that "delicious" is a word that's lost its strength, so they find new words—like "tempting" and "feather-light" and "crisp." Even proper nouns, like "Cajun" and "Yorkshire," have potential, as do combinations like "chocolate chunk cookies."

Hotels may focus on services, such as "morning newspaper" or "express check-in," but they may also juice up features with an extra word or two, like "Roman-style" tub or "European-style" services.

These literary tricks are refinements and require reading, practice, and imagination. They take copy out of the ordinary category, but the smart copywriter still knows that the message must be clear, comprehensive, and credible. Creativity may interest or excite the readers, but facts still do a better job of persuading, Figure 5–6.

The Close.   There are numerous ways to sign off on an ad. Some are clever, some merely serviceable. The important thing is that the close properly and forcefully identify the sponsor along with providing a means of action. "Write for a FREE brochure to _____." Or "Mail This Coupon Today." Or "Call Your Travel Agent." The company logo, address, and phone number(s) figure prominently in the close.

WRITING FOR RADIO

Travel and radio make for a happy marriage, primarily because, as mentioned earlier, sound is able to convey images, and the travel industry is blessed with hundreds of easily identified sounds, from train and ship whistles, to surf, bagpipes, and bongos. Radio copy is written for the ear. That means that commercials should choose language that doesn't confuse the listener. ("Did he say 'chief' or 'cheap'?") There are words that are hard to pick out, or difficult to say, and there are also words that have an appealing sound to them, like "macadamia" and "mimosa" and "slumber." The good radio copywriter *hears* the message, the way a composer *hears* the musical

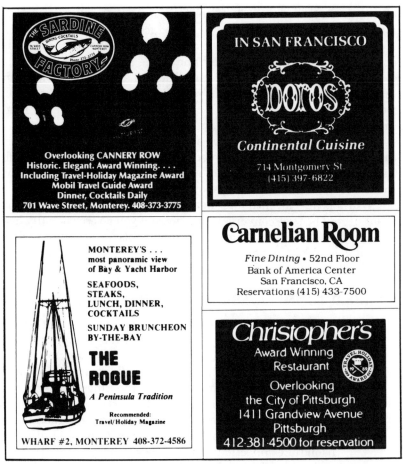

Figure 5–6. The trick in small space advertising is to focus on essential information and to design an ad that stands out. (Courtesy Carnelian Room; Christopher's; Doros; The Rogue Restaurant/Restaurants Central, Monterey, CA; and The Sardine Factory Restaurant/Restaurants Central, Monterey, CA)

notes. Again, the content must embody the requisite information, but it shouldn't sound like the reading of a schedule.

Radio—and television—are also media that place time demands on the writer. You can't script a thirty-three-second commercial, or an eleven-second identification spot. Both media program for ten-second, thirty-second, and sixty-second commercials, with some exceptions—like a combination of twenty-second spots, or a two-minute spot within a sponsored show. The writer must be conscious of this limitation and can't write "fat" so that an announcer has to hurry through the message or the producer has to cut copy on the scene. Practice provides a sense of timing, but the writer can also check by reading the spot aloud and using a stopwatch.

Radio commercials should also focus on a single main idea and make sure this gets across. If you want to announce a new low weekend rate for a hotel, don't clutter the spot up with too many distractions about the restaurant menu or the sauna.

Each radio spot should have a strong opening and a strong close. Since radio is a background medium, advertisers have to get the listener's attention. Later, they need to remind this listener about the name of the sponsor and about any action to be taken.

Radio is also an intimate medium, so the commercial shouldn't shout. Keep the tone conversational, even if you do occasionally hear some of the frenetic announcers on some stations screaming about what a good deal they have.

Here's a sample sixty-second radio script:

SOUND: AUTUMN LEAVES (INSTRUMENTAL). UP THEN UNDER.

ANNCR: You mean you've never seen New England in the fall? Incredible! That's what you'll say, too, as you view the scenery made famous by a thousand American artists. This two-week coach tour by Aspen Travel takes you from Chicago, across Canada, through the Finger Lakes region of Upstate New York, into the picturesque mountain ranges of Vermont and New Hampshire, and then to historic Boston, out on the beaches of Cape Cod, dip into friendly Connecticut, then across Pennsylvania, Indiana, and home. Two great weeks aboard a modern coach, with overnight stops in first-class hotels, a chance to sample great regional meals, and a thousand opportunities to take fantastic photos. Get the details right away from Aspen Travel, by calling 333-6666 or drop into our office at the Ranger Mall. Do it now—before the leaves start to fall.

SOUND: AUTUMN LEAVES (INSTRUMENTAL). UP AND OUT.

The radio commercial could be far more complicated, with several voices, sound effects (SFX), specially written music or jingles, or with certain talent specified, like an actor with a foreign accent. If the spot contains words that may be unfamiliar to the actor or announcer, the writer should provide phonetic pronunciations, like this:

"Visit the gardens at Xochimilco (SO - CHEE - MÉEL - KO) . . ."

Even difficult words that are not names can be phoneticized, although the aim in radio writing should be to use short, easily grasped words. Those reading commercials also appreciate an absence of *s* sounds and *p* sounds and, in particular, the avoidance of alliteration that comes off as a tongue twister. "Hospitable hotel hosts" would be a combination to delete. Slang is also out of favor, except when it makes a point. Normally, slang is not only dated but often sounds a little crude on radio.

Listen to radio commercials and try to type them. There are straight-sell commercials, ones integrated into the show by DJs, conversational spots with two or more characters, short musicals, humor, testimonials, and other variations. Travel is a subject for any of these.

One final suggestion. Figure in advance how many words can be used to fit a specific time format. Remember that content dictates pace to an extent, that numbers take longer to read than is apparent in print, and that you can't merely count words because some words are longer than others. Some experts suggest counting characters (each letter and space) and figuring sixteen characters to a second. Others work on the basis of two words per second. Still, when you consider the inclusion of music and sound effects, you should read it aloud for more accurate timing.

WRITING FOR TELEVISION

Television is written for both eye and ear, although the eye is generally considered to have the edge. If you can see something, there may be no need to explain it in words.

Because of the nature of the medium, television writing is more complicated and more demanding—even though it may take no more creativity than radio The writer must consider potential production problems, location shooting, talent requirements, camera possibilities, color quality, cost, and other factors. On radio, you can symbolize Germany's Oktoberfest with a few seconds of an oompah band. For television, you'll need film footage or an expensive recreation of the foreign scene.

Obviously, costs aside, television is a great medium for travel. Cruise lines and airlines make good use of its potential. So do a few hotel chains and, on occasion, tour operators and travel agencies. With the increase in tourism budgets for some states, you're also being asked to "Wake Up to Missouri" or to rediscover the Black Hills.

You could create a TV spot using slides and an announcer, but this would be as boring as your neighbor's vacation pictures. Besides, that spot is in competition with lots of other television advertising and must look as if it belongs.

To write for television, you have to think visually. Let the picture carry the spot. Show rather than tell. The language can still be crisp and colorful, but it doesn't have to do the whole job. And you should take it easy on the viewer by presenting a minimum number of scene changes.

Like print and radio, a number of different formats are available to the television writer. A few nights watching the tube should display all of them. Testimonials, straight talk, demonstrations, and conversations are all stable ways to sell products and services. There are also mini-stories, musicals, and, in the last several years, a lot of special effects spots. Like opera, which combines theatre, dance, and music, television combines elements of almost all other advertising media, including print, since information is sometimes superimposed on the screen and the identification is nearly always in type.

Again, research and planning should be the basis of the television commercial. If research determines that the two major reasons for taking Amtrak are concerns about flying and a feeling of nostalgia, then these principles should be woven into the spot. Whatever follows has to be interesting, credible, and natural.

Time constraints remain a factor. The thirty-second spot dominates, but there are also the one-minute commercials and the ten-second and twenty-second spots, although the latter are always part of a grouping, so you have to consider what comes before and after— if you can. The ten-second-spot is called an "ID" or "identification" spot and these generally come as part of the "station break" between programs or segments of programs. Obviously, you have to have a simple idea and communicate it quickly. Fifteen or twenty words are the rule, plus strong identification visually. The longer commercials give you more time to develop a story line and some sponsors, relying on the viewer's ability to fill in the gaps, can deliver a fairly complex tale.

Since television is complicated and expensive, it really pays to get professional help. Few travel firms have the expertise to do this in house. Since TV advertising is commissionable, advertising agencies may be willing to take on this chore, independent of other business. Hopefully, their creativity and production experience will give the spot a more polished look.

Frequently, the television script is accompanied by what is called a "story board," a sequence of pictures that outline the proposed spot. Special preprinted storyboard sheets make this task a bit easier and artists may sketch in the story line or, in some cases, may use Polaroid mockups. There are also after-the-fact storyboards which use scenes from the completed commercial. These may be sent to dealers or distributers to show what the campaign will feature. A cruise line, for example, could mail these to travel agents, along with a schedule of local showings, so the agency could tie in with the campaign.

Everything starts with the writing—which starts with research. After the script is completed and approved, sound effects have to be gathered, talent hired, locations lined up, a crew and director hired, rehearsals held, and everything else accomplished before taping (or filming) begins. Leaving things to the last minute causes expensive delays. When the crew reaches the studio or location, everything should be ready to roll.

Once the commercial is shot, it can still be edited and changes made. Some of this can be done at the time the spot is being filmed and some may be accomplished later. The advertising agency and the client have to be satisfied that this is the product they want.

In terms of the script, there are several ways of formatting the writing. If the technique to be used is film, then the script may resemble a movie script, with dialogue centered on the page and action running from margin to margin, in capital letters. The typical television script for commercials, however, uses a two-column format, with the visual elements in the left-hand column and the audio portion in the right like this:

MOTORCOACH ROLLING THROUGH NEW ENGLAND HILLS	SOUND: AUTUMN LEAVES (INSTRUMENTAL). UP AND UNDER
MCU SIGN ON SIDE OF COACH: *ASPEN TRAVEL*	
FOLIAGE. PAN FOREST, THEN DISSOLVE TO MOUNT WASHINGTON	DRIVER: To your left is Mount Washington, six thousand two hundred and twenty-eight feet. P. T. Barnum called this "the second greatest show on earth." It stands (FADE) . . .

DISSOLVE TO MONTAGE OF SCENES (LAKES, BOSTON, CAPE COD) CUT TO HOTELS. EXTERIORS DISSOLVE TO DINNER AT COUNTRY INN CUT TO COACH TRAVELLING (INTERIOR) DISSOLVE TO COACH STOPPED. TOUR- ISTS TALKING TO NEW HAMPSHIRE NATIVE, CU NATIVE.	ANNCR: Vermont, New Hamp- shire, Massachusetts, upstate New York, Pennsylvania—plus first-class hotels . . . . . . and delightful eat- ing experiences. All part of your two- week fall foliage motor- coach tour, aboard a modern, luxury- appointed stratoliner coach.
SUPER LOGO FADE TO LOGO, ADDRESS, PHONE	NATIVE: See Aspen Travel for details. ANNCR: Do it today. SOUND: AUTUMN LEAVES UP AND OUT.

Scriptwriters must not only know camera possibilities, they should also make themselves familiar with production terms and abbreviations. Shots may be closeups (CU), medium closeups (MCU), extreme closeups (XCU), long shots (LS), medium shots (MS), and so on. It helps, too, to be aware of things that may be done in the editing process, like dissolving from one picture to another, or fading in and out of a scene, or using a split screen, or slow motion, or other techniques. Inserting these directions into the script may not be necessary, as long as the writer can explain what is wanted, but it's an advantage to have some idea of the possibilities.

DIRECT-MAIL WRITING

The chief advantage of direct-mail advertising is its selectivity. That means the writer must make an effort to reach the right audience with the right message in order to get maximum effectiveness from this medium.

The term *direct-mail advertising* is a bit confusing. For one thing, this is not the same as "mail-order" advertising. With the mail-order ad, the writer tries to accomplish a sale *directly* as a result. You see these ads in magazines that ask you to send money in order to receive something through the mails. You could also have an appeal like this delivered to your door. Mail-order advertising attempts to do the *whole* job. Very few travel firms use mail-order advertising, unless you count travel accessories that are sold this way. Travel often involves big dollars, so prospects are reluctant to part with that kind of money on the strength of a single ad or mailing. Mail-order advertising is merely one form of direct-mail advertising.

Another reason for confusion is that flyers stuck under your windshield, handed to you in the street, slipped under your door, or hung on your doorknob are also categorized as "direct advertising" and even as direct-mail advertising. All of these techniques may be used at one time or another by some travel units, but the most common forms are brochures and appeals received through the mail, along with materials supplied as a result of a phone or mail request, a visit to an agency or office, or attendance at a travel fair.

Direct mail in the travel industry may have a variety of purposes. Marketing a tour could be one purpose, or getting a prospect to consider a hotel's weekend getaway package. An airline might want to announce a few new destinations or schedules. A cruise line could appeal to previous cruise members to get them to repeat. A travel agency may want to make clients aware of a new location, or could do an image piece to show what travel agencies do for people. Local tourist bureaus may want to enthuse their own citizens about features of the community or they may design their mailings for pass-along value to relatives and friends outside the city.

The typical direct-mail package has a letter, a brochure, and a means of responding—like a return postcard or envelope. Some have additional enclosures and some may be just a letter. It depends on what you are trying to accomplish. A tour operator, for example, may direct a mailing to those who used that tour company in the past. Perhaps the mailing will include an introductory letter, a large brochure outlining all their current tour options, plus a return postcard for requesting more information on specific trips. If the recipient had requested this main brochure, he or she would get a different letter, thanking the writer for the interest, and enclosing the proper brochure.

Each project calls for some adjustments in style, but all of them start with the promise of some benefit to the consumer and generally end by repeating this promise while explaining how the reader responds. In between, the copy expands on the benefits to be enjoyed, explains the product or service in detail, and builds in both confidence and persuasion—all in some logical order.

Everyone receives a lot of direct mail. Instead of throwing it away, study it, observe how the presentation is made, how one insert complements another. The best ones not only read well, they look good. The paper is slick, the art attractive, and there is ample color, plus many typographical devices (underlining, italics, boldface, and so on) to emphasize key points. Appearance communicates, too!

If the budget, the list, and your own mailing technique allow for personalizing the message, this can be a plus. Some advertisers overdo this, sticking your name in oversize type in several locales. You know this is phony. But printing is currently sophisticated enough so that a personal salutation may be perfectly blended with a mass-produced letter. If the letter is personalized, then everything in it should reflect the same sort of approach. Don't lose the impact of the individualized salutation by using body copy that is obviously addressed to the mob.

A travel agency could treat its regular client list this way, providing them with letters (plus brochures or newsletters) addressed to them and continuing in a warm and personal way through the body of the letter. It just requires that the writer think as if one individual were receiving the mailing.

There are many tricks to using direct mail effectively. *First,* you have to have the right list. *Second,* you have to be both persistent and consistent. This means that main points may be repeated in the message and also that there will be regular reminder mailings. You rarely get the job done in one shot. *Third,* you should simplify your pitch as much as possible, both in points covered and language used. *Fourth,* you continuously research and evaluate, trying to determine what elements of copy and timing worked best. You test your mailings and see what results they bring in. *Fifth,* you must be ready to act on recipients' requests. If you advertise a brochure, be certain you have plenty on hand. If you prompt phone calls, be sure people are available to answer and that they know what to say. *Sixth,* you must police the list regularly, making certain that all information is accurate, and you must clean the list as least yearly to keep track of our mobile population.

Writers who are able to produce successful direct-mail letters often command big fees, so it, too, is a specialty. These people are not only masters of the written word, they are also technicians who have expertise about what lists might pull best, and what gadgets or gimmicks might be included, and how the envelope might be used to guarantee readership. If you can't afford to bring these professionals aboard, you can still analyze the direct mail you and others receive, you can read up on the subject, and you can chat with people at direct-mail houses.

Like other media, direct mail—which can be expensive—requires that you know what you want to achieve and that you have included in your planning a way to check results against goals.

OTHER FORMS OF ADVERTISING WRITING

For the travel industry, newspapers, direct mail, magazines, radio, and television account for the bulk of advertising copy. Still, there are other ways of reaching a mass audience and these also require some communication skills.

Out-of-Home Media

What outdoor advertising calls for more than any other writing skill is the ability to create catchy headlines and to integrate these with illustrations. Billboards, taxi signs, bus-bench signs, subway posters, and others in this print family are all tailored for short messages and, normally, for quick viewing. Experts say you need to get your point across in three to five words, plus identification. After that, even for pedestrian traffic, the problem of readership declines. For outdoor boards in busy areas, this huge 300-square-foot canvas may appear no larger than a small ad in the Sunday travel section, and you're moving past it far faster than you turn a page. So brevity is the soul of success.

Many outdoor ads rely on word play—puns, double-extendre phrases, unfamiliar language, slang (YOUR HOME AWAY FROM HOME; OUR SUN, THE DOCTOR; COOL, MAN), but the message can also be factual (ROUND TRIP TO D.C. $288).

As with other media, the outdoor advertising should tie into the theme of the overall campaign and not go its own way. Outdoor is especially helpful for reinforcement of other media or for registering a name or idea. Backgrounds, like copy, are best when simple; colors should be bold, type large and readable (avoiding script and Old English, for example), and illustrations, if significant, should be sized accordingly.

Miscellaneous Media

The names and slogans of airlines, cruise lines, travel agencies, and tourist bureaus appear on pens, nail files, calendars, pocket calculators, napkins, coasters, matchbooks, and hundreds of other inventive novelties. The skill here may be more in deciding on the novelty form than in wording the message, but these gadgets can be effective, especially if appropriate and worth retaining. Firms may print schedules of state football giants, or include weights and measures with a calendar. Whatever is done, the gimmick shouldn't obscure the purpose, so sponsor identification is the prime consideration.

On-site signs and displays are common, from exterior marquees to interior ship models, wall maps, display racks, travel posters, exotic souvenirs, and other items. Some call for written communication skills, but most are more influenced by placement and utility. The suppliers who furnish such items to travel agencies, for example, are interested in visibility and use—and sponsor identification. Travel posters, as one genre, are more illustration than copy, but they are popular, both as travel office decor and as collectors' items.

Travel firms make wide use of directories, ranging from the telephone book to tourism guides. Often these are mere mentions or, perhaps, repeats of print ads used in magazines or newspapers. The rationale for advertising in these media is the simple fact that those who use such aids are already conditioned to looking for the appropriate service. Travel agencies, in particular, get a lot of business via the phone book, and so do airlines.

The list continues. Whenever a new medium becomes popular enough to make advertising feasible, someone will figure out a rate card. Perhaps the days of skywriting are passé, but advertising on video cassettes is just beginning to take effect.

PUBLIC RELATIONS AS PROMOTION

Airlines, cruise lines, and tourism bureaus, among others, have public relations divisions; very few travel agencies follow suit. They may argue that they don't need or can't afford a PR staff. However, *every* business has a public relations image. People think well of you, ill of you, or they think nothing at all. Two of these conditions are negatives.

Public relations is a planned *management* function which, aided by research, seeks to understand trends and attitudes and to accommodate the client or firm to these directions through programs of communication and evaluation. It is distinct from advertising and has many facets—media relations, financial relations, special events, counseling, community relations, lobbying, and dozens of other variations. It includes virtually everything that a travel unit can do to build and hold good will.

Some of these aspects will be covered in this and subsequent chapters, while other responsibilities of public relations will receive less attention than they may deserve. The emphasis here is on the communication phase of the profession. This means that the research, planning, and evaluation tasks are no less important but are victims here of space and focus.

Research and Planning

Like all communication skills, public relations starts with a gathering of data, using methods mentioned in Chapter 3, and remaining aware of social conditions and trends as outlined in Chapter 1. Armed with this information, the planning begins, resulting in a recommended course of action. Once this is in place, a determination is made as to what will be communicated, how it will be communicated, and to whom it will be communicated. During this phase and after, evaluation takes place.

Some written forms of communication have already been mentioned, from letters to brochures. These are also part of the public relations posture. For the travel industry, three more communication techniques involve the news release, the feature article, and the corporate newsletter.

THE NEWS RELEASE

For many areas of business, learning to work with the media is a prime consideration. Like all other aspects of public relations, this, too, should be planned. Otherwise, the only time the airline gets coverage is when there is a strike, an accident, or some serious schedule delays. In fact, disasters of various sorts make up a disproportionate share of the news about railroads, coach companies, and cruise lines. Travel agencies seem to surface only when a branch is opened or closed, while tourism bureaus do fairly well with publicity, thanks to a feeling of local responsibility.

This haphazard situation calls for a more organized approach to the media. As a starter, this means having some sense about news and what constitutes news, and having some grasp of the professional means used to convey these stories.

News is really anything that will interest the general public or a segment of that public. Not every news item will have the same impact on different individuals. Travel trade publications, for example, carry many stories on industry changes that have little news value for the layperson. There are readers who are keen on sports and others who devour every column in the society section. Media try to program for all of these groups.

Some subjects are almost always good news copy. Famous people, like Prime Minister Margaret Thatcher or singer/dancer Michael Jackson command headlines, even when they do rather insignificant things, like purchasing a new car. Dramatic stories—like crimes, disasters, romance, and everyday humor—have their following. So do accounts of innovations, like an experimental method of heart surgery, or ones with a twist, like the beauty queen who declines her crown. When information circulated is important, as in the case of threatening weather or income-tax deadlines, people also pay attention.

By its very nature, travel offers a lot of news potential. People are interested in travel and intrigued by it. The christening of a new ship is news and so is the maiden flight of an airline new to a certain locality. Tourism figures are sure things for local consumption, and a travel agency may capitalize on an open house or the certification of counselors. But astute writers don't have to wait around for something to happen. There are news possibilities everywhere.

Let's say national attention is being drawn to the recovery of the dollar abroad. A travel agency could comment on its effect on travel from that area. The results of a survey could be made public. A nation in the news might have been visited recently by a member of your travel staff. How about calling the media and suggesting an interview? Sometimes there are humorous little stories brought back by tour members, or a travel executive might get space or time to list some travel tips at the beginning of summer. All these take is a little imagination.

Well, imagination may spark the idea. After that it takes professional skill to put the news release in the proper context. In communicating with the media, the writer should adhere to the generally accepted format for a news release; be conscious of the deadline demands of the print and electronic media; treat all media equally, playing no favorites; be accurate in facts and in spelling; avoid sending out weak news stories or pure puffery; edit the copy carefully for errors or omissions; and be accessible to the media should there be follow-up questions.

News releases may be hand delivered to the media, mailed (if time permits), or fed from computer to computer. Whatever method is used, they must still arrive in time to make the desired edition or newscast.

Mechanics of the News Release

News releases should be typed, not handwritten, and on a decent weight white paper. Copy should be double-spaced, with margins of about one and one-half inches. Duplicate copies to various media should *not* be carbons, but can be mimeographed or the products of a copier machine. Carbons are taboo because the recipient wonders who got the original—emphasizing the need to treat all media alike. A company letterhead will do, or a special news release form, or just a plain sheet of white paper. Color stock should be avoided, along with garish mastheads announcing that this is a NEWS RE-LEASE!!! Keep the look and content professional.

Here are some other requirements:

Indicate the Source.   The editors and news directors must know the origin of the story, so the writer of the news release should put his/her name, address, and phone number on the release—usually in the upper left-hand corner, but sometimes on the bottom. If the company name does not appear elsewhere, then it should also be included. Many publicists also list their home phone numbers, so that reporters and editors may reach them after office hours, if necessary.

Indicate Release Instructions.   In most instances, the story will be for immediate release, meaning the medium may put it on the air or in the paper as soon as possible. Sometimes there may be a reason for specifying a certain date and time of release. Maybe you are announcing a new program to employees and you want them to hear it from their boss before seeing it in the news. However, you also need to get the release around to the media, so you put a release time on it that has it issued after or during the employee meeting.

The release instructions appear several spaces below the name, address, and phone, and are usually in capital letters and under-lined. For example, FOR IMMEDIATE RELEASE or HOLD FOR RELEASE FOR TUESDAY, JUNE 6, AFTER 3 P.M.

Unless there is a compelling reason, it's always wiser to mark the story FOR IMMEDIATE RELEASE, since other instructions may go unnoticed anyway and cause the story to be prematurely released. Or the story kept around too long could get lost in a busy newsroom.

May Suggest a Headline.   Daily newspapers and most magazines prefer to write their own headlines. This is partially style and par-tially for space reasons. However, smaller papers may appreciate having a suggested headline. So fit the headline to the medium, and, if you're not good at writing headlines, forget them for any medium. Between the release information and the body of the story, there

should be a space of about two inches. This remains blank if there is no headline, or, if a headline is suggested, it goes in this space.
Date the Release.   This is the date the story is being released. It may appear (month, day, year) right after the name, address, and phone number of the writer, or it may appear at the end of the story. The most professional way to include it, however, is right at the start of the copy, combining the date of the release with the site of the release, thus: (FILLMORE, MN, May 11, 1989). The locale used should be the place from which the story originates and not necessarily the location of the writer's office. This line is called the "dateline" and precedes the story's lead sentence.

When dates appear within a story, it's prudent to spell out the entire date (". . . on Thursday, June 11 . . .") rather than just the day (". . . on Thursday . . ."). This avoids confusion.
Use a Journalistic Style of Writing.   Journalistic style is a factual style, tightly written, using short sentences and frequent paragraphs, leaving nothing important out, and avoiding any cute phrasing that reads more like an ad.

There are other ways to write a news release, but the *inverted pyramid* format is still the most common. In this style, the key facts are up front, generally in the first paragraph, and sometimes in the lead sentence. These salient facts include the so-called 5 *W*'s—the *who, what, where, when,* and *why*—plus, on occasion, the *how* of the event.

Following this data, the news story evolves logically, adding less vital details. Paragraphs, which usually run no more than four or five sentences, are indented about eight spaces, and the language used is as uncomplicated as possible. If some technical terms are included, they should be explained. The structure of sentences and paragraphs is varied to avoid monotony.
Localize, When Possible.   A local angle is always welcome. A person in Detroit isn't that interested in a new hotel being built in New Orleans, but would be interested if the same chain located in Detroit. Even when the main thrust is elsewhere, tap any local ties.
Use the Proper Numbers and Symbols.   While it remains true that news releases should be confined to a single page, if possible, the nature of some stories requires more space. News releases should be as short as they can be and as long as they must be. When additional pages are added, there is a preferred system for numbering. Pages to be continued have "—more—" typed at the bottom of the sheet(s) and subsequent pages are designated in one of several ways:

Story ident (like "new hotel")—2

or

new hotel—2-2-2-2

or

new hotel—Add 1 (which means this is Page 2)

or

new hotel—Take 1

(Page 2 is rarely used for news releases. It is more of a feature story or book device).

When the writer reaches the conclusion of the release, one of the following is typed:

—END—

or

####

or

—30—

The last choice, an old telegrapher's sign-off symbol, is most common.

Indicate Additional Information or Enclosures.   If photos or maps or exhibits are attached to a release, mention this at the bottom of the final page of the release: PHOTO ENCLOSED. If you want to add details for the media, like the arrival and departure schedule of a guest or the fact that media are invited to a news conference, this, too, appears at the bottom of the final page.

News Releases for Radio and Television

Because the electronic media rely wholly or partly on sound, and because both radio and television demand much shorter stories, different news releases should be written for these media. While this is not often done (meaning that the radio and TV newsrooms have to rewrite the stories), it should be considered for every release.

Besides condensing the message, the news release for these media should be conscious of the audio requirements. The language should be easy to read and easy to understand, and difficult words should be provided with phonetic spellings. Since listeners can't see quotation marks, announcers should always make it clear that a person is being quoted.

For a visual medium like television, some pictures need to be provided. You see few still shots anymore, except where tape or film is not available. Television news directors may send a crew to cover significant events and travel units sometimes provide their own tape. Even travel agencies may offer visuals from their files or from supplier sources. For radio, *actualities,* audio tapes of newsmakers, may be part of the release package.

Here are examples of a print release and a radio release:

frank warren
warren tours inc.
114 warwick street
tucson, AZ 26778
(602) 294-9404
(602) 303-5444 (H)

FOR IMMEDIATE RELEASE

Tucson, AZ (March 4, 1989)—Named today to head a new division of governmental travel for Warren Tours (114 Warwick Street) was Barbara Cowdin, a veteran employee of the Tucson travel firm.

In announcing the appointment, Warren Tours president, Frank Warren, noted the recent growth in government travel.

"Since 1986, when restrictions on bidding on government travel were partially lifted, our agency has added several federal accounts," said Warren. "Government travel now makes up a third of our volume."

Among the agency's government clients are Johansen Air

Force Base, the headquarters of the Ninth Army, and postal units in Arizona, New Mexico, and Colorado.

Ms. Cowdin has been with Warren Tours since 1978 and is currently a vice president with the firm. Prior to 1978, Ms. Cowdin, a graduate of Arizona State University, worked for Anderson Cruise Lines and for a Phoenix travel agency.

The appointment takes effect immediately and will include management of existing government accounts as well as solicitation of future accounts.

—30—

(radio release)

frank warren
warren tours, inc.
114 warwick street
tucson, AZ 26778
(602) 294-9404
(602) 303-5444 (H)

FOR IMMEDIATE RELEASE

Tucson, AZ (March 4, 1989)—Citing the recent growth in government travel as a reason, Frank Warren of Warren Tours, a Tucson travel agency, announced today the addition of a new governmental travel division to be headed by Barbara Cowdin (COW-DUN), a veteran travel consultant.

Cowdin will manage existing government accounts, which

make up a third of the agency's business, and will also prospect

for new accounts.

—30—

News releases for television could also be in this form, with accompanying visuals, or, in some cases, they might use the TV dual-column style mentioned earlier. More and more, however, news releases for television are an attempt to get their news departments to cover the scene.

The News Conference

There are times when a story has sufficient importance and enough visual impact to warrant the calling of a news conference. This tactic should be used sparingly. Reporters are busy people and must allocate their time wisely. They don't appreciate being summoned to attend a news conference where the content is of marginal or little interest. A good rule to live by is not to call a news conference if you can effectively disseminate the news any other way.

If you do set up a news conference, select an appropriate day and time, when a majority of the local (or national) media can comfortably make deadlines. Keep it short, businesslike, and open. Have on hand any visuals or handouts that may help the media, including sample news releases and pertinent fact sheets or biographies. Attention should also be paid to the site of the conference, making certain it has sufficient room, adjacent parking, enough outlets for the electronic media, and an ambience to fit the occasion. It could be an office, a hotel meeting room, an airport lounge.

Media can be invited by letter or phone, and a reminder phone call the day before is a prudent idea. Everyone who has a legitimate interest in the story should be invited, including, occasionally, college newspaper editors or editors of company publications. The presentation should be compact and time for questions incorporated.

Some larger travel firms may have reason to conduct simultaneous news conferences in a number of cities. This is more complicated but can be managed via phone or satellite hookup. Again, it would require a very special occasion to justify the cost and work involved.

Photography

Whenever visual material accompanies a news release, the same sort of professionalism expected of the copy should be present. Don't

Figure 5–7.   Wise managers accompany the photographer to make sure the results are what you had in mind.

supply the media with amateur photos, tape, or film. Hire a photographer or cameraperson, Figure 5–7. Newspapers like photos with good subject matter, with strong black and white contrast (as against the art*y*, grainy look), and ones that tell a story or support a story. Persons shown should be identified, reading left to right, and this information, plus caption, should be affixed to the photo.

When mailing the photo, cardboard backing should be included in the envelope and the outside marked or stamped with the caution: PHOTOGRAPH: DO NOT BEND. Slides may be mailed in plastic sleeves or sheets, also protected by cardboard.

There are books and courses on photography that can help the individual, but it remains true that, if good pictures help sell a story, bad pictures detract from its marketability.

Miscellaneous Publicity Tips

❑ Don't try to push a weak story on an editor, and don't ever use your friendship with a friend in the media to argue for publication. At the same time, you should never complain about an editor not using your news release—although you should mention any inaccuracies caused by the media in printing or airing the piece.

❏ Don't nag editors about when they plan to use a story and don't send along multiple versions of the same news on successive days.

❏ Cooperate with the media when they seek further details or want to set up an interview with company executives.

❏ In cases where only one publication or medium is getting a story, mark that FOR SPECIAL RELEASE TO _____, but do this only when there is a special angle—like a piece in a trade journal.

❏ Consider the use of special syndicated services to deliver expanded coverage of news releases, and consider a clipping service to keep track of news-release utilization.

❏ Think of other ways in which published stories might be used—as promotional pieces to branches or suppliers, for example.

THE FEATURE ARTICLE

Feature articles are a mainstay of the travel industry. For writers, they offer a chance to expand, describe, and dramatize. Readers find them more informative and entertaining and, because they are often saved, they have an added permanancy, Figure 5–8.

Feature articles appear in travel sections of newspapers, in a variety of magazines, in books, and even as the basis of documentary films. Many are the work of staff or free-lance writers, but others may come from those employed in the travel field, especially in company publications.

Feature articles are not fiction. They rely for their strength on the same reportorial skills found in news items. They are simply longer, more detailed, possessing a different focus other than communicating straight news. Feature articles allow the writer more freedom in style and content and they give the writer an opportunity to develop a point more fully.

In the travel industry, as in other fields, ideas for feature stories come from the experience of yourself and others, from reading, from a curiosity that requires satisfaction, and from an imagination that sees potential in ordinary events. Some topics are always popular— health, lifestyles, wealth, mystery, entertainment, and love, with other subjects, from sports to the arts, having their devotees. Travel cuts across many of these themes, just as it cuts across features listed by type.

There are personality profiles, expanded news, how-to pieces, analyses of problems, exposés, informative articles, and many more.

Right: O'Connell Street after dark. The broad boulevard runs through downtown Dublin.
Below: Dublin's Viking heritage is recalled in a pub sign.
Bottom: Christ Church Cathedral is one of the Irish capital's notable buildings. Strongbow, the Norman invader, is buried here in his armor.

1,000 Green Candles For Dublin

By Robert T. Reilly
The author lives in Omaha

SOME CRITICS refer to Dublin as a city surrounded by Ireland, meaning it bears little resemblance to the thatched roof-turf bog images of the republic. Other observers find Dublin "dirty" or "dull," comparing it unfavorably to various capitals.

They're wrong.

Dublin has a character, a presence, of its own — but only if you prefer history and literature to restaurants and night life, only if you opt for humor over haute couture. Paris regards strangers with an aristocratic eye; London floods your path with relic-conscious tourists. Dublin is awkward, comfortable, like a class reunion in Des Moines.

It has its own smells — double-decker exhausts, fish and chips, snatches of turf smoke, the dark reek of Guiness, coffee aromas from Bewley's on Grafton Street, the sometime tang of the nearby sea.

Dublin's look also is singular. The horseshoe bay thrusts the city against its soft hills, some newly forested with geometric glades of beech, chestnut, sycamore and spruce. Buildings wedged against one another flank the River Liffey, that green and turgid stream more perfect in prose than reality.

Around Saint Stephens Green stand the Georgian cul de sacs with ornate transomed portals and glistening door knockers. The row houses evoke for me the memories of the Massachusetts town where I was born.

Writing in Life magazine many years ago, Shana Alexander traced her love for Dublin to its echoes of an earlier America, the America of her youth. Perhaps that resonance isn't as strong for a Midwesterner, but Dublin does bring back East Coast memories from the '30s and '40s.

While there are video games and rock concerts and credit cards, there are many pockets of Dublin where time stood still. Walking into the downtown Pro-Cathedral takes me back to Sunday Mass in Lowell, Mass., with our Irish pastor parading the aisles during the singing, urging volume.

Sunday World-Herald Magazine of the Midlands, March 13, 1988

Figure 5–8. Travel features try to place the reader on the scene.

All have a travel dimension. Profiles of people in the travel industry, for example, or features on how to pack for a trip, or articles on the best times of year to visit certain cities.

Everything that has been said about research and about knowing your audience applies here. Self-interest is the key to gaining readership, and a solid grounding in fact is the way to sustain interest and produce credibility.

The Lead

Unlike straight news stories, feature articles rely on catchy leads, on some sort of hook to pull the reader into the story. Headlines and illustrations may help, but good writers spend a lot of time crafting that opening sentence. There are numerous ways to approach the lead.

❑ A *summary lead,* which capsulizes the article, giving the reader a notion of what's coming. When the whole article idea is intriguing, this is an effective technique.
"Presidents of cruise lines worldwide are happy with the upturn in passengers, but they still worry that nine out of ten Americans have never taken a cruise and they wonder why this reticence occurs."

❑ A *narrative lead,* which tells a story.
"I crossed the small bridge, the railing still warped and delicate, and could smell the Alpine wildflowers before I could see them."

❑ The *descriptive lead* sets the scene or creates a mood. Good travel writing conjures up these images.
"Even in darkness the wave stole noisily toward the shore, and the shrouded moon revealed the ragged peninsula circling to the right, and, just before it, a man was breaking his horse in the surf, using the ancient way."

❑ *Quotations* suffice as leads, but they should be meaningful and not merely decorative, and they shouldn't be overused.
" 'I've lost my passport,' the young woman told me, fear in her eyes."

❑ A *question* often gets the reader thinking.
"Why do the roosters crow with the changing of the tides, I wondered?"

or

"Are you one of those Americans who's never taken a bus tour?"

❑ Some writers use a form of *direct address* to involve the reader.
"You may think you've tasted ice cream, but you really don't know what ice cream is until you've sampled Glennie's in Saugus."

❑ There are *gimmick* and *teaser* leads, ones that arouse curiosity. They could be poems or puzzles or puns or riddles or merely something provocative.
"*Cead mille failte* yourself, I thought. With your fake accent!"

or

"Want to know about the least-visited bathing beach in England?"

The Rest of the Story

Once launched, the feature story should flow smoothly, retaining the reader's interest and compelling him or her to read along. Colorful description helps, and so do amusing and enlightening quotes, and, especially, anecdotes. You don't merely present a series of events or ideas; you witness people acting them out. You are placed on the scene and you hear the dialogue and experience the action. All the senses come into play for the writer and for the reader.

> Those who named Ireland "The Green Isle" and "The Emerald Isle" didn't overstate the case. When the mists have lifted and the quaint villages fade and the castle ruins are forgotten, it is a memory of green that remains. Despite advertising and photography, the traveler is still startled by the richness of the landscape itself. On a single hill one might glimpse green the color of early apples, or ripe olives or aging moss—all interlaced like tweed, with low rock walls for seams. Here and there some yellow furze, or red holly berries, blackthorn hedges or golden stacks of wheat, or a tree twisted in the Atlantic wind. Even in the rain Ireland is a beautiful country and, when the sun follows rain, it sparkles as if newly minted.

> With the growth of senior citizens as a demographic unit, motorcoach travel has received a fresh impetus. Ease and economy of travel appeal to this age group.
> "I like the idea that I'm not really that far from home," explains Judy Newton of Hartford, Connecticut, who just returned from a trip by motorcoach to Williamsburg. "We were gone only three days and all details were handled by someone else."
> Short, inexpensive weekend tours are also gaining popularity with travel agents whose eyes have been on the more traditional cruise and air packages.

Even talented writers often have trouble ending a feature story. They get overly cute, or dramatic or, perhaps, they just stop rather than properly tying up the work.

The ending may return the reader to the beginning, book-ending the article neatly, confirming or resolving the opening statement, or answering the question that was posed. The story's conclusion might also summarize the piece or provide a twist or surprise, like a short story. Sometimes, the feature writer may leave things up in the air, the way the Italian films used to do. This latter technique is intended to make the reader think a little more.

Some additional feature suggestions:

❑ *Don't waste time looking for the perfect story.* There are many good travel tales to tell, and even weaker ideas can be enhanced by an appealing style.

❏ *Always have paper and pen handy.* You never know when you'll hear a good quote or get a marketable idea. Since inspiration fades fast, the writer should have a ready way to capture it.

❏ *Prime your imagination* by traveling, or reading, or visiting with others. Stay in touch with the topic.

❏ *Keep idea files* and rework them occasionally.

❏ *Consider sidebars and other attention-getting devices.* Sidebars are short items that extend the theme of the main article, even though they might not fit within the context of the original. A short biography of a person mentioned in the feature might be a sidebar, or a set of facts tied to the article topic.

❏ *Rewrite.*

Interviewing

Many features have their origin or derive their strength from interviews, so the able writer is also a skilled interviewer. Each interview is somewhat different than those that preceded it, but experience does help the interviewer get the most out of the encounter.

First, the writer should set a time for the interview, a time that is convenient for all parties, and one that allows for the eventual deadline. Once set, this time should become a duty and the writer has to be there as promised. If uncertain of the locale of the interview, take a test drive earlier to insure you are not late.

Before arriving for the interview, the writer should have researched the topic and individual(s), to be able to frame questions and to respond intelligently to the dialogue. This research may be in the form of reading or it could involve conversations with others. Preparation also includes practice with the tape recorder, if you use one. You must know how it works and you must have a long enough tape for the session. There should be no embarrassing delays for mechanical failures or confusion.

During the interview, the writer must listen, speaking only to ask questions, extend a topic, request clarification, or to keep the dialogue flowing. The writer is there to learn and not to expound. At the same time, the interviewer should not feel bound by some rigid set of questions prepared in advance. Interviewing requires flexibility. If something unforeseen but interesting is introduced by the subject, then the writer should follow this new path to see where it leads.

The interviewer should ask the questions that readers might ask if they had this opportunity. This means having a sense of the reading public, and it means being thoughtful and incisive with questions. Sidestep arguments but push for deeply felt opinions. During the questioning, the interviewer may also be noting mannerisms of the interviewee, plus surroundings and other external factors, in case these details are needed later to produce a concept of place and action. Comments that are not understood completely should be queried and clarified, and the writer should keep an ear open for good quotes and for possible leads.

Once the interview is concluded, it's smart to write the story as soon as possible, while the experience is fresh. Especially when the chat is taped, the whole conversation may get cold. During this stage, the writer can also check facts, spelling, and other items. It's not a bad idea to send a thank-you note to the subject, expressing appreciation for the time allotted.

THE COMPANY NEWSLETTER/MAGAZINE

The interview is certainly the mainstay of the company newsletter or magazine. Most of these publications are short-staffed and have to rely on information being funneled in from voluntary sources. The editor or reporter undoubtedly interviews various executives in order to get details for company stories, but may also interview others for profiles or for news of lesser significance.

Corporate publications should have definite goals. Is this printed piece intended to communicate management policy, or is it primarily a morale booster for employees? Even when the purpose is to transmit executive decisions, the copy should be free of obvious propaganda. Your first responsibility as editor is to get employees to read the publication, so it has to be couched in their terms and their language. Otherwise, even the most urgent CEO message will not be received.

Periodic readership checks should be conducted to make certain both content and vocabulary are appropriate to the audience. Editors may also experiment with entertainment features—crossword puzzles, quizzes, cartoons, and other ways to involve readers. Some magazines and newsletters also offer classified ads and print letters to the editors. These may not be essential, but they convince the employee to turn the pages where, hopefully, the key information will also be noticed.

More and more corporate publications are being shared by an external audience. If this is the case, the content may change, eliminating the inside-only cant to the copy. This is risky, however, since you could lose the closest readers. If possible, there should be different publications for different groups.

Company communications come in a variety of formats and price ranges. Some are simple desktop publications; some are miniature newspapers, generally tabloids; some are large and lavish four-color productions. Regardless of the look, the aim of the writers should always be to address the intended audience in a language they understand, but size and budget do make a difference.

A small travel agency, for example, may make do with occasional memos and regular meetings, while large hotel chains, faced with the need to reach geographically scattered staff members, require a more formidable publication. Even the small travel agency, however, may issue a more impressive newsletter, monthly or quarterly, to its client list.

One overriding factor should be considered. Nothing should be published that reflects poorly on the travel firm. Often, the expenditure of just a few dollars more can turn an unacceptable printed piece into a modest success.

CHAPTER HIGHLIGHTS

❏ Marketing includes product, price, place, and promotion, and both advertising and public relations come under the latter heading.

❏ Advertising, a paid form of mass-media communication aimed at influencing the purchase of goods and services, is not simply being clever; it's reaching the right audience with the right message.

❏ Advertising copywriters must understand consumer psychology and trends, and must also understand that all media have their plus and minus factors.

❏ If travel firms cannot afford professional assistance, the ad writer has to study a new style, based on the AIDCA formula (Attention, Interest, Desire, Credibility, Action).

❏ Headlines, illustrations, body copy, and signature make up the print ad, although all may not be present in every ad.

❏ Radio is written for the ear, while television scripts should emphasize the visual.

❏ Direct mail, second in popularity to newspapers for travel firms, considers selectivity its greatest asset.

❏ Writing for outdoor media demands short, catchy prose and large illustrations.

❏ Publicity is merely one facet of public relations, which is described as a management function, based on research and planning, that analyzes trends and data, and counsels clients on ways to adapt their conduct to today's (and tomorrow's) culture. The work of PR also includes communication and evaluation.

❑ The news release has a specific format and must be written in a professional way. News releases for print and for the electronic media differ, with the latter being shorter and more attuned to the listener.

❑ The feature article is a popular fixture in travel circles and relies on good interviewing techniques and strong descriptive skills.

❑ Internal/external publications must fit budget demands and reader needs.

■   ■   ■

❑ EXERCISES

1. Bring to class two print ads for the same field (cruise lines, airlines, hotels, and so on) but not necessarily the same firm, one of which is aimed at consumers and the other of which is aimed at professionals within the industry.

2. Select a print advertisement for any travel service and write a radio or television spot (thirty seconds long) based on this ad, making any appropriate adjustments but without changing the essential message of the print ad.

3. Pick up a tour brochure at a travel firm and write a news release announcing this tour. Make sure you have included all the facts and that you abide by the mechanical requirements of a news release.

❑ CASE PROBLEMS

1. You are a regular and somewhat substantial advertiser in your local newspaper. Occasionally, you send the editor of this metropolitan daily a news release. Out of the last four releases you sent, only one was used and that was cut. You're thinking about calling and reminding the editor how much you spend annually with that paper. Is this a good idea? If not, what should you do?

2. *You're the advertising manager for a New York City chain of six hotels and you plan to buy some forty outdoor boards strategically located around Manhattan. The representative for the outdoor advertising firm brings you a street map of the city with the proposed locations marked in red. Is this good enough for you to agree to these sites, or should you do something more?*

VERBAL COMMUNICATION

While the written word is a vital part of the travel business, the spoken word is far more common. It exists at a formal level—as with speeches—and an informal level—in daily conversation with employees and clients. The profession doesn't demand that you be an orator, but the ability to project ideas to individuals, small groups, and larger audiences helps considerably, Figure 6–1.

THE SPEECH

College and high school graduates can remember with a certain amount of pain their first required speech. Facing their peers was worse than a trip to the dentist. Few realized the value of the course until years later. As adults they learned that success often goes to the person who can articulate ideas, even though the ideas themselves may not be strikingly original.

In travel, the demands placed on individuals will vary. Executives field more speech requests than agency consultants or in-house staff members, but, on occasion, everyone may be asked to talk. A luncheon club wants to know more about travel; a university class requests a guest speaker; a professional meeting presents an opportunity. Sometimes the preparation time is curtailed, so knowing how to write and deliver a good speech is a great asset.

Before the Speech

Those who have a gift for public speaking may not want to merely wait for an invitation to appear somewhere; they may wish to trigger the request from an organization. Letters to local groups mentioning availability, topics, and background will produce leads. If you're really into this, then a brochure can be prepared citing the important facts. Word of mouth also produces leads. Good speakers get ample opportunity to perform.

Since travel sales depend to a considerable extent upon recogni-

Figure 6–1.   The ability to present a subject effectively is a valuable skill. (Courtesy Bill Ramsey Associates)

tion and respect, it pays to get around. Delivering an interesting . talk provides both familiarity and an opportunity to dispense information.

Each speaker should have an up-to-date biographical sketch and photo. The bio should be of reasonable length, written as tightly as possible, and containing only essential details. Date and place of birth should be included, plus education, military history, job experience, marriage and family, honors and awards, accomplishments (like articles written), travel background (places visited, tours led), public service and professional activities, extracurricular activities, and, perhaps, languages spoken. The bio sheets may also refer readers to other sources, like *Who's Who* volumes.

Because casual emcees may neglect to review the biography in advance and then just read the long version, speakers often supply a shorter version for introduction purposes. This should be confined to less than a page, whereas the longer "vita" may occupy three to four pages.

Sometimes, too, when the topic is specialized, the speaker may want to add material not usually contained in the biography. If the subject happens to be the South Pacific, for example, the speaker may wish to include mention of military service in that theatre, plus a record of tours led to that region, along with other proofs of expertise.

If there is an accompanying photo of the speaker, it must be recent. Pictures taken twenty years earlier appear deceptive.

Speech Titles

Speech titles should accurately describe the material presented and they should have audience appeal. The latter consideration is the more important.

Rather than title an appearance as a "Slide Program on Australia," why not say, "Touring the Land of Crocodile Dundee"? Use a little imagination and create a bit of excitement. Think in terms of newspaper and ad headlines and envision the speech title on a marquee. Would your choice arouse interest?

Occasionally, an organization will request a speech title long before you have had a chance to construct the speech. In these cases, it's wise to have a generic—but catchy—title handy. Like "Words from a Weary Traveler."

It's normally up to the sponsoring organization to promote the talk, but, if it doesn't conflict with their plans, a speaker may also do a little promotion, notifying friends, alerting columnists locally, posting notices in his/her own office area.

Researching the Speech

Gathering information on a speech topic is like digging up information on any topic. One's personal library may suffice, plus the public or college libraries, plus trade journals and cassettes and personal interviews.

Every speechwriter and speechmaker should have a small personal library containing such items as a good dictionary, a thesaurus, a book of quotations (Bartlett, Oxford, Peters), a standard grammar book (Strunk & White is handy, inexpensive, and popular), handbooks on humor, fact books and almanacs, atlases, encyclopedias (perhaps the one-volume Columbia edition), and even more unusual items like foreign dictionaries, books on slang and contemporary usage, and guide books to other nations. There are collections of travel writings and texts covering many aspects of the industry. All of these can be helpful.

Many speechwriters also retain copies of their speeches, as well as copies of other speeches they've admired. You request the latter from those who deliver or publish them, or you clip them from a variety of sources.

Speechwriters may also husband other helpful documents, from magazine articles to annual reports. You can't let this paper take over your files, but, on the other hand, you never know when something will prove useful. It's comforting to have a system that easily recalls a fact or a phrase, without you ever leaving your office or den.

Some of this material can be committed to disks for storage and later computer retrieval, and programs that satisfy some speakers' needs are also available.

Special Resources

Newsletters, reprints, indices, courses, workshops, and other speech services are pretty accessible.

Speechwriters Newsletter, a weekly compendium of speech excerpts, specific tips, and other pragmatic items is a major source for the professional speechwriter.

The Speech Teacher is another publication with basic speech materials, and *Communication Education* and the *Quarterly Journal of Speech* sometimes have articles dealing with speechmaking as well as speech theory. There are also journals published by state speech societies, at least half a dozen major scholarly publications relating to speech communication, and there is, of course, *Vital Speeches of Today,* a collection of the best current speeches.

There is no shortage of books on speech. Some are very technical and are of primary interest to scholars, but many are practical guides to speech improvement. A few that the occasional speaker may find useful are:

Principles and Types of Speech Communication, by Ehninger, Gronbeck, McKerrow and Monroe, Scott Foresman and Co.

Conversationally Speaking, by Alan Garner, McGraw-Hill

The Art of Public Speaking, by Stephen E. Lucas, Random House

Confidence in Public Speaking, by Nelson and Pearson, William C. Brown

Speak Easy, by Peterson, White, and Stephan, West Publishing

Oral Communication: Message and Response, by Samovar and Mills, William C. Brown

One should also be aware of publications issued by organizations like Toastmasters, plus pamphlets produced by corporations and organizations, and should be alert to seminars and classes that emphasize aspects of public speaking that satisfy certain demands.

Preparing for the Engagement

Every speech presents a different set of problems. It makes a difference whether or not this is a new speech on a new topic, or whether it is a rehash of one of your old speeches.

If you plan to reuse an existing speech with a few updates and some local anecdotal material, you'll spend more time getting familiar with the situation and audience than you will in the library. If the speech is new, and technical, the heavy commitment comes at the outset, involving both research and interviews. You have to decide. However, it's really foolish for someone in the travel industry to agree to a topic about which the speaker has little direct knowledge.

Always gather more material than you'll need. It's far easier to discard than to pad. Subtractions may be the result of time restraints, repetition, local taboos, inappropriateness, or incompatibility with the rest of the talk. Cut those lines that merely clutter the address, but retain items that are essential in terms of information, color, humor, or emotional impact.

Different speakers pull their materials together in different ways. Some employ 3×5 cards, some typed sheets (sometimes using oversized letters) in plastic binders, some use a form of teleprompter or cue cards, and some tie their remarks to visual cues on slides or overheads. To do any of these things sensibly requires a careful outline, so that thoughts may be intelligently organized. The key is to find something that works for the individual. Many speakers like to work directly from a complete text, for example, while colleagues feel comfortable with a list of cue words or phrases.

Defining the Audience

You have to know your audience. If you are invited to address a group of fourth graders on the romance of travel, that's an entirely different assignment than explaining about job opportunities in travel to college seniors. The nature of the audience dictates things like vocabulary, length, emphasis, and other speech features. The toughest audience is one that contains a mixture of people, ranging in age from toddlers to senior citizens, representing several income and interest levels.

The size of an audience is also important. Speaking to ten people is a different task than speaking to a couple of hundred, Figure 6–2. Each affects delivery, content and even the emotional level of the speaker.

If there are special considerations, like occupation or allegiance to a specific church or political party, these must be factored in. So must the site of the talk. Some rooms challenge the speaker because of their size, their acoustics, or their architectural layout.

What all of these cautions suggest is that the speaker do a little advance work, gleaning as much as possible about attendance from the chairperson or from calls to group members and, if possible, visiting the lecture hall. If this latter tour is not possible, allow sufficient time the day of the talk to get a preview of the facility and the public address system.

Once armed with these facts, the speaker should think through the presentation, envisioning the audience in place. What sort of expectations do they have? What sort of questions might they ask? What sort of visual aids will work? How should I vary the content?

The job isn't over. Even though you have categorized the audience and site in advance, there could be surprises. The wary speaker

Figure 6–2.   The facility, the size and nature of the audience, and other factors affect all performances. (Courtesy Bill Ramsey Associates)

should remain alert. Perhaps too long a cocktail hour precedes the event and you must deal with a more raucous set of listeners. Maybe some negative occurrence, like the shutting down of a plant or the death of a popular organization member, happened recently. The air conditioning could break down or the speaking system malfunction. Perhaps the meal was poor, or the program too long.

You can't anticipate everything, but you should visit with people prior to the talk, getting a line on their backgrounds, remaining attuned to clues that dictate what should or should not be said.

Once the speech is underway, you focus on a few people in the audience and try to read their reactions. There is a chemistry that exists between speaker and audience and the practiced speaker immediately picks up on interruptions in this chemistry. You *feel* a negative response to a comment, or you see evidence in the faces of listeners that tells you to desist, to cut things short, or to expand on a certain point. You know when an audience doesn't understand, or when you've told a joke that jars, or when they've heard that story before from another source, or when they feel patronized.

It's difficult to explain just *how* you know, but the professional does. Perhaps you can see the eyeballs glaze over when you start into a too familiar anecdote, or you witness the frowns and shifting when you touch on a delicate topic. You may hear a soft muttering, indicating approval or disapproval.

Any fool can tell people are getting tired of the remarks when a majority begin to consult their watches, or even shake them. Yet there is more subtle body language that provides similiar clues. Check them out. Did you mispronounce Reykjavik? Are you covering the same ground as a previous speaker you didn't hear? Have you said something embarrassing to some listeners? Regroup. Ad lib. Shift. Even a confession of your dilemma will probably work.

Although travel staffers should try to avoid such situations, you may also be confronted by hecklers, hostility, noisy drunks, inattentive chatter, and other distractions. The worst thing to do is to try to ignore these rude acts. Normally, you have to deal with them — or someone has to deal with them. No dissident individual or group should be allowed to dominate a meeting.

WRITING THE SPEECH

This chapter assumes you are writing the speech for yourself, but there could also be occasions when you write for another person. In these instances, you must be familiar with the speaker and with what he or she can handle. There's no sense in crafting an emotional oration if the proposed speaker isn't capable of this style. You need to know how the speaker deals with humor, with pronunciation, and you must have an idea of the way the speaker thinks and talks. It may take several meetings and several drafts before you reach a comfort level, but this exercise is necessary.

In writing a speech, for yourself or others, you should find a place where you can compose with a minimum of interruption. Some discover this milieu at their own desks and others may want to relax somewhere in the shade with a notepad. You have to be able to concentrate. Of course, if you compose on a typewriter or word processor, your mobility is limited.

Outlining

Any written work of any appreciable length can benefit from outlining. This plan sets up the route for you to travel and all you have to do is flesh out the details.

Here's how.

Decide on the General Purpose of Your Speech.   Do you propose to inform the audience, entertain them, or persuade them? Is this a lecture to a class, a luncheon talk, or a sales pitch to tour prospects? STATE YOUR PURPOSE IN WRITING.

Determine What the General Subject Will Be.   Suppose your purpose is to inform travel agency staff members on the proper methods of tour management. That could be the general subject. Or you might be somewhat more specific, but still broad, by selecting "Profiles of Tour Members" as a general topic. WRITE THIS DOWN.

State Your Specific Subject.   Staying with the tour theme, you might approach this by citing several case histories, or tracing the growth of tourism since the Grand Tour days, or you might discuss with listeners the way to deal with troublesome tour members, or you could compare American tourists with travelers from other countries. This is where you narrow the focus. STATE YOUR SPECIFIC SUBJECT HEADING.

Combine the First and Third Categories, Your Specific Subject and Your Specific Purpose.   To inform people about the growth of tourism. To entertain an audience with tales of tour member problems. To persuade people to represent their country better. SET THIS DOWN, TOO.

Write Out Your Central Idea.   This is the one notion you want to implant, the single most important idea you hope the listener takes away. It may be the concept that tourists are really ambassadors for America and should behave responsibly. It could be instilling the conviction that tourism is a major industry for the United States.

List the Main Points Springing From the Central Notion.
Give them a numerical order. In the "ambassador" example, you might make separate points of:

- [ ] Statistics on American travel
- [ ] List of complaints about American tour members
- [ ] Case histories
- [ ] Defense of this behavior and American complaints
- [ ] Suggestions for reform

Develop Each of These Points with Subheads. Thus:
- [ ] Statistics on American travel
  a. Number of foreign tours taken each year by Americans
  b. Most popular destinations
  c. Profile of the typical tour member
  d. Length of stay and details of accommodations, money spent, language abilities, and so on.

This is merely a way to add thoughts to the main thought, making it simpler to fill in the areas when you come to writing out the speech in its entirety.

Ordinarily, the main point is written out in a complete sentence, while the supporting points are clauses, phrases, incomplete sentences. Some speakers like to work from this outline alone.

Develop the Conclusion.   A call to action, perhaps? A final illustrative anecdote? An appropriate quote? A summary or convincing argument?

You can state this in outline form, if you wish. For example: "Conclude by showing listeners that international reputation is largely dependent on the impressions created by thousands of visitors, and that failure to project a positive image detracts from America's posture abroad. Spell out ways to improve tourist conduct."

Work on the Transitions.   The transitions are the sentences that smoothly link various elements of the speech. The audience should have a sense of orderly progression, which may be supplied mechanically, by using numerical prefixes for successive ideas, or saying "next," or using other connectives. While adequate, these grammatical forms are not too interesting. A more effective and subtle way to supply transitions is by obvious content relationships. The listener easily understands how you got from Point A to Point B because the sense of the message makes the connection.

Develop the Introduction.   Even though this will come first, it's normally written last. Now that you know where you're going and how you'll get there, you can write a beginning that properly introduces your remarks.

Reassemble the Outline in Proper Order.   Begin with the introduction, move to the first main point and the supporting points under it, then a transition to the second main point and its attendant subheads, another transition, the third point, and so on, until you reach the conclusion.

Once the outline is complete, you can begin writing the speech to the outline, fleshing out each point and subpoint. You build on the framework.

Beginning and Ending

Start your speech with something that will attract audience attention or win them over to you. Humor is fine, if you can handle it, but it's only one alternative. People who can't tell jokes well should not try. Humor should also be clean, free of any offensive ethnic references, and it should be relevant. It should also be fresh and, if possible, topical. And the speaker must be comfortable with the material or it won't work.

Comedy is merely one of many introductory techniques. Some professionals counsel that you need a provocative idea to open, a summation of the problem. Or you can pose a question to the audience, involve them personally, emphasize the importance of the topic, tease them, arouse their curiosity. A strong quote might serve as an entry point and some speakers employ visual aids to break the ice.

The ending of a speech should come naturally and should satisfy the listener. Terms like *in conclusion* and *finally* signal your intent to finish and are okay, but a summary statement, suggestion for action, or thought-provoking quote are better. You can leave the audience thinking by planting an idea and forcing the people to reflect on it.

Most writers and speakers find it far easier to craft a catchy opening than to construct a satisfactory close.

All That Time In Between

It's not enough to have a good opening and a telling close. The rest of the speech has to be interesting, too. You don't have to be slick and polished, although these qualities could help. All you have to be is somehow compelling. You are taking up the time of other folks, so you owe them a message that's worthwhile.

A speech is linear. It moves cleanly, without stumbles, without boring gaps, without repetitive statistics. It is replete with anecdotes and illustrations. The verbs bite and the adjectives startle or amuse. You drag the audience into each paragraph, making them nod in agreement, or frown, or smile, or cry. There has to be something in the speech for them, something they can identify with or profit from. As long as they can see a personal benefit, they'll stay with you.

Remember that a speech is to be heard, not read. Some very fine speeches don't read nearly as well. Certain words or phrases, while eloquent orally, may seem corny or overdone in print.

You can also claim attention by rhetorical skills, such as varying the pace and pitch. You can't thunder or whisper for half an hour, but each tone has its appropriate place. The delivery should be conversational, the way one would discuss a subject with friends, keeping the other vocal variations in reserve, to be used if needed. Here are a few additional tips:

- ❏ Keep stories, examples, and statistics current.
- ❏ Study radio techniques. Note how announcers use words like *now, and, but* and *then* to punctuate their sentences, giving the listener a clue as to what comes next and allowing the speaker a brief pause.
- ❏ Quotes should be short and appropriate.
- ❏ Prefer the short word to the long, Latinized word, and don't use words you have trouble pronouncing.
- ❏ Avoid jargon, confusion, and exaggeration.

Length and Other Considerations

Circumstances affect the length of a speech. A luncheon talk should be confined to twenty minutes, while a dinner speech may run a bit longer. Workshop presentations could be several hours, with timely breaks. A classroom lecture occupies the regularly scheduled period, from fifty minutes to ninety minutes or more.

The speaker must consider the audience and the situation. If in doubt, keep it short. Few people get angry because a speech is too short, whereas many wince at the longer talks.

Some presentations allow for questions at the end, or during the talk. Make this option clear at the outset and be sure that the speaker or the chair handles this part of the program effectively. Some starter questions may be planted, or written questions may be solicited in advance. Keep an eye on the time and on the interest level of the audience, and cut off the questions when either interest lags or the hour grows late.

DELIVERY

If you think about it, you realize that few speeches you've heard in your life are really spellbinding gems. You don't have to be a great orator to hold an audience; all you need to do is have something to say and say it effectively.

There are techniques to delivery, of course. Some of these are dictated by the purpose of the talk. Is it to entertain, to inform, to persuade? Are you discussing the comic things that occur on tour, or are you trying to convince a select audience to travel with you? Each purpose suggests a slightly different style.

One of the first steps in delivery is to conquer the universal fear of speaking in public, a fear that ranks at the top of admitted concerns. This anxiety stems from lack of confidence, lack of security. First, you must realize this feeling is common. Even experienced performers get butterflies each time they face a new audience. So, take comfort in the realization that you have a lot of company.

Being thoroughly prepared also helps. If you've spent time preparing the presentation, rehearsing it, and even envisioning audience reaction, this takes away the feeling of uncertainty. You'll know the talk is good and that you have the ability to deliver it.

Another psychological aid is the consideration that the audience wants you to succeed. They're with you. They empathize with your situation and, besides, they are hoping for something that interests, even excites, them. Only in rare cases will an audience be hostile.

Set some goals for yourself in the presentation. What do you plan to accomplish? Once you have well-defined expectations, you'll discover it's easier to work toward this purpose. This helps you assume control, and helps convince you that your talk will be of benefit to this group.

Some speakers warm up before beginning their presentation, engaging in a series of vocal exercises the way an opera star might run through the scales. Often, however, these exercises are not possible or practical. You're already in the hall and are part of a larger program. You can't suddenly erupt into some repetitive vocalization. But you can take a deep breath before you stand up. This helps relax you, and enables you to give force to your important opening comments.

For most talks, a conversational tone is to be preferred. This doesn't mean that the volume is low, but that you should sound as if you're talking to a few friends, even when you are addressing a huge congregation. You must project; you must be heard; and, if you are using a microphone, you must know how to adjust to its volume. The speech should appear effortless. If you look like you are suffering, the audience suffers too. Try to make your commentary natural, not forced, not overly dramatic.

While proper volume is critical, the speaker should also be flexible. Speech must be modulated. Some words require extra emphasis; some phrases deserve a quieter, intimate setting; sometimes you must almost shout. Again, these techniques must fit the message. Narrating a slide show would rarely call for any such histrionic effects, but conducting a workshop might. Varying the level of the speech keeps the audience alert and allows the speaker to maintain control.

Gestures are helpful in many ways. They stress certain points, they add life to the words, and they assist the speaker in subduing any nervousness. But gestures must be natural, not studied. You don't impose gestures on a speech; you allow them to grow out of the message, the delivery, and the pace.

Speakers may have to work on their pronunciation and enunciation. You have to pronounce words correctly, and, if in doubt, get help from your dictionary. You should also enunciate clearly so that the audience understands what you're trying to convey. Mumbling, dropping the ends of sentences, turning away from the mike, lowering your voice, stumbling over words — all of these may lose an audience.

Sincerity is important. You must believe in what you are saying and you have to communicate this conviction. Enthusiasm helps, too. If you appear uninterested in what you're communicating, how can you expect an audience to respond positively? You must have a sense of what's going on, a realization that you are interacting with your listeners. This affects delivery and sustains the speaker.

Part of this sincerity comes from the speaker's grasp of what the words mean. Often those who are working from a prepared text merely go through the language with little cognizance of what is being said. You may notice this about prayer. Sometimes you've been repeating the same prayers since you were a child. Then, one day, you say them slowly, listening to what the words say, and the meaning suddenly becomes fresh and revealing. As a presenter, you have to listen to your own message.

Public speakers suggest that you concentrate on a few friendly, responsive, faces in the audience instead of confronting an anonymous mass. Take comfort and take cues from these interested persons. This enables you to concentrate on what you are saying instead of worrying about what people are thinking of you. It's hard to ignore the faces that never change expression and look bored and uninterested, but you can always find some listeners with a more receptive attitude.

As mentioned earlier, you must also determine how you will deliver the talk. An extemporaneous approach works best, if you can handle it. Reading the speech is also acceptable, as long as you are not absolutely married to the text and lose all eye contact and sense of audience. Working from an outline may be a good combination of both methods. Memorizing the speech is tricky. First, it's not easy. More importantly, you work so hard on remembering words and sequence, you lose touch with the listeners and the situation. The effect seems canned and studied, rather than conversational.

Speakers should time their speeches in advance and should keep the remarks to a reasonable length. It's far better to leave an audience wanting more than it is to exhaust them with your rhetoric.

With practice, you find your own style, or styles. You learn whether or not you can handle humor, or dramatic renderings, or a heavier oratorical style. Get comfortable with the material, get familiar with it and with the audience, get control of yourself — and you'll do fine. If you feel good about what you are doing, the listeners will pick up on this conviction.

Practice Helps

Even the most seasoned speakers review their material in advance. This allows for more freedom at the event, more familiarity with content, and a sense of ease which comes with repetition and refinement. In rehearsal you learn how to pace the remarks, how to add interpretation to ideas, and how to pronounce words that may be difficult in themselves or in sequence. You can try varied approaches; correct awkward phrasing; and clarify muddled language.

Many speakers find it helpful to rehearse before a mirror, often with a stopwatch to ascertain timing. This is done aloud and not silently, because silent reading is inaccurate in terms of time. Pauses and emphases can be added and gestures tried out. This is also the time to practice departures from the script, if you plan to work from a prepared text.

During this preparation, the speaker also learns how to pace the speech, although not every interruption for applause or laughter can be anticipated. The pace must be comfortable for the speaker and must blend with the content. The typical travel talk is likely to be structured like friend talking to friend, the way you might introduce your vacation slides. But people in the travel industry may also be called to testify on bills that affect their profession and that pace will be more deliberate, more intense. They could be on television, where the delivery is even more relaxed than when confronted by a live audience. Common sense and personal style, together with audience reaction, dictate the flow of the address, but practice helps.

During this rehearsal period, the speaker may solicit the advice of others to whom the remarks can be delivered — friends, associates, family members. Or a tape recorder may be used to capture the essence of the talk and the speaker can do an individual critique. Even ad libs and pauses can be scheduled in at this time, and visual aids can be integrated into the presentation.

Handling Equipment

Every actor is terrified of props. The actor knows the set door won't open on cue, or the blank pistol will misfire, the cake won't cut, the lamp won't go out, the doorbell will fail to ring, the crown won't fit, and the wine carafe will be absent. When you're concentrating on remembering lines and moving gracefully and interacting with others, these items are an extra burden. The same panic can invade the speaker's rostrum.

Speakers should know what equipment is available, how it works, and who to call when it malfunctions. And people who have no affinity for tools should avoid the more complicated aids. Plugs can be pulled out, slides appear out of sequence, and microphones squeal and buzz. The speaker should ask questions of experts and should become familiar with the operation of projectors or overheads or the volume controls on the mike. Speakers should also check to see whether the lectern light works so they can easily read their notes and they should note lectern and microphone heights. If there are blackboards or flip charts in the presentation, the speaker must know how to integrate them smoothly. Video and audio tapes must be properly cued up and all other props, like awards or printed handouts, have to be readily available and figured into the sequence of events.

Other Considerations

The event itself influences the character of the talk. A travel manager addressing the annual picnic must look at the assignment differently than an airline president testifying before a Congressional committee. Still, homework is the key, followed by an ability to envision the situation and tailor the remarks accordingly.

Speakers should also be flexible. The program preceding the speaker may run long, forcing the speaker to curtail the prepared remarks. Room temperatures may change the routine. Local circumstances—some success or tragedy—sometimes suggest an alteration in the speech. Whatever the intrusion, it's unwise to calculate that everything will go exactly as planned.

THE SLIDE SHOW

Slide programs are a natural in the travel business. They combine the drama of sight and sound within the economic limits of small travel companies. Done properly, they can be entertaining, even compelling, and they cost only a fraction of the money expended on a decent film or videotape. (However, some of the multiscreen computer-run shows may have high price tags.)

The secret to good slide shows is the ability to come up with visual concepts rather than writing wall-to-wall conversation. If you can see it, you probably don't need to say it—except for reinforcement. The pictures flow through the professional scriptwriter's mind, just as they will appear on the screen. The writer feels a rhythm to the program, observes the procession of images, and adds words and sound effects to support this vision.

It's true that some slide shows begin with a collection of slides and the script is tailored to fit them. This can work, but it's risky. It's better to prepare a rough script, secure the graphics, see how the whole thing comes together, and then add narration and sound.

Script writers should be flooded with ideas, especially in the travel industry where so much is visual and where sound effects can evoke scenes and moods of distant places.

Any destination provides the opportunity for a brief travelogue, and some of these can be combined in a package to introduce an entire area. Slides can also be used to sell a tour, educate a group about the value of using a travel agency, convince individuals about the affordability of cruises or the economies possible in corporate travel.

There is no need to put words to every slide. Some may require no explanation or identification, while others need emphasis or clarification. Sometimes you introduce a dozen slides with a few words and let the music and sound effects do the rest. For example, if the narrator says that Northwest flies to dozens of foreign destinations, you can just run the music and show identifiable landmarks.

Writing the Slide Show

There are different ways to script slide shows. Some writers prefer the four-column method, with one column for the slide number, the next for the description of the slide, the third for narration, and the fourth for music or sound-effect cues. The problem with this format is that it leaves little room on a normal page for narration and forces you to use numerous script pages for even a short program.

More common is the two-column format, with the left column for the description of the slide (and, possibly, a number) and the right for narration and sound effects. Directions for changes of slides are indicated by an asterisk, or colored dot, whether the program will later be operated manually or automatically. These directions are added after the rest of the script has been completed.

Music and sound effects are available for purchase. The most expensive way to go is to commission original music and have it played by an orchestra. Radio stations and sound studios have their own music and sound-effects libraries, which are much cheaper to use. You can secure ships' foghorns, jet engines, surf, the swish of skis, the babble of a foreign marketplace, and you can locate mood music, ethnic music, even abstract or generic tunes.

Sound effects (listed on the script as SOUND or SFX) are usually indicated in CAPS and underlined. So are music cues. <u>SOUND: MARTIAL MUSIC</u>.

If there are directions as to how a line of copy is to be read, this information is usually written in capital letters and placed in parentheses in the appropriate script position. NARR: (WITH SUR-PRISE). Words requiring emphasis are generally <u>underlined</u> and pauses are shown by double dashes.

Most slide programs run ten to twelve minutes, with very few going beyond twenty minutes. After that, the audience is likely to get edgy. In writing to these time lengths, you can't be perfect, since pace and word length vary, but you might not want any more than two words per second. That means that a minute of a script probably contains less than 100 words (allowing for pacing),and that a page of two-column scripting probably amounts to half a minute, or a little longer.

After viewing an initial version of the proposed show, the speaker (or creator of the show) may want to add slides or narrative, or cut both. At this point, electronic pulsing may be added to drop the slides automatically, and the sound track can be recorded to allow for more versatility in sound and for more control over narration.

If the individual speaker operates the projector manually and accompanies the slides with live commentary, the delivery should be crisp and interesting and free of amateur hesitations. While a canned narrator is safer and easier to use, there are some advantages to a live narrator — like the chance to pause for longer periods or to respond to queries during the presentation.

SLIDE SCRIPT

	SOUND: SURF PLUS FIJIAN CHORUS
GOVERNMENT BUILDING AT SUVA	NARR: A member of the British Commonwealth since 1970, Fiji remains one of *
SEASCAPE WITH ISLAND BACKGROUND	the last unspoiled places on earth, still reflecting the Saturday matinee image of the South Pacific, *
BEACH AT KORELEVU	with white crescent beaches, blue water *
	lagoons, and a culture that echoes a romantic past.
FIJIANS IN MEKE COSTUMES	Scattered on the perimeter of the two main islands are hundreds of *
SMALL, ISOLATED ISLAND	smaller islands, most uninhabited, but crested with coconut palms and protected by coral reefs.*
*Slide changes	SOUND: CROWD NOISES

TRAVEL CASSETTES AND TELEVISION

Virtually all travel cassettes are done professionally, although some travel units do manage to produce their own. Involvement of staff members might come more in terms of preceding or following the visual presentation. Unless the sole purpose is entertainment, few cassettes can stand on their own. They require an accompanying sales pitch.

Like cassettes, television programs on travel also employ tapes that were produced elsewhere, but the travel manager or staff could be asked to participate in a travel show. On the local level, these shows rarely run in prime time and are more likely to be seen on Sunday mornings. Even though audiences are small, some travel agencies find such programs a source of leads and prestige.

Typically, the travel show will focus on a destination and incorporate film, slides, and interviews. While some television stations may furnish more than a production staff, it's likely the travel agency person involved will have to construct the show and provide the visual materials. In addition, this person will probably host the program. It's work, and the manager or staff member should not think otherwise. It takes effort to come up with decent programming week after week, and scripting, production, and hosting can take ten to twelve hours for the simplest formats. The individuals involved should continually evaluate the TV show to determine whether or not it is worth the time and money expended.

Those in the travel industry may also be asked to appear on news or interview shows. Sometimes these appearances can be touchy, as when some airline disaster or weather delay requires the presence of airline personnel. At the start of the summer tourist season, local agency personnel may be interviewed about tourist plans or the decline in the dollar's value. Tourism bureau employees can count on periodic TV queries about the prospects for visits and conventions in their area.

Appearing on television requires a cool presence, a sense of humor, and an ability to avoid long, complicated responses. Guests should dress properly, avoiding loud patterns in suit or dress, and should not bring along a lot of notes which later prove difficult to find. Remain conversational; listen to the discussion; pause before replying. Keep in mind the impression you wish to make, an impression of professionalism and candor. Think before you speak and couch responses as succinctly as possible. Many TV guests get into trouble because they talk too much. If you know your field and can keep your dignity and can exhibit a friendly on-the-air personality, you'll succeed.

MEETINGS

Executives spend between half and three-fourths of their time in meetings. Some might fit in the large audience category, but most are small group assemblies. The small group is described as three or more persons, and both college courses and seminars have been designed to help communicators better understand the dynamics of these congregations.

While groups are composed of individuals with diverse personalities and interests, most of them do share some common facets. When such gatherings take place in the travel industry, they generally have a specific purpose, one that involves all of those present, and members probably recognize their interdependence and their ability to influence or be influenced.

There are many reasons for assembling. One could be to transmit information, such as a new program, the results of a sales campaign, a planned move, some alteration within the travel industry, or other important data. Meetings may be convoked to solicit ideas, like thoughts about marketing, or a name change, or prospects for a tour, or solutions to some internal problem. Sometimes individual assignments are made at meetings, so that all can be aware of the overall picture. Meetings provide support for management or for employee goals, or they may be convoked to honor team members, or to conduct routine business. The aims may differ, but many of the principles remain constant.

To begin with, meetings require planning. They should have a purpose and should not be called at someone's whim. The time should be selected carefully, paying attention to work schedules and to other conflicts. While a Saturday morning meeting may find many employees available, they could also resent this intrusion into their weekends. Night meetings present the same problems. Luncheon meetings often have too much waste time involved. Breakfast meetings are getting more popular and, if sufficient notice is provided, meetings that occupy a regular part of a working day can also succeed.

The locale is another consideration. Normally, convenience is paramount, but seclusion may sometimes take precedence, arguing for a spot distant from the office. Regardless of the site, it should offer some assurance of lack of serious interruption. Group members are supposed to concentrate and to interact, so they can't be sidetracked by telephone calls or staff visits. Some meetings require special tools, like TV monitors or projection screens, and such demands will limit the suitable space options. The meeting room should be chosen with care and should be booked well in advance.

Everything else must also be organized, from water glasses and note pads to the selection of someone to take notes (or tape the proceedings). Most important of all, an agenda must be developed and, if possible, circulated to members prior to the meeting, giving them an opportunity to gather information, if necessary.

The agenda should cover the topics that need to be covered but should also be concise enough to be comfortably handled within the time frame allowed. If supporting data would help in understanding or discussing the agenda, it should be provided.

For each meeting, the appropriate people should be invited. A staff meeting in a small travel agency may include everyone, while a larger agency may call a meeting of its sales staff alone. Hotel chains may have periodic gatherings of managers, while local tourism bureaus may avail themselves of volunteer boards who regularly assemble. The point is that all persons who should be there should be invited. Errors of omission generally result in suspicion and hurt feelings.

The Chair and Team Members

At some meetings, a chair emerges by vote or by the natural dominance of an individual. Most meetings, however, have a person designated as chair, probably because of corporate rank.

Chairpersons manage meetings in diverse ways. Some are timid and hesitate to impose their views on the audience. Under their aegis, things can get out of control. Other chairpersons may be democratic but still in charge, allowing sufficient discussion but still maintaining a grip on proceedings. Chairpersons may also be autocratic, permitting very little discussion and very little opposition. Chairs can be weak, strong, light, serious, organized, scattered. The best ones can lead, but they also know how to listen.

Good chairpersons are also good psychologists. They can diffuse conflict, and draw out shy members, and they can stick to an agenda. They use their talent for summary and they avoid stepping on the thoughts and egos of others. They keep things moving and they achieve results.

Members also have contributions to make. First, they should do their homework before attending the meeting and should come prepared with questions and suggestions. If given assignments, they must fulfill them. While in session, they should listen, contribute, share the dialogue, avoid conflict, and accept responsibility.

Success in persuading others is often characterized by the knowledge and confidence of the speaker, and with the ability to present facts without antagonizing others. There is a way to introduce information without sarcasm, criticism, or elite posturing. The able communicator is always under control.

Following the meeting, the decisions arrived at—if any—should be disseminated to those attending and to all others on whom they have an immediate impact. Speed and accuracy in the drafting and communicating of information is always appreciated.

Meetings have the potential of producing fresh ideas or of gathering latent public opinion. They may also relieve stress among employees or executives. They can be used to train, to motivate, or to check on the progress toward objectives. They can also result in anger or frustration and meetings are sometimes used to avoid dealing directly with problems. In any event, they do take time.

Because of the time factor, travel corporations with national and international offices may turn more and more to teleconferencing instead of assembling a lot of busy people in one physical spot. Hotel chains already do a lot of this, tying their properties together via satellite or by phone hookup and dispatching problems in this manner.

Some Types of Meetings

Meetings with prospects will be covered in a later chapter, under sales, but there are other forms of meetings that challenge the ability to effectively communicate.

Staff meetings are common to every industry, and most of them are boring. They needn't be. A solid agenda helps, and so does the ability of a chairperson to make efficient use of the time. Managers should be committed to listening to the ideas and complaints of subordinates and discussions should be open and productive.

Normally, staff meetings are not suitable for critiquing the specific performances of individuals. These comments should be reserved for more private discussions, although general reviews of staff problems may be introduced to the entire group.

When a manager does decide to summon an employee for disciplinary reasons, every effort must be made to ascertain all of the facts in advance. Experts counsel that before the criticisms are leveled the employer should focus on some of the positive attributes of the employee, then single out the negative behavior. These same experts also remind us that there is little sense in criticizing a staff member unless that approach will do some good. This meeting should not be solely an opportunity for the manager to vent anger. If the fault is irreversible, then dismissal may be the only solution.

There are all types of one-on-one interactions and each requires tact and understanding. Personalities inevitably intrude. Some individuals just seem to clash; some don't trust each other. The wise administrator senses these volatile situations and does whatever can be done to remove them from the discussion. Fruitful exchanges result from a high comfort and credibility level, from the conviction that this dialogue is being conducted by two sensitive and intelligent adults. Just as the task of addressing a huge convention audience represents one species of challenge for a speaker, the insightful management of a two-party conversation may have its own set of obstacles, Figure 6–3. Appreciating the nuances of communication helps

Figure 6–3.   Speaking skills involve not only formal public address but also the many daily discussions with fellow employees. (Courtesy Tim Fitzgerald)

here, but success starts with the individual's own desire to be fair and open.

Nonverbal Signals

Along with the ability to speak and listen comes the power of observation. Gestures help the speaker deliver the message, and less obvious gestures provide clues to audience reaction. We know many of these signs already. Frowns signal disagreement; tears may be tokens of fear, guilt, shame, or sympathy; a rising volume in response normally denotes anger. A person who thrusts his or her face close to yours, invading your space, represents a challenge, a confrontation. A hand on your shoulder may mean encouragement or unwarranted affection.

Some signals are not as obvious and a whole school of body-language theory has grown up around them, Figure 6–4. Listeners lean forward when they are interested or involved, lean back in their chairs when less concerned with the content. Folded arms is a sign of some resistance, while tilting the head may signify consideration, disbelief, or tentative agreement. The tightening of one's lips may display an inner hardening of attitude.

Some 125 of these nonverbal signs have been identified and categorized, and they are used in venues as diverse as courtrooms and singles bars. As mentioned earlier in this chapter, the speaker

Figure 6—4.   Positions of the hands and body can show concentration or relaxation.

should be attuned to shifts in audience behavior, warning of lagging interest or growing hostility. In one-on-one situations, too, hunched shoulders and averted eyes may convince the speaker to let up a bit, while a certain rigidity in the eyes may announce that the employee has no intention of altering the conduct being discussed.

Veteran salespeople get very good at reading these signals and can often tell whether a prospect is serious or merely killing time. Experience gives them this ability to discern and the same gift can be earned by any speaker, any communicator.

OTHER COMMUNICATION ENCOUNTERS

Most of the examples studied in this text are somewhat formal. The individual sets out to write or deliver a speech; the brochure or itinerary writer has a result in mind; the chairman of the meeting develops an agenda. Yet we're all aware that a majority of our communication is spontaneous or without the more elaborate preparation that goes into more organized exchanges.

Managers, at all levels, are teachers, communicators. Their styles differ. Some lead by sharing power, by involving others in the planning and execution stages. Others jealously guard their authority and pass along only what they feel needs to be said in order to allow the firm to function. Still others are unpredictable, sometimes appearing unreasonably demanding, sometimes seeming to be weak and uncertain.

Consistency is a virtue, and so is the ability to make subordinates part of the team. The leader is responsible for helping to form and articulate company goals, and middle management also passes along details of personnel policies and expectations. All sorts of communication situations involve the leadership, although not every executive will be in on every decision. Among the supervisory jobs are personnel selection, training, evaluation, remuneration, security, discipline, the handling of grievances, recognition, opportunity, promotion, transfer, dismissal, and other chores. Each takes some variant skills and it's the rare individual who is good at all of these challenges. But each executive must develop techniques to deal with such responsibilities. They can't be continually handed off to subordinates.

Guest Relations

Much of the travel industry is concerned with making clients, passengers, or guests feel at home. To accomplish this, communication is the principal ingredient. The host supplier already has an advantage — these people chose to travel or stay with you. All you must do is reinforce the wisdom of that decision. Genuine concern, the ability to listen, and the willingness to extend yourself in the rendering of service — these are the keys.

At a hotel, the desk clerk is a focal point. Even when harrassed, or tired, or when confronted by a difficult guest, the clerk must remain polite, efficient, and professional. Airline stewards and stewardesses are normally models of cordiality and effectiveness, as are their counterparts on cruise lines. Passenger agents at airline ticket counters, even when internally frantic, must keep their composure and serve the passengers amicably. Even the airline pilot can humanize a flight by injecting periodic comments that explain delays or point out landmarks. A creative first officer, stuck in a holding pattern over O'Hare, used the time to conduct an aerial guided tour of Chicago, even recommending restaurants and plays.

Tour members form a special group. The tour manager must maintain control and must be able to quietly convince individuals to stay on schedule, to cooperate with the itinerary, and to get along with one another. Even when this may become a chore, the tour manager keeps smiling, stays calm, and puts everything in perspective. Verbally and nonverbally, the tour leader is setting the standard while setting the pace.

Most travel companies are aware of these communication needs. They conduct training sessions or workshops, or they publish literature, all aimed at improved guest and client relations.

CHAPTER HIGHLIGHTS

❏ Oral communication is far more common than written communication and this skill needs to be part of the travel industry's tools.

❏ Speakers can initiate opportunities, circulating their biographical sketches and speech titles to likely organizations.

❏ Once a speech has been arranged (or even before the commitment is made), some research should be done on the sponsoring organization, the event, the audience, and the subject. Knowing the resources available saves time, and some of them should be part of the speaker's own library.

❏ The speaker must know the nature of the audience to be addressed.

❏ Each speech should be carefully outlined, fitting the details to this outline. Strong beginnings and endings should be provided, along with interesting content containing ample illustrations.

❏ Each speaker should rehearse the speech until the exercise feels comfortable, and each speaker must also work with the visual aids or other tools that will be used.

❏ Slide shows generally use a two-column format and are written to a subject rather than to existing slides. Cassettes and TV shows have potential for meetings but should be skillfully, professionally prepared, and the material carefully selected.

❏ Meetings serve a variety of purposes, from information gathering to persuasion, but all must be planned in detail, with time, place, and agenda key considerations.

❏ Strong, open chairpersons are a plus, along with meeting members that listen and contribute. Staff meetings and one-on-one confrontations call for special tact and understanding.

❏ Some 125 body-language signals can help speakers understand audience reactions.

❏ Internal relations with employees and external relations with guests, clients, or passengers all require communication skills.

❏ *EXERCISES*

1. Spend an hour in some busy place — student center, mall, res-
    taurant — and catalogue the nonverbal signals you observe
    and what they probably mean.
2. Assume you are trying to sign up some of your family friends
    for a cruise and you want to accompany your pitch with a 10-
    minute slide show. Also assume that you must put this slide
    show together yourself but that you do have a source of supply
    for the slides, music, and sound effects. Outline the purpose
    and general theme of the slide show and write the first page of
    the script.
3. You've been asked to give a talk to college sophomores about
    the advantages of travelling while you are still young. The
    meeting will take place at 4:00 p.m. in a room in the student
    center, with an anticipated audience of about 40 students. Out-
    line this speech and write the opening and closing paragraphs.

❏ *CASE PROBLEMS*

*1. You're the manager of a large urban hotel that caters to
business travelers. Room rates are competitive, recent renova-
tions have substantially improved the facility, and the restaurant
gets rave reviews. One of the few areas of complaint involves the
reception desk and, in particular, one of the veteran desk clerks.
This person is knowledgeable, dependable in an emergency,
scrupulously honest, and is willing to work long hours. However, the clerk can also be curt with guests, sometimes even rude,
and has provoked numerous phone calls and letters of complaint.
How do you handle this situation?*

*2. You are the public relations director for a major airline,
one that a recent survey identified as having the worst on-time
record of any of the twelve major air carriers. To make matters
even worse, your airline was also among the airlines with the
highest percentage of traveler complaints. A local television
station has requested an interview with your boss, the airline
president, in order to get the company's response to this survey.
Do you agree to the interview? If not, how do you get around
this? If you do agree, how do you prepare your boss? Be specific.*

7

VISUAL ASPECTS OF COMMUNICATION

The written and the spoken word are challenged today by the graphics that pervade our lives at every level. Even as the literacy rate improves, the reliance on pictures increases. Almost subconsciously, we have come to accept certain visual symbols as communication, Figure 7–1.

In the early days of the motion picture, when there was no sound and when impressions had to be communicated quickly, numerous devices were used to cue the viewer. The black hats and white hats in the westerns, for example. Or the checkered tablecloth which said that poor but honest folks lived here. Or the overly dramatic tears and sneers. Music also helped even then, letting the audience know when something dreadful was about to happen.

Figure 7–1. Even objects like plaques are used as visual evidence of achievement.

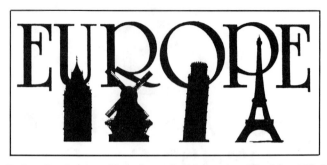

Figure 7–2.   Certain national symbols are readily identifiable.

Today we recognize all sorts of international road signs, warning us about the possibility of landslides or the existence of a nearby school. We can identify hundreds of products by package shape or logo. We've become familiar with weather maps from television news and we even accept the commercial interruptions of TV drama without any question. The Eiffel Tower characterizes Paris and the Arch symbolizes Saint Louis. Pictures are everywhere and they form an important part of modern communication, Figure 7–2.

Because appearance is part of communication, the smallest unit of the travel industry still has a stake in producing a visual look that matches the image it's trying to convey. Circulating sloppy newsletters or creating inept print advertising—even for high school play programs—is a serious mistake. For some readers or viewers, that single example is the impression they take away. Not every company or agency can afford to hire an expensive designer or even to employ an advertising agency, but, hopefully, at least one staff member has acceptable taste and should pass on the look of the communication.

DESIGN

There is much about design that is natural. We arrange a room in a pleasing manner or group pictures in a certain way on a wall. Pictures pasted into a scrapbook are organized for effect or for neatness. People who can handle these chores rather readily may panic when asked to put a print ad together or lay out a poster. They shouldn't; the principles are the same.

Design really means the arrangement of elements to produce an attractive and effective result. It's a pattern, a plan, and it should serve a purpose as well as influencing a viewer. Three characteristics of all design, from fine art to supermarket tabloids, are *harmony, sequence,* and *balance,* Figure 7–3.

Figure 7–3.   Harmony, sequence, and balance are the three basic elements of design.

Harmony refers to the interaction among elements. In singing, we think of harmony as being good when all voices blend well. The same criterion applies to art and layout. The elements work together. This may involve color combinations, relationships between illustrations, the way different parts of the brochure complement one another, or even the way all of the elements match up with the theme of the communication. If there is dissonance—type style clashing with message or illustration, a mixture of unrelated graphics—harmony is destroyed.

The smooth transition from one element to another is called *sequence,* and this enhances reading and viewing. A comic strip is a sequence, and so is a film strip, slide program, or film. In static forms, like paintings or print advertising, there should be a sequential relationship among elements, so that one flows into the other, leading the eye where the creator intended. In an advertisement, for example, the eye may take in the headline, move through the illustration and copy, and end with the logo or coupon.

Balance is sometimes evident, sometimes subtle—and the subtle phase is more interesting, Figure 7–4. Symmetrical balance occurs when elements on both sides of an ad or illustration perfectly balance with other, the way you'd add weights to a scale to keep it steady and horizontal. Two mirror images on either side of a vertical line would be in perfect balance. But asymmetrical balance is more pleasing, more original. Even though elements may be of different sizes or colors, they somehow appear to be in balance. A bright color may balance a large object, and several small units may equal one big unit. Imbalance bothers people, like pictures hanging askew on a wall or the tilting room in the Fun House.

These three factors are essential to design, but there are all sorts of variations used in implementing them, Figure 7–5. Designers may work with color or black and white; with line, flat shape, art, or photography; in small space or large space; with or without type; and dozens of other options.

Figure 7–4.   Informal balance is demonstrated in this small space ad. (Courtesy of Windjammer Barefoot Cruises)

Some Considerations

☐ Something must dominate in print communication. It could be a headline, a picture, a logo, a price. If every element has equal weight, the reader doesn't have a place to focus.

☐ Copy is part of any layout and must work together with the illustration(s). The type is a shape that figures in the total look of the layout.

Figure 7–5.   The rectangle, circle, and triangle are the three basic shapes used in design.

❏ Don't feel you have to fill every corner of every layout. White space opens things up, helps the reader concentrate on the key areas and items.
❏ Watch the visual cliches. Avoid using the same tired old photos and illustrations you see in half the print ads.
❏ Experiment with different arrangements of the elements by creating small "roughs" of the ad before you get too firm with the layout.
❏ Once you've established a workable format, stick with it for a while. Repeat your winners.
❏ Learn to work in a small space. Many travel ads are relatively small and making them stand out is a challenge. Clip ads that do this successfully. Envision how your ad will look on a page with other ads. Give it a different look. If surrounding ads are in reverse (white on black), then your black on white ad is more visible. And vice versa. Photos usually don't work well in small space ads, so consider line drawings. Many advertisers also opt for some sort of border to define their space.
❏ Know the mechanical requirements of the publication in which you are advertising. Tailor your ad to fit that space. A newspaper column, for example, could be two inches (twelve picas) wide, while a magazine or play program might well be the quarter page, which could be three to four inches wide.

FORMATS

Everyone in the travel business should have a *swipe* file containing samples of materials you might use for inspiration. Included in this file should certainly be the different possible formats for print ads. These are numerous, but there are nine major types which are used alone or in combination.

Types of Formats

Picture Window.   We're familiar with this type of layout from ads for cigarettes and beer and for magazine ads for travel companies. In its simplest form, a photo forms the background with some type generally superimposed in strategic places. Full-page color ads for cruise lines are a good example of this genre. See Figure 7–6.

Frame.   A border fences in the copy, separating it from adjacent ads. Sometimes the border is a simple line, but it could be dots, flowers, hearts, or any design. Sometimes the frame takes the shape of a ship, blackboard, or notepad. Examples of frame ads are shown in Figures 7–7 and 7–8 (pages 168 and 169).

Mondrian.   This format, echoing the Dutch painter, employs different sizes of rectangles in some pleasing patterns. The rectangles may enclose photos, copy, or tint blocks.

Multipanel.   Using a series of same-size panels, this format can resemble a comic strip, except that the spaces may not contain cartoons, but could also feature photographs or type. This works well for the telling of a story, like a recap of a trip, or explaining how to do something, like packing a suitcase.

Silhouette.   In this format, all the elements combine to form a shape — which could be recognizable or abstract. The copy and illustrations could form a diamond or the outline of an airplane, or they could merely unite to create some less-defined contour.

Copy Heavy.   There's a place for ads that feature a lot of print copy and a minimum of illustration. Ads trying to interest buyers in vacation real estate may fit this mold and so do print ads that simply list schedules of airlines.

Typeface.   Here, some type element is the star. Usually, this is a headline that employs some distinct typeface, oversized, or that may take a common typeface with a catchy message and blow it up. See Figure 7–9 (page 170).

Rebus.   Remember those picture puzzles in the magazines for youngsters, where pictures symbolize words or letters? They've even used this technique on game shows. While a rebus ad doesn't normally do this, the format looks a bit like the puzzle, with small photos or illustrations sprinkled among the print copy.

Circus.   Not a common format in the travel industry, this type of ad (a favorite of supermarkets) combines a lot of different elements — headlines, copy, illustrations, tint blocks, large dollar figures, and other elements. Rarely attractive, the circus ad does get read, especially if the prices are competitive.

Other designations are also assigned to formats and, as mentioned, many of the preceding formats can be combined (picture

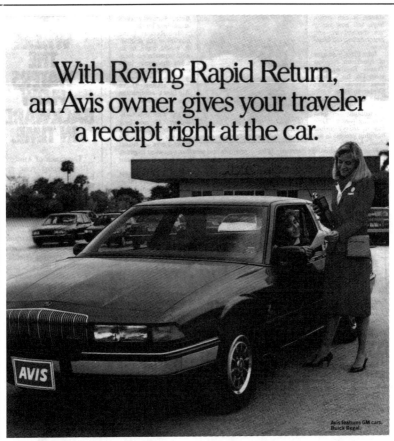

With Roving Rapid Return,
an Avis owner gives your traveler
a receipt right at the car.

Avis features GM cars.
Buick Regal.

Ever since the employees* took over Avis, Inc., we've been trying harder than ever to make it faster and easier for your travelers to return their cars.

Now instead of having them come to our counter, we've brought the counter out to them.

Our Roving Rapid Return representative calculates your traveler's rental charges and provides a printed receipt right at the car.

It's all done with our Avis Carside Computer.℠ And because it's electronically linked to our Wizard® III computer system, it does all this in seconds.† Your travelers can save time and get to their flight ahead of schedule.

And Avis also makes travel planning easier. Your travel consultant can give you instant confirmation and last-car availability information through Avis Total Access in SABRE, Complete Access in System One and Inside Link in Apollo. And the Avis Rate Shoppers Guide℠ guarantees our lowest applicable rate.

So next time your travelers need a car, rent from Avis.

Because now that the employees own the company, it's not just our job to make you happy. It's our business.

AVIS®

SEE US AT NPTA BOOTHS #529 AND #628.

We're trying harder than ever.℠

*Employees at all corporate locations.
†During peak periods at select airport locations for charge card customers who do not require modification of their rental charges. © 1988 Wizard Co., Inc.

Figure 7–6.   A variation of the picture window format. (Courtesy Avis Rent A Car)

Figure 7–7. Formal balance is achieved when the elements on either side of an imaginary center balance perfectly. This is a frame layout.

window and frame, for example) to produce a different look, Figure 7–10 (page 171).

Besides Print Ads . . .

Besides print ads, many other visual forms used by the travel industry communicate successfully or unsuccessfully to clients. Admittedly, many segments of this profession are frequently under

Figure 7–8.   In this frame ad, the coupon is actually integrated into the design. (Courtesy Princess Cruises, Tracy-Locke)

duress, and the temptation to issue something—anything—is common. But these items may hang around for a while, continually announcing that the sponsors are careless, cheap, or without taste. Remember that it takes only a little more effort and money to produce something presentable than it does to create something tacky.

Even a routine item like a poster or sign should be as good as it can be. Scratching out something in pen or crayon may work for selling "FRESH EGGS," but it doesn't belong on any travel corporation's window, door, or bulletin board.

In Response To Your Complaint Letters, Virgin Has Expanded Its Upper Class By 60%

Address Your Letters Of Thanks To: Virgin Atlantic Airways, 96 Morton Street, New York, N.Y. 10014.

We've just added 60% more cabin space to every Upper Class flight between New York and London.
Which means we have 60% more fully reclining sleeper seats at your disposal.
And in November, we'll be expanding our Upper Class between Miami and London. By 100%.
You're very welcome.

Virgin Atlantic Airways
Take us for all we've got.

Figure 7–9. Headline layout format. (Courtesy Virgin Atlantic Airways and Neil Leinwohl, Associate Creative Director, Art Director; Kevin McKeon, Associate Creative Director, Copywriter; and Korey, Kay and Partners)

Why Puerto Rico is
The Shining Star of the Caribbean.

No other island has the unique Spanish heritage of Puerto Rico.

No other island has preserved the beauty of its past more than Puerto Rico.

No other island offers a wider variety of places to stay than Puerto Rico.

No other island offers more to water lovers, sports enthusiasts and clients with a sense of fun and adventure.

No other island has Le Lo Lai, Puerto Rico's year-round folklore festival.

No other island will welcome your customers more warmly than the Shining Star of the Caribbean.

For more information, write: Puerto Rico Tourism, 575 Fifth Avenue, Box Y, NY, NY 10017.

PUERTO RICO/The Shining Star of the Caribbean

Figure 7–10.   This print ad exemplifies elements of formal balance, the Mondrian format, and the silhouette format. (Courtesy Puerto Rico Tourism Company)

Each printed assignment has its own peculiar requirements, but the basic notions of design and layout still apply. Because a poster is generally larger than an ad but more likely to be given only brief attention, it features fewer elements, oversized art. Travel posters are famous within this genre, often consisting of a compelling scene and just the name of the locale. Many have become collectors' items. A brochure must not only consider how each page lays out, but must also plan for an overall uniform effect. If a series of brochures is issued, the sponsoring firm may wish to give them a family look, indicating they come from the same source. Newsletters and company magazines are, again, a different assignment. Generally, magazines are more open, with more and larger illustrations, perhaps even a variety of headline styles, whereas newsletters tend to be more formal, geometric, based on an interesting, balanced rectangular format. Again, each page must work with opposing pages and must also present a cohesive appearance.

COPY BLOCKS

Those assembling the printed piece should always remember that blocks of copy are also part of the layout, Figure 7–11. You may have to squint your eyes to discern this, but the clusters of printed words contribute to the design as much as the illustrations.

Copy must also fit the layout mechanically. If space is a factor, as in a small ad, the writer has to accommodate that space. There's no sense in writing 100 words when only 50 will fit the space. There are numerous ways to "copy fit," ranging from working from a mathematical chart calculated for different type designs and sizes to counting characters within a square inch of copy. Once a format has been established, as in a regular monthly newsletter, the simplest way to copy fit is to count the number of characters in a line of printed copy and the number of lines that occupy one column inch. Then, all one has to do is set the typewriter or computer for that number of characters (letters, space, and punctuation), type the copy, and then count the number of typed lines to determine the approximate number of column inches that will be filled. Some editors, after determining the proper number of lines from their typed copy, cut out a matching block from a previous publication and paste it on the layout. There are also pages of adhesive type which can be applied to the layout and, if hard copy of equal size is produced by the computer, as in desktop publishing, one copy of this can also be inserted into the layout.

Figure 7–11.   Design of an 8½ × 11 flyer, with masthead at top and copy blocks ruled out. Copy blocks can also be used for pictures.

When typed copy is being sent to a typesetter, it is normally marked up by the designer or production person. Most travel units do not have such a person on staff, so it's likely these things will emerge from discussions with the printer. Even the amateur may include some indication of size and type style by attaching samples of what is wanted. The more one can do to present an idea of what is desired, the better the chance of this being accomplished. Most printers will cooperate and contribute, but a few are careless and unimaginative and need to be shepherded.

TYPE

Again, the average travel person can't be expected to understand the nuances of typography. Even those who regularly deal with this pragmatic science can't usually tell at a glance either the size or the family of type, so such expertise is even less likely in the travel business. The important thing is to have some idea of what you'd like, to deal with a good printer, and to listen to the counsel of those who are competent.

Another caution is that the typeface chosen should be compatible with the message, fitting the mood of the story you want to convey, and the headlines and subheads and other elements should all work together. You don't want a mix of type that looks as if it were just splayed from some print shop.

Basically, there are five general styles of type, Figure 7–12:

❑ *Roman* type is characterized by *serifs,* or little extenders, on the letters, making reading simpler and easier on the eyes.
❑ *Gothic* or *block* type is without serifs, giving it a modern appearance, but making it less effective for long blocks of copy.
❑ *Script* type resembles a stylized handwriting and would almost never be used for long messages. It is handy for invitations, headlines, and other copy calling for a delicate approach.
❑ *Text* refers to what used to be called Old English type, the sort you see on "shoppe" fronts or on diplomas.
❑ *Ornamental* type pulls together all of those other styles, from those affecting Oriental characters to those presenting the look of the Old West. This is a catchall category.

Within each of these general classifications, there are many *families* of type, distinct variations that sometimes bear the names of their creators, like Bodoni or Garamond, or a descriptive title, like Hellenic or P.T. Barnum. Each may have a slightly different feel, a different character.

Roman

abcdefghijklmnopqrstuv
wxyzABCDEFGHIJKLM
NOPQRSTUVW 1234567

Script

abcdefghijklmnopqrstuvwxyz 123
ABCDEFGHI
JKLMNOPQR

Text

abcdefghijklmnopqrstuvwxyz
ABCDEFGHIJKLMNOPQR
STUVWXYZ& 1234567890

Block or Gothic

abcdefghijklmnopqr
stuvwxyz ABCDEF
GHIJKLMNO 12345

Ornamental

abcdefghijklmnopqrstuvwxyz
ABCDEFGHIJKLMNOPQRSTU
VWXYZ&   1234567890S c..

Ornamental

ABCDEFGHIJK
LMNOPQRSTU
VWX 123456789

Figure 7–12. The five basic type styles are Roman, Script, Text, Block or Gothic, and the catchall Ornamental.

Breaking the organization of type down still further, there are *series* or a complete range of sizes in one specified face, and *fonts,* which are composed of a single size within the series — like twelve-point Futura.

And, of course, many type families offer italics, boldface (where the letters are darker than normal), small capital letters, condensed type squeezed together, or type letterspaced out for an open effect. There are also numbers and punctuation marks and, sometimes, a collection of decorative items called "dingbats."

Printers are normally happy to supply copies of their type books to clients and you may also purchase one of many books on type. In a local situation, however, it's wise to see what's available before specifying some rare and exotic type for a job.

MEASURING TYPE

There are two terms common in the measuring of type — *points* and *picas.* Points measure height and picas are used to determine width. There are 72 points in an inch, so 36-point type would be half an inch high, and 18-point type would be a quarter of an inch high. These figures are approximate, since type styles have some variance. Ten- and 12-point type are more common in body copy.

There are 6 picas to an inch, so a column that is 15 picas wide is 2½ inches wide. A pica is a simpler measurement to use than fractions of inches. In publications, columns are generally between 12 and 18 picas wide in order to facilitate reading.

When a more open effect is desired, extra space may be allowed between lines. This is called *leading,* or ledding.

Being able to measure type, while not a necessary skill for the travel staffer, is easy enough to do and adds to the person's graphic abilities.

PRINTING METHODS

In simplest terms, there is *hot* and *cold* type. Hot type refers to the older method of typesetting where characters, first individually and then by line, were cast in metal in much the same manner as people used to cast ammunition or tiny lead soldiers. This type was then arranged and locked into a frame, inked up, and blank sheets were pressed onto its surface by rollers to imprint an image. Later, after setting type this way, molds were made of the entire page and this could be affixed to a giant roller which ground out impressions on paper fed to it.

A modern method of printing involves cold type, which occurs when typefaces are "imaged" directly on paper. This could be accomplished by photocomposition, typing, electronic composition, pasting transfer letters on paper, or producing hard copy from computers. Multiple copies may be kicked out by computer, of course, but the most common method is to start with a page already imprinted, followed by a metal or composition plate of this page, affixing the plate to an "offset" machine which transfers the impression to an inked roller that, in turn, repeats the image on succeeding sheets of paper.

Although some printing is still done by the hot metal method, offset lithography is more common.

There are other ways to transfer images, like laser printing; silk screening, which is employed for posters; gravure printing, which uses a recessed rather than a raised surface; and some offset variations, like web offset.

The chief thing for the nonprofessional to remember is that you start with clean and accurate copy that properly fits the allotted space; you suggest or discuss the appropriate type faces and sizes; you select paper, color, and illustrations; you work with someone on layout; and you proofread the copy carefully before it gets to its final stage. You'll also be concerned with the reputation of the printer, the cost, the quality, and the delivery schedule.

COLOR

Besides the physical abnormality of color blindness, some people have no real sense of color, no notion of what color can achieve. People with these failings must trust color decisions to others. Again, listening to printers, paper salespersons, and others familiar with color choices is a wise idea. On the other hand, if your instincts tell you something is wrong, don't settle for it without some querying of the professionals.

Don't view color as merely decorative. Color triggers emotions, and color mirrors purpose. For fall foliage tours, a design emphasizing warm autumn hues makes more sense than cool greens or blues —which might make sense for an Irish journey or an Alaskan cruise. The human eye also reacts differently to a vivid red than it does to a mild lavender.

A knowledge of color includes an appreciation of what color can do, of what hue is appropriate for a specific goal, of how variant colors work together, and how certain inks work on certain papers. Red, blue, and yellow (or magenta, cyan, and yellow) are usually seen as primary colors, with other colors appearing as combinations of these primaries, plus, perhaps, white or black. There are at least 7500 different commercial inks available, with many of them part of a series of color swatches which printers or paper companies may supply. These color samples can be matched for compatability and tried in various combinations.

Experience quickly shows you that a green ink on blue paper is not a good idea, but a red ink on green paper may also look too Christmasy. What you are after is, first of all, legibility, and, after that, appropriateness, attractiveness, and emotional impact.

PAPER

There's both a visual and a tactile aspect of paper, along with its ability to handle type and illustrations. For example, newsprint, used for your daily paper, absorbs ink, so it won't do as good a job as a coated magazine stock in reproducing photos. Papers with marbled surfaces may appear rich but make for harder reading. Some projects may call for a flat, uncoated surface rather than a high gloss, and, always, you have to consider both availability and cost. The paper stock you'd like may not be on hand locally. Can you afford the time delay and cost to secure it elsewhere? Perhaps the boss suggests a paper with an expensive finish? Does the boss understand the premium price placed on this?

Salespersons for paper mills and their sales outlets can provide samples and may also advise the nonprofessional on what papers will best handle a specific job.

Paper comes by the ream—500 sheets—so the weight designation given to a sheet of paper is indicative of what 500 sheets will weigh. These sheets are $25'' \times 38''$ or $17'' \times 22''$ or similar. Smaller sheets, for letterheads, book pages, and the like, are cut from these larger sheets. Obviously, the thicker or heavier an individual sheet is, the more a ream of these sheets will weigh.

When we speak of a 20-pound offset paper, that means that 500 sheets of the large size would weigh 20 pounds. A cover stock of 80 pounds means that 500 of these sheets would weigh 80 pounds. Common sense dictates that pages of a book or magazine would not normally be cut from a cover stock sheet.

Again, the paper that looks right, feels right, is of the right color and the proper weight, is the one you want for each particular printed piece.

PHOTOGRAPHY

Travel thrives on photography. Tourists generally tote their cameras, neighbors show their slides, brochures are crowded with lush scenery, video cassettes are growing in popularity. Photography is very important in this industry. That's why it's unwise to trust it to the amateur.

Sure, anyone may take the occasional good—even great—photo, but when you want consistency and dependability, you're better off to stick with those who make a living at the art. Even for items like the newsletter, where black and white is the rule, it creates a poor image to display a lot of crude, out-of-focus, overexposed or underexposed shots. These reflect on the company. Any art should be as good as it can be.

If someone in the firm happens to be a professional photographer, that's a rare plus. Normally, the travel company staffer will be content with explaining what pictures are needed and, in some instances, even supervising the shooting. In the latter capacity, the travel person should not interfere with technical aspects but may certainly have input in terms of subject matter. Cliche shots should be forbidden, and the sponsoring firm should make certain that elements in the picture present the image the firm desires.

Even after the photos have been developed and delivered, there may be decisions to make. Which ones will be used in the brochure? What size will they be? Should we crop any of them for enhanced effect?

Photos may be enlarged or reduced. Making the picture smaller may sharpen the elements in a good photo, while enlarging it could bring about a grainy effect. Cropping a picture is the process of eliminating part of the original photo, either to create a different effect, get rid of unwanted detail, or prepare the photo to fit a different set of measurements. Crop marks are always made on the margin of the photo and never on the photo itself, while directions to the printer or engraver about reduction, enlargement, or cropping are printed on the back or typed onto a piece of paper affixed to the back of the photo. Directions should not be written on either side of the photo with a ballpoint pen, since that might show up when the picture is printed. Ditto for the use of paper clips on photos. These may scratch the surface or could leave a mark that could also be seen after the photo is reproduced.

Screening Photos

In order to transfer a photo from the print stage to a reproduction on some other surface, the photo must be *screened*. Before the picture becomes part of the printing plate, it is reshot, with a screen over the camera lens. This screen imposes a series of dots over the photo, and these dots subsequently pick up the ink and prevent it from puddling in one spot. The number of dots per linear inch is determined by the paper on which the photo will be printed. Since newsprint is absorbent, a coarse screen must be used, meaning fewer dots per linear inch — perhaps 55–85. So your daily paper may use what would be called 65 screen. For a coated surface, perhaps you'd choose a 120 screen, resulting in finer definition and a reproduction closer to the original.

With color photography, before printing can be accomplished, the photo must not only be screened, it must also be *separated*. Color separation is done by using filters on the lens when the photo is reshot. The primary colors are isolated by using filters composed of complementary colors. To produce the yellow tones alone, a purple (red plus blue) filter is used; to obtain the blue, an orange filter is used; to get the red, a green filter is employed. These three plates (yellow, blue, and red) are printed in sequence, all in perfect register over one another, and a final black plate is used to provide definition. The picture is, in essence, reassembled on the printed page, one primary color at a time.

Many other things can be done with photos. Instead of relying on the familiar square halftone, the main element(s) can be outlined by masking or retouching, resulting in a silhouette look. Or, in the development process, a soft ellipse may be used to surround the main figure, creating a "vignette" photo. In the screening process, all sorts of screens can be used to superimpose a stipple effect, an antique effect, a "target" effect, and other variations. Sometimes, too, one additional color may be printed over the black, giving you what is called a *duotone*.

Again, printers and engravers can explain these possibilities. Since every little wrinkle normally costs extra, there should be a reason for the variations and not merely some whim of the designer.

ARTWORK

Just as you might buy *stock photos* from some supply house—photos that are on hand and might serve your purpose—you can also buy *clip art,* drawings that are immeasurably less expensive than commissioning the original art. Several art services offer books of clip art for sale, including several instant art books specializing in travel, like the Delmar series by Louis Mercurio Associates. When using clip art, you should make certain the art fits and that it is not too familiar.

As a glance through any magazine will convince you, there are innumerable art styles. High fashion is easily identifiable, and it's a far cry from the realistic illustrations in supermarket ads. There are pen-and-ink drawings, scratchboard work (where white lines are etched out of a surface bathed in black ink), wash drawings (using a paintbrush to achieve various shades of black and gray), colored pencils, oil paintings, pastels, and so on. Some art is ultrarealistic; others are ethereal, even abstract.

In a newsletter or brochure, drawings may provide a change of pace from photography and, in small ads, sketches may reproduce much better. As with photos, amateur work has no place here. If you can afford to hire an outside art studio, do so—unless you have your own in-house art department. If the budget isn't there, look into clip art. But don't settle for the inept work of some over-zealous staffer.

One good thing about travel art is that numerous travel landmarks are immediately identifiable, from Diamond Head in Hawaii to Mount Fuji in Japan.

COMPUTER GRAPHICS

Only the larger travel entities—airlines, cruise lines, hotel chains —can afford to invest in the equipment necessary to produce state-of-the-art computer graphics. For most of those who use this medium, the source will be outside their offices. While some static art, like logos, is accomplished by computers, the major use for this technique is for television—or for the composing of all sorts of charts, from annual-report-type graphs to others with an engineering purpose. Many of the latter results will not be seen by the public and are used only internally.

Someday, when pricing is more reasonable, computer graphics may be in more common use for even the smaller tasks, like laying out an ad or designing a brochure. Even now, however, the computer generates considerable communication within the travel industry, and the possibilities have scarcely been tapped.

Everyone is familiar with the ability of the computer to retrieve data instantly, like airline schedules and prices, hotel availabilities, VIP clients' preferred rental cars, weather details, billing information, and other items. Computers can be utilized in the scheduling of employee hours, recording of corporate donations, evaluation of publicity clips, and shopping for Christmas presents for employees or clients. They can be used in place of the mails, to talk with each other, or can be linked with libraries to access material on foreign destinations, or may be programmed to correct spelling errors.

In so many ways, including the delivery of sophisticated artwork, the computer has become an indispensable adjunct to even the smallest office. There are, however, some cautions. A small travel agency should think twice before loading up on computer systems just because the bigger agencies have them. This could be expensive, unnecessary, and might even disrupt the firm's previous efficiency. Another concern is the effect of computers on those who must face them all day—on their personalities, their eyes, and their general health.

FILM, TELEVISION, RADIO, AND SLIDE SHOWS

As they are fond of saying in government circles, the operative words here are "Get help!"

All of these media present production problems beyond the ordinary layperson, unless you opt for the simplest one-projector slide show. Even then, the photo and taping assignments call for expertise. Because of the requirement of professional help, it makes little sense here to do more than review what transpires in these areas, rather than conduct a how-to-clinic.

With the improvement in the quality of video-taping, *film* has declined as a commercial medium. There are still some things a film crew does better, but these advantages are diminishing. Even the flexibility and portability arguments have been defused and there is often little to choose from between the finished products visually. Normally, the film begins with a script or, at the very least, a shooting schedule, and the travel employee or executive may have considerable input at this stage. Then, cinematographers and sound technicians go on location or work in a studio setting, capturing on film and audio tape the action and dialogue (if any). They'll shoot far more footage than will finally appear on screen, in order to provide them with options and transitions. The raw film is developed, screened, and a rough sequence formulated. Further screenings are held, honing the film to meet script, timing, and quality demands. The sound track is similarly edited and then added to the visual track, using a special editing machine. More decisions ensue, and, again, the travel industry personnel should be involved. Once the film is approved as edited, it is sent to a film laboratory where "optical effects" are added, dissolving or cutting from one scene to another, fading in and out of black, and employing all of the visual tricks that are part of the medium. Before the final print is made and duplicated, there are additional steps and additional opportunities to add, delete, or refine, but as the process progresses, these changes become more complicated and more expensive. As with print material, catching lapses early on is least expensive.

Although television crews also shoot on location, much of what we see on the air is produced in a studio. The news, game shows, even the soaps. Travel shows are generally set within a studio atmosphere, with film, video, and slides to spice up the programming. Two or three cameras may be employed, with participants fitted with lapel microphones. The set is likely to be tight, restricting any broad movements, and there could be a rear projection (or front projection) screen as part of the arrangement, to facilitate the showing of visuals. A director, seated in a nearby control booth, runs the show, cueing different cameras, introducing music, integrating the film, making certain time limitations are observed. Often, the show will be taped in advance. One good thing about tape is that it can be viewed and edited immediately. If something goes wrong, the director can call for another take right away.

As far as involvement of travel personnel is concerned, unless they help write the script or anchor the program, their input will be minimal. The director is in charge once the cameras start rolling. If you are not satisfied with the finished product, you may, of course, request another shot or sequence.

This scenario also applies to the production of TV commercials. The travel client, their advertising agency, and the production (or television) studio team up in production, agreeing in advance on what will be shot. Once the shooting is underway, the director should be left alone until there is a natural break, or until the segment is complete.

Radio production is considerably simpler than either film or TV. A talented neophyte might do a credible job. However, it's still a good idea to involve the professionals. Just as a lawyer who represents himself or herself has a fool for a client, so, too, the travel employee who plays the role of writer, on-the-air announcer, engineer, and editor is making a big mistake. Production costs for radio, including decent talent, are not great. Even a small radio station is likely to have a small music and sound effects library, and their staffers can normally handle copy better than the amateur. Everything the client can bring to the recording session is welcome, from script ideas to special sound effects and performers — but all should be of broadcast quality.

The production of slide shows is varied. You may start with either script or slides, but even at that early stage, there should be some idea about the complexity of the programming. Single- or dual-projector shows call for different photo and copy decisions than multiprojector, multiscreen extravaganzas. The latter is most effective when it has some sort of stability, like being set up in an office or company auditorium. Transporting a battery of equipment and synching it at each site is expensive, time-consuming, and risky. The simpler slide show versions may feature a single projector and narrator, a single projector and a pulsed audiotape that electronically drops the slides, a pair of projectors linked by a dissolve unit that more artistically blends one slide with another while employing taped narration. All of these options may be produced by the intelligent amateur, except for the multi-image types, which are far too technical for the nonprofessional.

Every other promotional technique, from outdoor billboards to electronic marquees, is best left to those who understand the medium. Ineptness in production destroys an otherwise effective message, the same way dissonant body language may counteract an otherwise positive speech. This applies to little things, like a knowledge of the proper use of brochure shells supplied by larger carriers, a grasp of the variant ways mailing pieces may be folded, and the talent to devise an attractive ad layout or brochure dummy. This is especially true for items like logos or signatures that have real permanence. Companies often spend hundreds of thousands of dollars to develop a symbol for their firm, so even the smallest travel agency should commit some funds to this important and long-lasting element.

OTHER VISUAL CONSIDERATIONS

Besides the communications that emanate from travel firms, consideration must also be given to the physical impression the firms themselves present. Some travel agencies are cluttered and messy, hardly conducive to convincing a client that ticketing will be error free. Other sites may be clinically neat but have no character, no ability to suggest that traveling is enjoyable. There should be a compromise. Any office can combine warmth and efficiency, Figure 7–13. Posters, brochure racks, wall maps, ship models, and other artifacts have their place, but employees and clients shouldn't find them more distracting than helpful.

Travel agency employees, too, contribute to the look of an office. This isn't a newsroom or typing pool; it's a place where emphasis is on meeting the public. Many agencies prescribe a uniform, or least some attractive and identifying apparel. Airlines are the prime ex-

Figure 7–13.   The decor in travel offices can add a lot to the impression of ability and efficiency. (Courtesy Travel and Transport)

ample of this, but when you think about it, every mode of transportation tries to spruce up its representatives.

Tourism bureaus are typically busy places, especially in major cities. They attempt, through appearance and personnel, to convey hospitality and the promise of solid information. Often, there are chairs for weary tourists, dozens of helpful brochures, book racks, schedules, posters, even souvenirs. The whole scene must be inviting.

In areas that are not normally open to the public, like the offices of a major hotel chain, the external aspect may be less critical but should not be neglected. Prospects do visit and people have to work in this atmosphere. It should be as congenial as possible.

In short, planners should be aware that all of our senses are involved in communication, and we make a mistake when we concentrate mainly on the audio portion of messages. Everything should work together.

CHAPTER HIGHLIGHTS

❑   Visual impact is an important consideration within the travel industry, so attention should always be given to the way any communication looks.

❏ Design embraces harmony, sequence, and balance.

❏ Among design considerations are dominance of one element, white space, working with small formats, a knowledge of mechanical requirements, and avoidance of visual cliches.

❏ Among the design possibilities are these nine common formats: picture window, frame, Mondrian, multipanel, silhouette, copy heavy, typeface, rebus, and circus layouts.

❏ Besides print ads, brochures, posters, newsletters, and other printed items have their own design demands.

❏ Copy blocks are part of layout and must be treated as such. Copy fitting is part of the layout technique.

❏ The five general categories of type are Roman, Gothic or Block, Script, Text, and Ornamental. There are also type families and, within these families, there are series, fonts, and individual characters.

❏ Height of type is measured in points, of which there are 72 to an inch, while width of typed lines is measured in picas, with 6 picas to a linear inch.

❏ Letterpress and offset are the two main printing methods, using hot and cold type, but there is laser printing, silk screening, gravure, and variant forms of offset.

❏ Color, which triggers emotional reactions, requires skill in its printing application, with attention required in selection and combinations.

❏ Choice of paper affects both visual impact and the reproduction of graphic material, especially photography. Its weight is figured on the basis of the weight of a 500 sheet ream of large, uncut sheets.

❏ Consistently good photography is the province of the professional, but the travel staffer should be aware of the possibilities and requirements of screening, cropping, and reducing pictures.

❏ Artwork can be found in a variety of styles and media, and it may also be purchased as clip art.

❏ Although expensive, computer graphics are becoming more common, especially in the electronic media.

❏ Because of the technical nature of radio and slide programs, and especially film and television, the production aspects of these forms of communication are best left to the experts.

❏ It's worth remembering that the physical appearance of a locale and its staff also makes a visual statement.

■   ■   ■

❏ *EXERCISES*

1. Find a travel ad for each of at least five of the nine formats listed in this chapter.
2. Find examples of all five type categories (from any kind of print advertising), identify the category, and give the size of the type in points.
3. Collect two examples each, from travel advertising, of photography and art work, and tell why you think each item chosen is effective.

❏ *CASE PROBLEMS*

1. You're the creative director of an advertising agency and one of your clients, a tour operator specializing in Europe, wants you to develop a brochure promoting a new tour on "Ghosts on the Continent." The ten-day tour visits a haunted chateau in the Loire Valley of France, the Viennese sewer system made famous in The Third Man, *the fabled castle of "Dracula" in Transylvania, Mount Olympus in Greece where the mythic gods lived, and the catacombs outside Rome. Let's hear your thoughts on the size and type of brochure, colors, type style, photography, and art.*

2. As the manager of a medium-sized travel agency, you are trying to interest a local television station in scheduling a weekly program on travel. The station would handle production, but you would determine format, provide talent and props, and arrange for film or slides. Write a letter to the program director of the station, pitching this idea, and giving the director an idea of what the program might contain. Remember that you're selling the director on the idea.

8

PERSONAL SALES

Regardless of the vocation, salesmanship is part of any career. Even when not selling a specific product or service, the individual is often faced with the need to sell an idea, promote a cause, or convince a colleague. Knowing how to sell enhances even the most personal transaction and the wise individual never forgets this.

In marketing, personal selling is an important component in the mix. For many products and services, the presence of an individual to close the sale is essential. Price and quality may attract a buyer, and promotional campaigns may direct this buyer to a source, but often it is a person who has to conclude the transaction. Within the travel industry, for example, a business traveler may routinely book personal air with a minimum of contact with an airline staff member. Perhaps there is no real selling involved here. But there could be. Maybe the airline representative talks the traveler into enrolling as a frequent flyer, or, in cases where the corporation that owns the airline also owns a hotel chain, the representative may inquire about choice of accommodations. If the business passenger books through a travel agent, these options, plus inquiries about rented cars and other items, could be discussed. The choices mentioned by the travel agent may themselves be the result of salesmanship by a carrier representative.

More salesmanship is evident in vacation travel and in the solicitation of commercial, government, and incentive travel accounts.

Salesmanship is communication. Every aspect of the sales strategy involves communication, from the advertising and the packaging to the ability of the person on the scene to wrap up the purchase. All of the communication skills mentioned earlier come into play in sales.

PERSUASION

In this book's opening chapter, the value of persuasion was outlined. Persuasion is at the root of salesmanship. Even when a prospect may demonstrate real interest, even when this person may show up at a travel agency or cruise line office, there may be lingering doubts about the impending decision, or some unresolved options offered by competition. The salesperson has to erase the concerns and reinforce the decision.

To be effective, the source of the persuasive communication must be perceived as trustworthy. If the client is suspicious of the salesperson, conversion is unlikely. If, however, the salesperson is credible, a sale is more likely to result. The message must also be clear to the prospect, must offer something of value, and works best when some action is proposed—like making a deposit on a tour or agreeing to a request to make a business travel presentation.

Obviously, different persuasive techniques work with different people. Some travel prospects react to a bargain, while others may succumb to the snob appeal of an exclusive but expensive option. There are people who want to be told what they should do and others who prefer a more subtle approach. The good salesperson senses what works and follows that route until it either succeeds or proves inadequate.

MOTIVATION

Motivation is tied to persuasion, since a person's motives for making decisions lie at the root of his or her ability to be persuaded. A young traveler interested in making new friends and having fun will not respond well to a sales pitch touting Mayan architecture. A business traveler whose chief concern is scheduling and comfort may not be keenly interested in tales about the airline's cuisine.

The salesperson can't know the motivational keys to enthuse each prospect or each group, but should rely on experience and on general assumptions, and should also be alert for early clues that would help expose these motives. It's just another way of saying that a successful sales presentation talks in terms of client interest.

SALES THEORY

As with other aspects of communication, sales must be planned; there needs to be an overall strategy. Strategy begets technique and technique drives the way a salesperson presents the product or service. More attention may be given to these sales options when time is not a major consideration, but even with instant over-the-counter sales, theory should be instinctive.

Sales theory really answers the question about *why* people buy certain goods or services, and *how* they can be conditioned to make a positive response.

The *stimulus-response* strategy, for example, is at the root of all those sales track pitches, the kind common to insurance salespersons or telephone solicitors. These memorized speeches are designed to provoke predictable responses. This routine is difficult to apply to the travel industry, mainly because the choices are so varied, but some of the principles are good to remember—including the fact that a majority of people are likely to respond in the same way to the same positive appeal (a price reduction, for example). Tactics that work in one situation should also be husbanded for future reference.

A second strategy recalls the AIDCA formula mentioned in Chapter 5. Prospects often go through a series of fairly predictable states before coming to a decision, and the salesperson may take them through these stages, much as a coach trains an athlete or a teacher explains a problem. The *attention through action* formula works here as well as in a print ad. If you think again of the insurance salesperson, you'll recognize that, after attention and interest are secured, the salesperson works on desire and credibility and then initiates some action. More flexible than the stimulus-response theory, this strategy works best when you have a little time and few distractions.

Theorists also promote the *problem-solution* approach, where the product or service is suggested as a remedy for the difficulty. Many television ads for household products adopt this scenario. Your kitchen floor is grimy and guests are due to arrive. Solution? A cleaner that makes the linoleum glitter like a starlet's teeth. Although this strategy may be more common in the selling of larger industrial items, it could apply to travel. A football fan can't find a vacant hotel room in the bowl game city. Can you solve the problem with a spot in a nearby town? A seasoned traveler is looking for a totally different kind of tour. What can you suggest? A handicapped group wants a trip that accommodates its special needs. A businessperson has to attend a luncheon in Tucson and be back home for a dinner engagement. A dozen travel writers are due to visit your city and want to crowd as much as possible into three days. Dealing with the problems effectively is good salesmanship.

There is also a sales theory that echoes the notion of motivation and benefit. The prospective traveler has a need that should be filled. If the salesperson can zero in on that need and provide satisfaction, a sale should result. Sometimes the individual may not initially recognize the need and the salesperson may have to suggest it. "What you need is a cabin at Fort Harmony, which will be inexpensive, secluded, giving you peace and quiet and a chance to get your work done," or, "Have you ever thought about a cruise, because it sounds like that's just the therapy you need?"

All of these theories have potential and all might work in different situations. But the salesperson has to be alert for clues and skilled in communication. This requires listening and thinking and analyzing and responding.

CONSIDERING THE ENVIRONMENT

This topic was also discussed earlier, but like so many other elements, it also affects salesmanship. You have to be abreast of changes in the traveler's attitude and aware of concerns and trends. Twice as many people now fly compared with 1976, the year that airline deregulation began, and the growth in the number of airlines mirrors that. Health-conscious Americans are booking into hotels with spas and demanding meals with fewer calories. Because of scheduling problems in families where both partners work, shorter, more frequent vacations are becoming popular. Adventure is back in, and cruises continue to appeal. Travelers expect more when they travel and are often willing to pay the difference. Moreover, those who travel are more sophisticated and they understand more about the process.

The salesperson must be familiar with all that is going on in this volatile industry, because people talk about travel and read about travel, and they expect those in the profession to be expert in a number of areas.

SELLING SERVICES

The travel communicator needs to be reminded again that selling an intangible is quite different than selling an identifiable product. Travel is transitory. True, you have slides, photos, and purchases as reminders, but the trip itself is gone, like a favorite stage play or a classic concert. You can't park travel in your garage, wear it to the office, or serve it to guests. It's difficult to evaluate. Maybe that's why tourists are more relaxed about spending money while in this environment. It seems a bit unreal and short-lived and prices that might make you gulp at home cause more of a shrug abroad.

Selling travel is really selling an experience. Even business travel, which relies less on emotional appeal, remains experiential. For the vacationer, the salesperson tries to evoke visions of what the trip may bring while providing the concrete details. That's why the salesperson is such an important element in the service marketing mix.

SALES PLANNING AND MANAGEMENT

Good companies—successful companies—have marketing plans and sales goals. They revise these periodically, keeping them realistic but challenging. Salespeople need something to shoot for, some targets to assail. Some plans for sales may be very sophisticated, segmented into not only the main areas, like vacation and business and incentive, but also into many smaller units, cataloged by definition and geography. Small travel agencies will have fewer categories and more modest goals, but all members of the travel industry must look ahead at their potential for sales growth. These targets are a mix of experience, trends, competitive strength, the economy, a firm's own financial needs, and sales force stimulation.

To achieve goals, the right people must be part of the team. That's why an aptitude in selecting personnel is helpful. It's not easy in the travel field because the salary levels are relatively low and the work demanding, especially for travel consultants attached to agencies in busy locales. Even so, when choosing salespeople, the travel executives usually look for the right attitude, some evidence of determination, communication skills, and the ability to be self-motivating. A bright person can learn the business, but it may be too late to develop the essential character traits. New employees may be graduates of travel schools or they could move into sales from some other area of the firm. They could come to the profession with experience in other sales work, or they may just possess the requisite qualifications and be worth training.

Once aboard, salespeople should be properly schooled in corporate or agency policies and expectations, should be supplied the information required to do a good job, should be part of the marketing team, and should have their work checked on a regular basis. Salespeople need encouragement and direction, and they should be rewarded for production.

The normal reward is usually monetary, but that's not the only way to recognize achievement. Praise, promotion, and challenging new assignments are other ways. So are trips, a chance to attend seminars and conventions, contests with cash or other prizes, and even a simple thing like dinner or having your name affixed to a plaque. Suppliers also offer incentives to salespersons, often in-kind rewards like hotel space or vacation travel.

Whenever a firm institutes a reward program, the enterprise should be carefully thought out, with company executives making certain it's fair, that it promises benefits for the company, that it's affordable, and that it's manageable. In the fairness category, for example, modern firms now recognize that merely saluting the top dollar producer may not be equitable. Location and population may have a lot to do with success. So many companies have adopted a formula that matches achievement against reasonable expectations, so a salesperson that builds up accounts in a small or difficult market may be regarded more highly than one who accumulates more sales in a more promising territory.

Companies work differently with sales personnel. Some offer commissions only, some salary and commissions, some only salary, and some have more complicated contracts with floors and ceilings and other conditions. In many ways, selling is the most fair job available. If you produce, you are compensated. No amount of connections, luck, or personal charisma sustain you unless you actually move goods and services. So a salesperson with an outstanding record is always in a strong bargaining position with an employer.

Retaining capable salespeople isn't easy. Money is one problem, but benefit packages (except for travel) may be lower than in other businesses, working conditions are often crowded and hectic, stock options and profit sharing are relatively rare, and a majority of travel firms have no clear career track.

WHAT MAKES A GOOD SALESPERSON?

There are numerous sales styles and a variety of sales personalities. Some salespersons are aggressive, almost intimidating, while others are more laid back, letting the prospect take the lead. Today's professional is likely to be less frenetic than past sales staff members. The image of the loud used-car salesman is passé. Americans don't like to be pressured into a purchase, so a new type of salesperson has emerged—one that knows the product, knows the client, and knows the route to pursue to bring about a sale.

Facets of Two Winning Techniques

Knowledge.   The salesperson understands the product or service. In travel, this is difficult. There are so many destinations to know, so many routing options, so much differential in pricing, so many variations of all kinds. That's why you must be a good listener and reader. The salesperson is always a student, picking up anything that will help with the job.

Let's start with geography. The successful agent or representative should be familiar with the nations of the world, their major cities and attractions, approximate travel distances and weather conditions. Going even beyond that, a basic grasp of physical geography would be a plus, enabling the salesperson to calculate climatic changes and make intelligent suggestions as to appropriate clothing or accommodations. Even a small island like Jamaica can feature dry weather on one side of a mountain range and wet weather on the other. The salesperson should also be familiar with the specific demands of tours. Older passengers have sometimes been surprised that they had to wade ashore in certain locales. If the tour is a walking tour, how many miles do they walk on an average day? Are there special rules for dress at places like the Vatican? Can you purchase Waterford Crystal at the factory itself? Will the traveler have any difficulty finding people who speak English? Are shots required? How safe is it in Country A?

The salesperson can't know everything, but he or she should be able to find the information quickly and there shouldn't be any erroneous guesses about details.

Schooling helps. A local university probably offers courses in geography, history, and culture. There are thousands of helpful books, from volumes about every nation to the half dozen or so popular guide series. There are film cassettes and brochures and trade journals and travel magazines. The federal government issues newsletters on other countries and so do some travel services. Larger cities have citizens who come from abroad, and other travel personnel may have visited the place you need to learn about. Ask. Listen.

One of the ways those in the travel industry acquire knowledge is through familiarization tours, trips sponsored in whole or in part by carriers, hotels, tourist bureaus, and tour companies. Trade journals often carry lists of available trips for travel agents, for example. While such "fam trips" can be enjoyable, they are often packed with visits to properties and amenities. To get the most mileage out of these journeys, the fam tripper should make the scheduled visits, ask questions, take notes, fill out a report, and share experiences with colleagues. Many travel firms require these steps before approving any familiarization tours, and executives seem increasingly willing to pay part of the employee's travel costs when real benefits can be demonstrated.

One *Travel Weekly* writer, concentrating on fam cruises, suggested that clients who have used the cruise line be contacted in advance of the trip and questioned about their opinions so that these specific points can be checked out. Once aboard, the writer counsels asking a lot of questions (including questions of fellow passengers—but without revealing your purpose), taking photos, experiencing everything available, trying to see the cruise through the eyes of a consumer, and then compiling a scrapbook on the experience for use by others in the firm.

Besides the lists that appear periodically in travel trade journals and the communications from suppliers, there's a trio of directories issued annually by GTC Fam Facts (1454 E. Hinchman Road, Berrien Springs, Michigan 49103) that list all sorts of discounts on carriers, for hotels and car rentals, plus details on specific costs, dates, and availability of spouse travel. The same organization also publishes a monthly *Update* on familiarization tours.

One of the best ways to improve one's knowledge of the travel industry is to achieve CTC (Certified Travel Consultant) status, which is the result of a minimum of five years of experience, and the successful completion of a five-part course. Even reviewing the CTC study guides helps.

Analysis.   Just as the successful salesperson must continue to acquire knowledge, this same person must also get in the habit of analyzing both the travel market and the travel prospect.

Building, updating, and expanding lists of prospects is essential. Some travel units do a poor job of compiling lists of those who use their facilities, while others have remarkable computerized rosters for easy retrieval, complete with all sorts of personal information.

Building a list may be accomplished in numerous ways. You can start with your own contacts, plus club and parish lists (when available), directories, items carried by the media, magazine articles, and other sources. Salespeople may also secure leads from friends or from individuals in a position to hear about prospects and influence their decisions. Advertising produces leads, and so does attendance at social functions, sponsorship of prizes, and even the scheduling of film showings or other social events. The professional salesperson tries to match offerings with likely interest. A trip to European shrines could use a lot of parish directories, while a weekend football package could appeal to students and alumni. A list for potential commercial accounts may come out of a Chamber of Commerce directory or clippings from the newspaper's business pages or from word of mouth at civic and professional meetings.

No list should be allowed to get too old. List companies "clean" their lists at least annually, correcting addresses, name changes, title changes, and other variables. The list must also be worked. No sense in having information unless someone utilizes it.

In addition to analyzing sources of leads, the salesperson should become adept at analyzing prospects. Psychology and experience play a part here. Old hands in the travel business can nearly always spot a "shopper," a person who may already have booked with a competitor but is checking out the deal in terms of price. They recognize a situation in which one partner is less enthusiastic about a tour than another. In a presentation situation, they are conscious of which one of the business executives is really going to influence the decision. They ferret out fears and motives and desires.

One agent asks prospects a lot of questions about their previous travel, noting whether people use the pronoun *I* or *we,* sometimes revealing whether they would be more comfortable with an independent FIT trip or with a group package.

Asking questions is another tactic in analysis, allowing the salesperson to "qualify" the prospect, ascertaining what the person is really after and what he or she is willing to pay for it. Here's a young couple, both employed, living in a rented trailer. Despite their relative youth, they could be prospects for an upscale trip, simply because they may have an above-average disposable income. Here's a company whose officers are politely listening to a proposal for their business travel but who are all unwilling to offend the veteran employee who has been handling their travel for years.

The salesperson gathers information as quickly and subtly as possible and builds the message on this data, structuring the persuasive elements for maximum effect on the decision makers.

Sales Track.   You've heard these on the telephone or when visited by certain salespeople. They often sound canned, and even the replies to objections have a hollow echo. Still, there are positive aspects to a practiced routine. At the very least, it serves as a checklist to guide the salesperson. Notice the way many insurance firms school their sales staffs. The salesperson begins by gathering data on the prospect, including lifestyle clues and needs, then analyzes the current insurance situation, pointing out shortfalls. A solution is proposed and explained, questions answered, and objections neutralized. Often, the salesperson will try to reduce the negatives to a single one. "So, if I understand this right, you would like to have more insurance and, in general, you like our company and the policy I've just explained?" Getting assent or hearing no serious challenge, the insurance salesperson may then say, "Then I guess the only problem is whether or not you can afford more insurance." (Pause) "Would you believe that this policy I've just described costs less than fifty cents a day, just about three dollars a week?" By then, the hook is in.

Travel may be sold the same way, relying on a progression of logical and emotional topics to bring the sale about.

Enthusiasm, Confidence, and Appearance.   The way information is presented is sometimes as important as content. Every teacher knows this. If a salesperson can generate enthusiasm about the product or service, this communicates itself to the client. Some travel consultants have the ability to convey a vigorous interest in what they are selling, convincing the prospect that they wish they could take this journey themselves. Enthusiasm is contagious and makes the undecided patron more excited about the potential. Confidence is also a key, not only in adding credibility to the presentation, but also in sustaining any salesperson through the slower, more frustrating days. The solid salesperson embodies belief in the product or service and belief in self.

Another factor is appearance. Not everyone can have a Hollywood visage, but those who meet the public should be suitably dressed, clean, neat, and amiable. Dress and demeanor should not be a barrier to sales but, rather, a help. When you know you look good, you feel good, and when you feel good, you gain poise and confidence. You look professional and you strive to match that image.

Focusing on Benefits.   This topic has been mentioned several times in this text and it is absolutely vital in selling. Prospects don't really want to know how long you've been in the business, or how large your company is, or how many cruises you've sold. They want you to talk about them and their interest. They need to know how purchasing this product or service will make them happier, healthier, smarter, wealthier, or more fulfilled. The best selling techniques always rely on benefit strategy. Mentally, you place the clients in some exotic setting or you show them how they save money or you convince them their corporation's travel will be handled far more efficiently.

In many respects, selling is informing. You give individuals the information they should have in order to make an intelligent, satisfying decision. But you should be more than an order taker; you can sell creatively, using your imagination to attractively package verbal or written proposals.

For example, some consultants are skilled at *cross selling,* querying the traveler about the need for options like hotels, car rental, and insurance. Others have a knack for *selling up* a tour by upgrading the purchases by an individual. This latter strategy should be used prudently, because the prospect may well react negatively to any semblance of high pressure. On the other hand, a sensitive travel consultant who really knows the business and who really understands the client, may realize that this particular individual will not be happy in the accommodations selected and that he or she could afford better, so an upgrading is not so much a ploy to increase commissions as it is an attempt to provide adequate service. Talking someone out of a too-cheap cruise could even be necessary in order to protect an agent's reputation.

Overcoming Objections.   Once the prospect has been qualified, the information supplied, and credibility established, the salesperson must be ready to field objections or eliminate concerns. Many of the objections can be anticipated, and others can be predicted during the initial discussion phase.

Successfully responding to objections calls for careful listening, including attention to what isn't being verbalized, and a reluctance to interrupt until the prospect has finished speaking. Don't contradict the people directly or put them on the defensive. Treat each concern seriously, even if it's outrageous, and respond as briefly as possible. You must always make certain you fully understand the objection. Perhaps you are asked about hotel location but the real concern is security. The prospects may ask about the kind of equipment they are flying in, because of an expressed interest in adequate leg room. The bottom line, however, is a worry about flying overseas. Concerns about cost are common, and could mean that you have not properly qualified your prospect or that you have not adequately stressed the benefit package. It's always best to tell the individual what the money buys before you get to the price. Otherwise, you spend your time merely justifying a stated cost.

People who are really not interested may invent all sorts of reasons for not buying. Some of these may be off the wall. "What if the bus is hijacked?" "I just can't eat any foreign foods." "I'm not sure what to do about my dog." When you can counter these, you do so, but gently. When you see it's a waste of time, move on.

Corporate clients may object that they are well satisfied with their present method of handling travel internally. The salesperson must bottom line the differences. The tourism bureau manager has a potential convention chairperson worried about the summer weather in North Carolina, so the manager must reply with facts and, perhaps, testimonials. Those who sell cruises have discovered long ago how to respond to the objection that there's nothing to do once aboard and that the traveler will be bored.

The salesperson must also consider stalling tactics as an objection. If they say they want to "think it over" or "will call you later," you have to figure out if they really need time or if you have merely failed to make your case. If the latter, then you should quickly review the main points. Take the blame for not making things clear and try to resolve the issue before the meeting is concluded.

The salesperson may have to work at extracting some hidden objections. If you sense these are hovering around the conversation, ask questions.

- ❑ "I'm sure you've had some experiences that cause you to feel that way. Would you mind telling me about them?"
- ❑ "Obviously, I haven't done a good job of explaining all this. Are there still some questions or concerns you might have?"
- ❑ "I think I saw you react when I talked about the walk through the Tower of London. If that's your concern, let me put it in perspective."
- ❑ "I guess it comes down to this. If I can show you that you can handle all of the company travel needs at a lower cost and without any loss of efficiency or the personal touch, then you'd consider our proposal?"

The salesperson brings out the objections, isolates them if possible, and answers them quickly so that he or she can move ahead with the presentation. Actually, objections can be very helpful and they shouldn't frighten the agent or representative. Answering them well lends a lot of credibility to the proposal.

Objections may sometimes be complaints. An airline lost their luggage. A travel agency neglected to book first-class space. A cruise line representative takes the heat for a company policy on the payment of commissions to travel agents. A hotel representative is scored because of one rude incident by a desk clerk. The salesperson must listen sympathetically, offer to look into the complaint, and then do so, following up with a response to the prospect.

Closing.   Sales manuals have a lot to say about closing the sale. After all the information has been passed along, all the motivational buttons pushed, and all of the objections answered, the prospect must be asked to make some sort of commitment. You can't back off and let opportunity slip away. You *close*.

DIFFERENT TYPES OF SELLING STRATEGIES

Obviously, there is a major difference in selling techniques among those who are dealing with drop-in prospects across a crowded travel agency counter and those who appear by appointment before a group of executives. While the underlying principles may still hold true, their application varies according to the situation.

Inside Sales

Travel employees who staff the desks and counters for walk-in traffic have to be alert to a variety of sales opportunities. Besides mastering the selling techniques mentioned earlier, the inside salesperson must be adept at quickly analyzing prospects, watching for telltale body language signs or familiar questions. The best salespersons don't force sales; they help the customer sell himself or herself. They present information, respond to queries, lead the prospect through the decision process, but allow the client to develop the convincing reasons for buying, Figure 8–1. Using this strategy, salespersons learn that prospects often buy things they don't really need but which they want. And, even though the inside salesperson doesn't have time to prepare for the individual client, there are some additional lessons experience teaches:

Know When To Stop Talking.   Some salespeople continue selling past the point of client conviction. This overkill can produce second thoughts in the prospect and may result in delay or loss of the sale.

Have the Ability To Relax People.   Every sales situation embodies a certain amount of tension. While this is present, it's difficult to close a sale. The salesperson should put the prospect at ease— by a nonthreatening demeanor, by refraining from sounding superior, by giving the prospect a chance to talk.

Sell Creatively.   With a little thought, the salesperson can express benefits in a more compelling way. Instead of saying the price includes a couple of dinners, a train ride, and hotels, it's more effective to say: "The one low price covers first-class hotels, a buffet dinner featuring foods from all regions of Italy and a Neapolitan cabaret, and a leisurely train ride through the picturesque Dolomite Alps." You shouldn't overdo the poetry, but imagination is contagious.

Be Tactful.   Times and customs change. In the past, a travel agent or passenger agent might query an unmarried couple booking travel together, but no longer. Current counsel suggests that the agent's job is not to judge or preach. Other situations that call for tact might be when an agent feels that an elderly or handicapped person could

Figure 8–1.   Travel agents try to be helpful to clients, often talking them through tour material. (Courtesy Travel Careers Institute)

have problems with a certain tour, or when some alternative method of payment is proposed, or when a restaurant must refuse a certain credit card. The salesperson can be firm, but pleasant.

Don't Let Your Frustrations Show.   On busy days, counter sales can be tiring and frustrating, and there's a temptation to take out these feelings on the client. But the client doesn't know what kind of day you're having and doesn't care. The professional is able to subdue the negative emotions, smile, and do the job.

Consider Future or Repeat Business.   Even though a sale may be missed on a specific occasion, the stage may be set for a later sale. A positive experience may bring the prospect back and may also extend the relationship after a successful sale. The good salesperson will work on the immediate prospect but also take the long view.

Practice.   Every vocation requires practice. Salespeople may role play situations, ask friends or colleagues for critiques, talk into a tape recorder, make notes on strong and weak points.

The sales manager, or branch manager, should set the standards for the sales force, keeping track of individual achievements, and providing training and encouragement for the staff.

Outside Sales

This term is used in two senses, to describe the independent salesperson who functions outside the travel agency, and to delineate the company employee whose activities are focused on calls outside the firm. Here, "outside sales" is used in the latter sense.

This type of sales takes various forms, from contacting organizations as part of group sales to selling management on the value of incentive trips, and from lining up corporate clients for business travel to successfully securing government contracts. Each assignment differs from the others, and all vary from inside selling tasks.

As with other manageable sales situations, you begin with a thorough job of prospecting. Active salespeople are always thinking about their work. You don't see them sitting around waiting for things to happen. They are investigating numerous opportunities, combing files, making phone calls.

Where do they find these prospects?

Use your head. Assume you have a file of vacation clients. Many of them are in business and may even manage businesses. How about booking their business travel? What about businesses located in your immediate area, if you are a travel agency, or in your market territory if you represent an airline, cruise line, or hotel chain? Develop the habit of reading newspapers and magazines, looking for clues about new businesses or significant changes. Many cities also have breakfast clubs that swap tips on industry newcomers. Other elements of the travel industry may supply leads—not to competitors, but, perhaps, to travel agencies. Some agencies regularly talk with representatives of carriers, hotels, and car rental agencies about business leads. There's the possibility of customer referrals, comments from friends and relatives, key directories (even the telephone book), Chamber of Commerce business lists, membership lists from clubs and organizations, plus your own presence at service club meetings. Those in the travel industry who give periodic speeches find they often hear from prospects in the audience, while others mention making sales while riding in an airplane with strangers. Salespeople may visit bridal shops or luggage shops or caterers, to let them know they're around. And what about the printer who does your printing? Would the printer take some of your cards to give to other customers?

There are other ways to promote leads—through advertising, public relations, and through special events. What about mailings, open houses, cruise nights, destination parties? Can you develop a relationship with a travel editor or local travel columnist, hoping for occasional mention?

If you can look at every new contact as a potential client, and if you use a little imagination in developing lists, the sales will follow. Of course, you must then apply the sales techniques you know, adding in these extra outside-sales suggestions:

Make Certain You Talk To The Right People.　You want to be certain you are talking to those people in the company or organization who are able to make a buying decision. Others in the firm may be friendly, and they could help, but you have to get in touch with the prime movers. While you're at it, you might also keep a weather eye out for those people who could be a thorn in your side. Perhaps some executive has a relative who works for a competitor. Perhaps another person feels he or she may lose a little status if a travel agency takes over bookings. You have to be aware of this danger and you must find ways to neutralize this threat.

Keep in mind that the "right" person in a firm may not always be the CEO. Many executives would delegate matters like travel to a subordinate. You have to learn who that subordinate is, how he or she thinks, what concerns this individual has, and what the best way is to make an approach.

Make the Calls.　In the selling of some products, sales managers practically assure staff members that if they make the calls, they'll make the sales. While it's not quite that easy, it's certainly true that if you don't get out for face-to-face meetings, you won't sell many travel services. For presentations to large firms or organizations, appointments should be made—and kept. Salespersons should be on time, properly dressed, with all the visual aids and material they may need. They should know as much as they can about the prospect company and should know names (including pronunciations) and titles of those they'll contact.

Know What You Have To Offer.　This means not only knowing your own service but also understanding the competition and having an idea about the needs and desires of the prospect firm. A travel agency, for example, could talk about convenience of location, qualifications of personnel (like schooling, years of experience, Certified Travel Consultant ratio), sophistication of equipment, and reputation. The agency may also have a system of rebates for travel volume or some other inducement. The sales representative must know what can be deliverd so that the resultant arrangement is beneficial to both client and agency. You have to meet the competition, but you can't give away the store.

Have Selling Tools on Hand.　The tools must fit the situation. You can't very well show a film at a restaurant lunch, and table-top flip charts aren't too effective with a large group. There's a whole catalog of helpful items, from overheads to cassettes. Whatever seems logical should be brought along. But there still needs to be some printed material, some concrete proposal, something to leave with the client if that seems appropriate.

Suggest an Office Visit.   Again, this is a judgment call, but if you have an office that will impress, especially in terms of personnel and equipment, try to get the client to visit the premises. It's easier to demonstrate the answer to questions here.

Don't Neglect Opportunities in Present Accounts.   A sales force will often spend a lot of time on getting new accounts but fail to consider the possibilities of adding more business from existing accounts. Perhaps a business client might become a prospect for incentive travel. You may currently serve a firm that has branches elsewhere, in locations where you also have offices. Perhaps the firm might be encouraged to consolidate its travel, using these other centers.

Maintain Contact With Clients.   Immediately after a sales call, there should be a "thank-you" follow-up, then a later follow-up if no word is heard. If the client is signed up, the travel unit should stay in touch, with periodic visits and mailings. Printed items of interest can be forwarded to a client, or a note sent when the client firm or its principals accomplish something noteworthy. The salesperson shouldn't become annoying, but there are ways to subtly remind the client that you are there and ready to serve. Staying in touch also helps insure that you'll be able to react quicker to potential problems and that you can respond to and rectify complaints with a minimum of delay.

Keep Good Records.   Regardless of an individual's ability to recall details, it's necessary to keep thorough and updated records of sales calls and client contact. To avoid making embarrassing errors, there needs to be some ready file that can be consulted.

Some Outside Sales Situations

While travel agencies interested in corporate, group, and government business will call on appropriate companies and organizations, sales reps for airlines, cruise lines, and other transportation suppliers will consider travel agencies as among their most important clients. Just as media representatives make calls on advertising agencies, so, too, do the carrier reps contact those who can recommend or purchase travel space from among a variety of choices. These representatives stay in touch by mail or phone and they also drop in on travel agencies, perhaps taking key people to lunch. They also invite agency personnel to parties or film showings they might host. Of course, these same carriers also feature counter sales, so these more immediate skills must also be developed. In the one case, the sales rep acts as an intermediary, and, in the second instance, the sale is direct, requiring all the skills mentioned earlier.

Airlines (and those who sell airline space) have had a tougher time since deregulation, primarily because there are so many different fares to the same destination. There is also the temptation to get complacent, since a major portion of the calls or visits to airline counters are by people who have already made up their minds to go somewhere, Figure 8–2. Still, there is missionary work to be done here. These same people will travel elsewhere in the future and you want to create a good impression.

Individual hotels and restaurants rarely make sales calls, although it wouldn't hurt some of them to become better acquainted with travel agents and tourism bureau personnel. Major chains do make such calls, again in a soft sell manner, merely alerting travel agents and potential client firms to new facilities, programs, or prices. They'd like to be considered for incoming business, especially the convention trade.

Figure 8–2.   While counter sales for airlines may be substantial, the client has normally decided already, so the emphasis is on service more than persuasion.

Convention and tourism bureaus for the city, state, or country make calls on groups and organizations that might consider meeting in that locale. They also stay in touch with travel agents, hotels, restaurants, and local attractions. If supported by local government, tourism bureaus must also look upon elected officials as a special public and do a regular selling job on them, too.

THE PRESENTATION

Often, you may get only one chance to make a favorable impression on a prospective client. If that's the case, then there is no excuse for sloppy preparation and shoddy material. This should be your best shot.

Elements discussed previously under speech communication and special events also apply here. The person(s) who presents the case for the travel company should remember all the public-speaking tips, from a strong opening to the proper use of explanatory anecdotes. And the presentation—which really is an event—deserves the same attention to detail that would be expended on a company banquet or awards ceremony.

The presenter should be chosen carefully. Product knowledge and ability to articulate are essential, but there are traits beyond those. The person who leads the discussion should have a presence that impresses the listeners, should be alert to audience reactions, and should be willing to share the platform when other expertise is called for. The presenter should start on time and should keep the program moving. The language used by the presenter should be free of anything potentially offensive or gramatically incorrect. The presenter is the chief salesperson and must run the show with intelligence and tact.

Checkpoints in Preparing and Delivering the Presentation

Clearly Define the Reason For the Presentation. Perhaps this may seem unnecessary. Travel executives may assume the purpose is to sell their services, period. Not true. The purpose may be to save an existing account, or to convince the audience that your small agency can handle things, or to showcase your computer hardware, or even to set the stage for a later sale. After discussing your aim and agreeing on it, the elements of the presentation should be ordered in a way that fulfills this purpose.

Organize the Presentation.   You want the delivery to be smooth. You want to control its progress, even anticipating the questions. This requires an outline geared toward accomplishing all those steps a good ad attempts, from attention and interest to desire, credibility, and action. It usually works better to speak from an outline rather than relying on a completely scripted text.

Envision the Audience and Situation.   You should find out where you will meet and who will be there. Know all you can about the audience, their titles, experience, their likely attitudes toward your firm and the proposal. If you get a chance, visit the meeting room in advance, noting the location of wall plugs for equipment, determining where you'll stand or sit. Some sharp salespeople are even able to predict where each member of the listening group will be located. If the situation changes when you get there—if someone is added, for example, or the room is changed—be prepared to adapt.

Simplify the Visuals.   Any visual aid should be appropriate to the situation and should not be a cause of worry for the presenter. This is no time to experiment with equipment with which you are unfamiliar. If the presenter is nervous about threading or running a projector or if several pieces of equipment require delicate coordination, another member of the presenting team should be assigned the task. It's best, however, to work with aids that are not confusing or subject to breakdown. Besides, you don't want to overpower an audience; you want to inform and motivate them.

Focus on Details.   Small details can ruin a presentation. You may not be able to prepare for all eventualities, but with a little imagination and organization, you can deal with most of them. You must work on things internal to the presentation as well as potential external interruptions or distractions.

Prepare for Questions.   Political candidates preparing for debates have their aides assume the roles of opponents and interrogators, hitting them with issue or personal questions that may be asked. The candidates work on their answers, settling on the most acceptable ones, and then try to keep these in mind so they emerge during the heat of the contest. Presentations are similar. What will the audience ask? How can you defuse or respond to these queries? What objections might surface and how will you deal with them? Should you turn certain questions over to other members of your team? What do you say if no one knows the answer? The give and take of this exchange should be anticipated.

Rehearse.   All those involved in the presentation should participate in a dry run. Don't merely skip through it but work through the entire event, from opening handshakes to farewells. Some organizations set up a meeting room to resemble the eventual site and practice delivering the pitch to the appropriate "chairs." Equipment is set up and used, questions answered, and adjustments made. Each rehearsal should be evaluated, amended, and repeated.

Enter the Meeting Room With Confidence.   The knowledge that you have a good product, that you know the product or service, that you have adequately analyzed the audience and rehearsed the presentation—these factors help a person exhibit assurance. Perhaps you need a deep breath before you begin, or you could start with some anecdote that will relieve the natural tension. However it is accomplished, the presenter should be in command from the outset.

Consider a Summary Opening.   In situations where the audience is under certain time pressures, it helps to begin with a summary of what will be covered, so that listeners have some notion of the progress of the meeting. A summary also helps prospects organize their own thoughts.

Know How To Maintain Interest.   A sense of progression alleviates boredom, and so does a lively delivery style, with more examples than statistics (even though statistics also fit). The presenter should note reactions and body language and should speed up, slow down, explain, repeat, illustrate, or do whatever is necessary to make the presentation clear and compelling.

Retain Your Own Perspective.   The presenter shouldn't panic, shouldn't get angry or impatient, shouldn't neglect the agreed-upon purpose and organization. While staying flexible as to time and continuity, the presenter wants to keep cool and work toward the original goals.

Know When and How To Stop.   Don't allow a strong presentation to dilute its message with a weak and awkward closing. Remain businesslike. You've made your points and now, respecting the crowded schedules of your audience, you take leave graciously— after, of course, precipitating the action you sought. Perhaps all you can hope for at this juncture is consideration, or an agreement to visit your offices. Perhaps you could close right now. You don't neglect opportunity, but you also avoid standing around, making small talk, causing the audience members to forget the solid program you just completed. Be polite but professional.

TYPES OF PRESENTATION GROUPS

Although the types of groups to which a travel organization might make a presentation are legion, ranging from a college travel club to a Fortune 500 industry, there are four major categories that should be considered: business travel, group travel, incentive travel, and government travel.

You could divide and subdivide categories. Making a presentation to a large corporation is different than calling on a small business with a handful of employees. Knowing a little about the company and its travel potential is wise, and you shouldn't assume that even a successful CEO really understands the travel field. This meeting may be an educational process, but the bottom line is likely to be some savings in time or money. Rebates may be in order, or VIP treatment, perhaps the operation of an in-house company travel department. The travel firm must also decide whether the work, time, and discount policies are worth the effort.

Group travel could involve a client corporation, but it could also mean a presentation to an organization. A college alumni group may want to embark on a Caribbean cruise, or an insurance firm could opt for an employee vacation package. Regardless of the audience, you want to reach the decision makers and you'll want to approach them on the basis of travel that will be both popular and affordable. Sometimes a promotional session may be arranged for the entire club, if the numbers are manageable, but the normal appeal is to the core leadership.

Incentive travel has become increasingly attractive to corporations, who often find this the best way to reward performance. Pyramid companies may hold out a New Orleans vacation as a lure for signing up the most distributorships, and insurance companies offer a week in Switzerland for top performers. The incentive package should have built-in appeal. Hawaii would make a more attractive destination than Houston, although the Texas city might have some added features that would raise its vacation stature. Again, the travel organization might help the company sell the trip to employees by staffing meetings, providing brochures, supplying promotional materials.

In recent years, selling of travel to governmental units has opened up, and many of these contracts are very tempting. An estimate of travel expenses by the Fifth Army, for example, were calculated to be over $85 million a year. To secure such a lucrative account, travel agencies had to bid against one another, with the list finally narrowed to the "best and final" group. The Fifth Army provided proposal forms which had to be filled out and documented. Presentations were made, followed by on-site visits. It took well over a year for the decision to be made and additional months to implement the winning program. Some competing agencies offered rebates on volume; another firm promised a substantial annual contribution to a military personnel fund. Government presentations entail a lot of paperwork and a lot of waiting—but they're often worth it.

SELLING OTHER THINGS BESIDES TRAVEL

In addition to merchandising transportation and accommodations, all sorts of other items may be sold. An airline could offer items from its in-flight store and the editors of its magazine would solicit advertising for the publication's pages. A cruise line may have gifts for sale, some of them souvenirs of the trip. Hotels not only pitch conventions but may make appeals to local service clubs and luncheon groups. A travel agency may offer travel insurance or passport photos. There are even experts in the selling of travel agencies themselves.

And everyone in the industry should remember that the selling of ideas is always current. Many of the techniques used in selling other items also work here, like knowing your audience and rehearsing your presentation. Perhaps psychology comes into play even more, especially if you are one-on-one with those you must convince, or if you are dealing with a small group. Some listeners are intensely logical; some resist innovation; some welcome new ideas; some may be jealous; some may struggle to see how the fresh proposal might work. There must be something in it for each of these individuals before they will acquiesce. Making an idea universally popular isn't always possible, but all you really need is consensus or executive approval and you can get under way. The point is, you have to work at communicating your fresh approaches to problems. You can't expect to have this notion unearthed and implemented unless you help it along.

THE TELEPHONE AS A SALES INSTRUMENT

This topic will be discussed in more detail in the next chapter, but a lot of selling is initiated this way, either through a cold call or through the solicitation of a personal appointment, Figure 8–3. In many ways, travel has lagged behind other industries in the use of the telephone to sell, even though they rely on this form of communication for so much else.

Figure 8–3.   Good telephone sales technique is a significant plus.
(Courtesy Travel Careers Institute)

ETHICS

In the short run, an unethical salesperson may prosper, but in the long run, this strategy inevitably fails. There are enough problems in the travel industry already, from the plethora of fares to the vagaries of weather, without adding a controllable practice like your own behavior. The temptation to exaggerate, to denigrate the competition, to cheat on an expense account, or to doctor a report may be strong. Once you surrender to this form of behavior, your value as a salesperson begins to diminish.

To be credible—and a salesperson has to be credible—you must first be honest. Travel conditions should be described as they are, without embellishment or concealment. Hotels should not be advertised as first class if they are really substandard. An airline can't brag that it has the record for on-time arrivals if that is untrue.

Ethical behavior should be a way of life. You don't lie; you don't take unfair advantage of others; you don't misrepresent the product or service; and you don't compromise your own moral sense.

The salesperson is the company to most clients, so care should always be taken to insure that this representation is honorable.

CHAPTER HIGHLIGHTS

❏ Selling is communication and it's always an important element in the marketing mix. It subsists on persuasion, which must be trustworthy and must be geared to the motivational drives of individuals or groups.

❏ Among the common sales strategies are those labeled stimulus-response, logical progression, problem-solution, and motivation-benefit.

❏ As with advertising and promotion, attention must be paid to the reality of the environment and the trends that are currently operative when an individual is selling. And this person must also appreciate the fact that selling an intangible like a service requires a different technique than selling a tangible product.

❏ Sales goals, sales management, sales training, and a system of rewards should be part of every travel firm's sales plan.

❏ Characteristics of a good salesperson include: knowledge, ability to analyze, adherence to some form of proven sales presentation, enthusiasm and confidence, appearance, benefit-oriented sales talk, ability to overcome objections, and the ability to close a sale.

❏ Those charged with responsibility for "inside sales" must know when to stop talking, must listen, must be able to relax others, must be tactful and creative, must conceal frustations and consider long-range goals, and must practice.

❏ "Outside" salespersons build prospect lists from a variety of sources, contact the right people, work their sales calls, know their business, bring along selling aids, maintain contact with clients, and keep good records.

❏ Among the many situations addressed by outside salespersons are work with corporations and government agencies, private organizations and groups. Besides business travel, vacation and incentive travel are also responsibilities.

❏ A successful travel sales presentation keeps these items in mind: purpose, organization, audience, visuals, details, questions, the need to rehearse, confidence, audience interest, proper perspective, and timing.

❏ Besides travel and accommodations, travel companies may sell everything from gifts and insurance to selling the business. Ideas must also be aggressively sold.

❏ As a basis for all selling, ethical behavior should be the standard for all salespersons in the travel industry.

■   ■   ■

❑ *EXERCISES*

1. Interview a salesperson for any product or service, inquiring about their training and sales strategies. If they are willing to share their prepared sales track, bring it to class.
2. Select a company within your geographical area and assume you are attempting to sell them on adding an incentive plan involving travel for their top producers. Write a memo to your boss (who could be a travel agency manager, head of a cruise line or resort, or a tour operator) and suggest—in outline form—the way you believe this prospect should be approached. Demonstrate that you know something about the prospect firm, and about its best contacts, that you have a good package in mind, and that you have some ideas on how to make the presentation.
3. Working with a classmate, set up a role-playing scenario that will involve counter sales in a busy travel agency. The salesperson should suggest a certain tour and the prospect should be ready with objections. To make this fair, the salesperson should not know of the objections in advance, even though he/ she might anticipate them.

❑ *CASE PROBLEMS*

1. As an outside salesperson, you call on the alumni director for a large state university. This school, with over 100 thousand alumni on its list, wants to start marketing annual trips—perhaps two a year. Your job would be to help construct the itinerary and also help prepare the promotional material. The potential is substantial and you are eager to get the account. So is your boss. At a private luncheon, the alumni director tells you that for each trip he not only expects a free ride for himself and his wife, but that he also wants a percentage of the profits—but quietly, without the University administration's knowledge. You are told by the alumni director that other travel agencies have already agreed to these terms if they are the successful bidders. When you get back to your office, you reflect on the situation, on the substantial nature of the account, and on the fact that other agencies—your competition—are evidently willing to provide these incentives in order to get the contract. Write a memo to your boss giving your recommendations, explaining the reasons for them.

2. You have just transferred from a travel agency in your hometown of Philadelphia to a post as sales manager for a medium-size travel agency in the Midwest. In your initial search of business prospect lists, you realize a high percentage of the firms in your territory have an agricultural base—packing houses, grain products, farm machinery, and similar products. You also realize that your background is urban and that you understand little of the farm and ranch environment. How would you improve your knowledge of this audience? What impact do you think this environment might have on the business executives in the region? What sort of differences would you expect to find in making presentations? Outline your plans for your initial year, combining both your own "education" and your ideas for building sales.

9

TOOLS OF THE TRADE

Although the human element is the key to strong communication in the travel industry, the individual is not expected to function alone. In recent years, many aids to communication have been introduced to the travel field, helping to make things move faster and with added accuracy, and allowing those in the profession to accomplish things that were impossible a quarter century ago.

Each tool is, however, only as good as the person who uses it, so it's worthwhile considering some of the items that can assist — if properly utilized, Figure 9–1.

Figure 9–1. **Drums, an ancient means of communication, are still used in Native American ceremonies.**

THE TELEPHONE

Even with the new technology, the telephone remains the indispensable travel office adjunct, Figure 9–2. Even the smallest company is equipped with multiple phones and the larger units are linked into sophisticated systems that pick out respondents, search for alternate respondents, permit the dialing of frequently called numbers with a few digits, even track individuals to their home phones. Each travel office should carefully choose the system that best fits its own needs and budget.

As a communication tool, the telephone can be used for everything from information to sales, but it can also serve as a means of discrediting a firm or turning away a client. Wise and prudent use is essential, and telephone systems will help school employees in proper technique.

Regular Telephone Etiquette

Every office must understand that the telephone is often the sole link between the firm and key publics. Individuals who have never

Figure 9–2. Though hardly a new tool, the telephone remains one of the most indispensable instruments in travel. (Courtesy Travel Careers Institute)

been on the company's premises may form an impression of the organization from the way a phone call is handled.

Some of the receptionist sins are losing a caller, answering the telephone in an unprofessional manner, or forgetting about the caller. Here are some tactics callers complain about:

"May I Say who's Calling?"   True, some secretaries are instructed to screen callers in this manner, and the construction of this inquiry is at least polite. However, when the sequence is the request of the caller to talk with someone and then the counter-request for identification, the suspicion is that any later statement that the person called is not available is really an indication that he or she doesn't want to speak with you. The person who answers the phone could first tell the caller that the boss is in and then ask for identification. That helps.

"What's the Nature of Your Business?"   More and more secretaries seem to be asking this question and almost every caller resents it. The caller has business with the individual called and not the secretary. This question should never be asked, except in situations where screening is absolutely essential, as in some sensitive government areas. If the person called is out, the secretary may then ask if he or she may be of help — but not in advance.

Long Wait.   No caller should be left hanging without periodic checks back to see if this person wants to continue to wait. Otherwise, they may think they've been cut off.

Annoying Musical Interludes.   Ordinarily, background music during a wait is welcome, but some firms employ sound tracks of monotonous tones which make the delay seem even longer.

Rudeness.   Some people who answer telephones just sound irritated or overworked or indifferent. Their responses may be curt and impolite, and they may even argue with the caller.

Inattention.   The receptionist or secretary puts you on hold and then forgets what or who you wanted. They might also lose you while attempting to transfer the call.

Failure to Take and Record Messages.   From the viewpoint of those within the firm, another error is the lapse in transmitting the message. Some secretaries fail to ask for message or identification, neglect to get a phone number, transpose digits, write illegibly, garble the content, misspell the name, or commit some other lapse.

Recorded Messages

Predictably, after a few years of standard taped responses on answering machines, people began experimenting with variant types of absentee answers. Some are clever, some overly cute. These offbeat messages may amuse some callers, but there's also the danger of annoying some serious people who are already irritated at not reaching you. The safest solution is to be businesslike, clear, short, and sufficiently upbeat. The idea of this equipment is to collect messages and to reassure callers and not to entertain.

Another thing users of these machines need to remember is to be consistent in turning on the machine and proficient in properly setting the tape to record. Messages should also be collected as soon as the individual returns and jotted down, just in case the tape is subsequently erased.

Long Distance

Since the breakup of AT&T, the long-distance emphasis seems to be on what system works best for the individual. It's always a good idea to check this out, fitting the system to the firm's profile, but even with the new fiber-optic appeals and other innovations, some elements of long-distance calling don't change.

For example, in order to save time and money, smart communicators often jot down in advance a list of points they intend to cover in the conversation, and they have pen and paper ready to record data. These people are also conscious of the most favorable times to call in order to budget most economically, and they have handy materials they might need for reference. Those in the travel industry find it helpful to have an atlas nearby, plus a clock or chart that shows time differences across the globe, and several guides or directories of specific interest to the profession.

Cellular Phones

The sale and use of cellular telephones is a growing business, with more and more cars installing these communication tools. Executives stuck in traffic find them useful for getting work done. They can be used to set up appointments, collect data, alert people at the office, verify details, and perform dozens of other tasks. True, they become a toy for some individuals and a few owners also consider them a bit of a driving hazard, but the convenience can be great — especially for the mobile employee. When the combining of lap-top computers and cellular phones becomes common, it may be tough to get people out of their automobiles!

Other Phone Variations

Phone lines are used to transmit facsimile copies of letters or documents. A FAX machine is required at each end of the line and, although the technology currently exists to have the receiver and sender units both unattended, most places currently have older machines that require operators. FAX transmitters are categorized and priced according to both function and speed, with the more expensive units operating five times as rapidly as the cheapest units. These machines can be rented as well as purchased.

The FAX machine is particularly handy for the travel industry. Tour member lists can be FAXed to hotels, and itineraries can be checked with tour operators. Hotel confirmations can be supplied immediately. Many key documents can be reproduced in hard copies for examination and filing, rather than relying on copying down details.

Teleconferencing has been popular for some years now, although, like anything else, it has its drawbacks. The primitive form resembles the old party lines, where several phones are tied together, allowing anyone on the line to listen in and join in on the conversation. These can be set up by an operator or through some of the new in-house switchboard systems. Taking this a step further, the office may be equipped with a speaker phone which allows several individuals at each station to participate in the conversation. Today, we even have picture phones which allow others to see the speakers as well as hear them. This latter device is used not only for meetings but also for occasions when an executive might wish to address a group of employees or the media.

There are complaints about the hollow sound of the speaker phones, about the more impersonal atmosphere (compared with face-to-face meetings), about the tension created by this method, about the cost, and about the limitations of the system. Users remind others that the way to make teleconferencing more successful is to plan well for it. Those involved should have time to consider their input and to organize their questions.

The Telephone as a Sales Tool

From minor utilization a few years ago, confined mostly to awning and cemetery lot sales pitches, the telephone has become a major force in sales. Telemarketing is a high-growth industry. In the travel industry, hotels, while not engaging in much cold solicitation, often marry sales points to reservation information. Other elements of the profession don't use these techniques as much as they might. If there is slow time at a travel agency (and that's a big "if"), consultants might make calls to their lists of regular prospects or go through a roster of potential travelers. Couldn't cruise lines contact subscribers to certain travel magazines with emphasis on such voyages? Local attractions could build clientele by some judicious telemarketing.

Experts remind telemarketers that the caller must be distinct and precise, exhibiting the ability to listen as well as to speak effectively. The more successful phone salespersons are able to generate interest and rapport, while keeping the conversation on target. Still, they are flexible enough to vary the pitch to prevent rigidity and they can field questions with skill.

There is a growing resistance to telemarketing as the incoming calls increase, so future callers will have to be even better at this trade. It helps telemarketers to be aware of the negative reactions and to be able to put themselves in the position of the person being called. Consider what things irritate you about such calls and remove them, if possible, from your own sales presentation.

Handling Phone Complaints

There are many reasons why travel agencies are called, but chief among these are to obtain information, to check schedules or prices, to actually book a trip, and, finally, to lodge a complaint. The first three instances call for knowledge and, perhaps, salesmanship, but the final task requires patience, tact, and skill.

When a complaint is lodged, the travel consultant must listen, must not contradict or argue directly, must eventually let the caller talk to someone else if that is the demand. The person called should be sympathetic, courteous, and professional and, if some remedy is indicated, the response must be prompt.

CONSULTANTS

Perhaps another human being shouldn't be included among the travel tools, but the mission of consultants is to assist travel firms. We're talking here of outside consultants and not the professional agents who bear this title. Outside advice and support isn't always the answer and it may prove too expensive for some firms. Care should also be exercised in choosing consultants. In order to secure business, the consulting firm may use its heavy guns to solicit your account but later dispatch a less experienced and gifted individual to actually service your needs. You should know what you are getting and what this person will do and how much all of this is going to cost.

There are many positive aspects of outside assistance. At the very least, you may be provided with an extra pair of hands to help you accomplish tasks you were unable to get at. You also buy knowledge of the particular field and, probably, a variety of case experiences that can bear on your situation.

In particular, you buy objectivity. Outsiders arrive on the scene without the prejudices or personality conflicts insiders face. They can look at a problem dispassionately, working only from the obvious facts. Friendships, organizational fears, predictable frustrations born of years of service — all of these won't deter the consultant. Of course, this independence also means the consultant will not be as familiar with the local scene or as concerned about the individuals involved. The consultant may also regard you as only one client among many and, perhaps, even a minor client.

Another benefit of the consultant is the ability to tackle areas that require special skills. The writing of government contracts comes to mind, along with the occasional task of selling or buying an agency or other travel business. It helps to have people who have been there and who can review the elements you need to consider.

When considering the services of an outside consultant, it's advisable to check references, to inquire about past success, to discuss fees up front, to insist on meeting the individual who will work for you, and to have a clear idea about just what you expect. The more you can do in advance and the most concrete you can make your requirements, the better relationship you'll have.

COURSES, SEMINARS, BOOKS, PERIODICALS, ORGANIZATIONS

Because the travel business is often a hectic career, it's tough to schedule time for personal advancement. Still, that sort of commitment must be made. In order to progress, individuals have to discover convenient ways to expand knowledge and skills.

With the increase in the number of travel schools and travel programs, relevant textbooks are on the increase, covering everything from the business side of travel to tour management. In addition, there are myriad books outside the industry that also have value. In the communication area, there are texts that cover every topic treated in this book. Volumes on writing and giving speeches, on crafting news releases, on assembling slide shows, on mastering the new technology — all are available.

There are also the numerous guides mentioned earlier under research, books that cover countries, cities, modes of travel, different types of accommodations, and even the history of travel.

The newcomer should visit some well-run travel firms and inquire about their personal libraries. See what they have on hand, what books they find most useful.

For more current information, travel agencies keep on hand brochures from hotels, carriers, resorts, and other sources and they may collect everything from ferry schedules to pamphlets on packing tips. They also keep handy current issues of publications like *Travel Weekly, The Travel Agent, Business Travel News, Tour & Travel News, Travel Management Daily, Travel Management Newsletter, ASTA Travel News,* the weekly *Travel Trade* and bimonthly *Travel Marketing and Agency Management Guidelines,* and the four regional editions of *TravelAge.*

There are annual directories listing tariffs and timetables; a series of cruise guides (like *Ford's International Cruise Guide*); the indispensable *Official Hotel and Resort Guide*; a variety of guides to air, bus, and train schedules; plus a dozen other handy reference volumes.

Formal training, which is becoming increasingly necessary for entrance into the travel field, takes many forms. Many community colleges offer a two-year course of training in travel and at least a dozen colleges and universities feature a four-year degree program. And there are the specialized travel schools, some weak, some very good, Figure 9–3. Communication is certain to be part of the curriculum. The American Association of Travel Agents also offers a correspondence course as well as periodic seminars spotted around the country. The Association of Retail Travel Agents schedules seminars and the Institute of Certified Travel Agents has developed a comprehensive course leading to accreditation as a Certified Travel Counselor. Airlines conduct their own educational sessions and, of course, there are numerous seminars and conferences sponsored by other organizations that may prove helpful in the travel field. There are, for example, regularly scheduled workshops under the aegis of the Public Relations Society of America, the International Association of Business Communicators, and private groups like Lawrence Ragan Communications Inc.

Two organizations already mentioned (ASTA — The American Association of Travel Agents, and ARTA — The Association of Retail Travel Agents) are helpful to the professional travel person, as are the World Association of Travel Agencies (WATA), the Universal Federation of Travel Agency Associations (UFTAA), plus numerous organizations catering to tour managers, travel writers, incentive travel executives, and others. There are also some regional consortia and other groups allied by specialties. Carriers have their own

Figure 9–3. Many university programs, technical school offerings, and studies in specialized schools focus on travel education. (Courtesy Travel Careers Institute)

different organizations and there are even social clubs for members of the profession.

All of these sources assist with learning and communication.

Some Informal Communication Aids

Besides the collection of books and periodicals and supplier-generated brochures, the travel industry professional also maintains a "swipe file" consisting of materials that may provide layout suggestions, copy ideas, creative events, and many other starters for the communication process. When some printed piece or news item on a promotional success comes across your desk, you clip it and husband it for easy reference. Also collectible are good speeches, the results of surveys, special editions of travel publications, information on government programs, lists of sources on tours and information, consumer news, data on equipment and technology, plus anything else that may one day prove helpful.

Allied to the details provided by the "swipe file" are the results of conversations with other professionals. Visit a print shop; talk with paper salespeople; take an ad executive to lunch; spend some time with magazine sales reps; pump the airline representative for insights and trends; listen carefully to the pitches of attraction salespersons; read the reports of colleagues who take familiarization tours. Pick up information wherever you can and devise a means of storing it for efficient retrieval.

THE ADVERTISING AGENCY OR PUBLIC RELATIONS FIRM

If you're ailing, you probably head for your physician's office. But you don't go there for every cold or stomachache. You use the medical professionals when you really need them.

Ditto for the communication experts in ad agencies and PR firms. They should be able to give you an assist with the more difficult tasks but needn't be summoned when you want to tack up a poster for employee scrutiny.

Still, money is a factor in these relationships. The small travel agency can't afford sophisticated professional services and the outside communication pros will not normally be interested in a miniature account. The larger travel entities probably have some ties with these professionals, even when they may staff communication departments of their own. The advertising and public relations people are valuable for the same set of reasons mentioned earlier about outside consultants. If employed, the PR people are paid by a fee arrangement, by the hour, or by the job. The advertising agency may also impose some fees, but most of their revenue will be derived from commissions on the advertising the travel firm places.

Without question, a good public relations or advertising agency can boost the communication level of any travel company. They may redesign a logo, or brighten an advertising campaign, or expand an image. Their contributions may not easily bottom line, like the results of a commercial sales call, but the influence is there.

Any professional communicator will want to tackle more than a single ad or brochure or an isolated branch opening. Both advertising and public relations require a more long-term commitment. They focus on campaigns and goals rather than the impact of a lone example. If the travel firm decides to employ such help, it should allow enough latitude to permit the communication experts to function.

How to select these firms?

Reputation is always a starting point. What do other clients say about them? What is their standing with the media? Who are their principals and what is their experience? Is their financial rating solid? Who will be your contact? Can you see some samples of their previous efforts? What do they know about the travel industry or about related service industries? How will they charge? What ideas do they have about your particular firm's needs?

Once you have satisfied yourself on these points, you may enter into a written or oral agreement, usually with a specific time frame stated, after which the success of the partnership will be reviewed.

THE NEW TECHNOLOGY

Conventional wisdom says that there are only four responses to the thrust of the new technology: innovate, automate, emigrate, or evap-

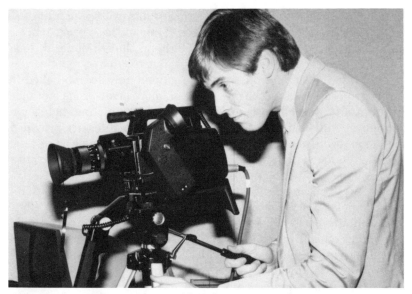

Figure 9–4.   Video equipment has become much more portable and flexible. (Courtesy Travel Careers Institute)

orate. When your competition is taking advantage of the latest automation features, you have to match this advance or chance falling behind, Figure 9–4. Commercial accounts will gravitate to those travel agencies that are the most efficient and cost effective. But technology cuts both ways. Carriers and suppliers, also equipped with the latest technology, will be in a position to bypass agencies if they so desire, and interface directly with corporations.

The major growth in technological application to the travel industry has occurred since 1970 and many travel agencies were slow to accept the full impact of this revolutionary set of tools. Even today, some segments of the industry, like meeting planners, are lagging considerably in this area, and most experts predict that the improvements in technology in the next two decades may make much of today's hardware and software obsolete. Committing anything about computers to print is risky because the innovations are arriving faster than type can be set.

Still, there are some basic elements that are and will be characteristic of technology advances and the travel industry should continue to be a prime candidate for these changes.

Computers

Over $80 billion a year is spent on computers in America, with a fifth of that sum expended on software. Approximately 300 different manufacturers produce a wide selection of hardware and offer well over 5000 different software packages. Some of these programs are specific to the travel industry, while others, though general, have application to certain industry needs, Figure 9–5.

Consider the numerous travel functions now accomplished by automation rather than the much slower, more error-prone methods. Reservations systems instantly pull up data on airline, hotel, and car rental availabilities and costs. Current schedules are provided. Individuals who are part of commercial accounts can also be selected from the memory file and reviewed for preferences in hotels, rental cars, seating arrangements, and other travel aspects.

Besides booking details, computers also capture information.

The potential for information has scarcely been tapped. Right now, computers are being used to duplicate traditional travel functions, from scheduling to billing, but future use could include office design for agencies, displays of cruise line cabin configurations, storage of promotional pieces, an inventory of geographical data, and hundreds of other applications.

Right now, in travel agencies alone, about 25 thousand personal computers are linked to one or more of the five basic airline

Figure 9–5.   Everyone in the travel industry must become computer literate. (Courtesy Tim Fitzgerald)

reservations systems, all of which have some built-in restrictions, Figure 9–6. Many of these PCs can do far more than they are currently accomplishing, but vendors want to limit use to functions related to their own sales intent. Still, some travel agencies do load other, perhaps competitive, programs into their systems. Sabre and Apollo are the leaders in reservations systems, but System One, PARS, and Datas II are also capturing a share of the travel business.

Software (like the Office Management System from PARS) may include word processing, electronic mail, graphics, calendar capabilities, and spread sheet proficiency. Sabre promotes the ease of switching from bookings to other office functions, "with the touch of a key."

Experts list a number of guidelines in purchasing computers and software:

❏   Consider the most complicated task you need to accomplish in your office and eliminate all of the systems that can't do this.

❏   Carefully review all the features offered by the systems you are considering and retain for further screening only those that have features you can actually use.

❏   Now that you have narrowed the choice, talk to people who are using these remaining systems and get their preferences, comments, and criticisms.

❏   Choosing the right software also involves knowing precisely what you really need.

Figure 9–6.   Travel office computers are linked to airline reservation systems. (Courtesy Travel and Transport)

❏ The descriptive materials provided by vendors should be carefully studied and a demonstration requested. It's a smart idea to invite others to this demonstration, especially those who will be involved in the use of the equipment and programs.
❏ Items like cost, availability of service, and provision for training must also be factored in.

Some Computer Uses

As a communication tool, the travel industry computers bring an immediacy to the functions of the industry. Some insiders have argued that deregulation of the airlines would have been impossible without the speed and skill of the new technology. They credit automation with sustaining fare wars and allowing such frequent schedule changes. They point out that Frequent Flyer Programs are possible because of the accumulative logging of applicable flights and that international travel has been greatly enhanced because of compatible systems. Computers make the search for the lowest fares much simpler and they display rates and rules for more than 3 thousand types of rental vehicles. Current programs allow travel agencies to interface with credit card data, merging it simultaneously into expense account reports.

Computers may lock in company travel policies so that individuals in those firms may not deviate from corporate rules about types of hotels or cars that are specified. PARS software includes maps, photos, films, and printed information which can be viewed, then quickly replaced by booking modes. The major systems are also moving quickly toward enhanced international connections, permitting travel agents to access information on foreign airlines as easily as they secure data on domestic ones. This global concept still has many bugs to be worked out, not in technology as much as in local rules and regulations.

New programs provide tour and cruise bases, outline upcoming special events, and give details on items like shopping, dining, and theatre tickets.

Word Processing and Desktop Publishing

Trade journals and seminars have contributed a great deal to the travel firm's knowledge of high tech and its specific and generic utility. Writers and consultants circulate advice on shopping for systems that are flexible and reliable and that have adequate memory and speed. Best-selling WordPerfect features a spelling checker bolstered by dictionary and thesaurus entries, while Word-Star and MultiMate Advantage seem to have an edge in processing form letters. There are drawing packages and even clip-art programs. Some software, supported by a linking modem, can transmit over telephone lines and, of course, disks themselves may be mailed or delivered, saving countless pages of documentation.

Many offices are becoming more adept at desktop publishing, designing and printing their own newsletters, brochures, proposals, reports, and other materials. Besides the appropriate computer, you might add the laser printer with up to 75 different typefaces, and then the right software—the WordPerfect program, for example. Today's printers are a vast improvement over the first models, with their slow pace and characteristic-type style. Current units offer speed and high quality and can be made to work with just about any computer.

Electronic Mail

Although this innovation is not yet a major device in the travel business, the trends point in this direction. The principle is that computers may be linked to other computers and can transmit messages electronically in minutes. The computers must be linked via some system (like MCI, Western Union, GTE) which may set an initiation fee, minimum rates, and charges based on time or message length. Published directories list all subscribers to the system. Phone companies compete with their mobile phones, teleconferencing, and "voice mailboxes" where callers can leave messages for later client retrieval.

Some Problems

Every communication plus is certain to have a few minuses. Although travel needs are greatly expedited by the new technology, the system is not without its flaws. There are the usual glitches, like overload or power failure or other malfunctions which cause the system to go down or lose data. There are problems in reconciling a variety of disparate factors.

Then there are the people problems.

These problems include not only the dangers of human error but also the real possibilities of burnout or other physical difficulties. Some studies are tying miscarriages and birth defects to continued use of the video display terminals (VDTs). Even barring these grimmer results, agency personnel who spend hours at their VDT stations may report neck strain, headaches, eye or back problems, and, perhaps, hand and wrist ailments. Some firms furlough their pregnant VDT operators and others may provide radiation shields, and still others are working on ways to minimize dangers, from specifying VDT position and distance along with the type of chair to be used, to requiring annual eye and physical exams. There is more attention being paid to overhead lighting and non-glare keyboards, and some states have proposed legislation to ensure safety in this particular workplace role.

Also indicative of problems created by the new technology is a 1988 case involving an Oklahoma father and daughter who accessed American Airline's computer reservation system, created a fictitious group of frequent flyers, garnered their free air tickets, then sold these to others—including other travel agencies. Having someone illegally tap any computer system is always a fear.

COMPUTERS AND THE FUTURE

When you realize that there are already portable computers on the market that are more knowledgeable than the average high school graduate, you can appreciate how difficult it is to predict future growth in this communication field. Today, a bright and creative person, equipped with a sophisticated lap-top computer, can perform the functions it once took a small company to accomplish. Will more of the travel business move to the streets? Will automation constrict the number of jobs available in the industry? Will travel agency salespeople calling on corporations carry pocket computers that are tied into mainframe systems to kick out schedule and cost data? What effect will the transfer of government travel accounts to private agencies have on the interaction of their often-sensitive computer banks? How will areas like incentive travel and group travel benefit from further advances?

What we do know is that there have been more changes in the way we live and work in the last twenty years than in the previous 600 years, and futurists are predicting that the next two decades will see more changes than occurred in the past century. There will always be resistance to change because once you have learned how to perform a task, it's hard to abandon that knowledge. Your mother may continue to clean her house in the same general way her mother taught her. But we have to be open to change, to use it to our advantage.

At the turn of this century, there was a movement in Washington to close down the Patent Office because some administrators were convinced that everything that could be invented was already invented—and that was only four years before the Wright Brothers took off at Kittyhawk, and only decades before a man walked on the moon.

Theorists also argue that future generations are going to be divided not so much by money and social class as by education and information. Less than a quarter of Americans will have high communication and verbal skills and they will have their choice of nearly two-thirds of the available jobs. Nearly three-fourths of Americans will compete for the remaining positions. These same theorists posit these skills as requisite ones for the future:

- ❏ *Ability to communicate.* With the information cycle at a peak, those who both understand the technology and can construct the message, will be in demand, in the travel industry and elsewhere.
- ❏ *Ability to negotiate.* This isn't meant in the narrow sense of labor/management discussions, but in the wider context of bringing people, ideas, and even companies together.
- ❏ *Ability to learn.* Acquiring knowledge is lifelong and those who cease to learn will be left behind. When deregulation arrived, some professionals surrendered, claiming they could never

Figure 9–7. Batteries of operators working at computer terminals service clients in large travel agencies. (Courtesy Travel and Transport)

master the complications of choices, fares, and fare bases. But most survived, and learned, and may even have prospered.

❑ *Ability to adapt to change.* Not too many years ago, some jobs were advertised as requiring strong typing skills. Today the expectation is that applicants are computer literate, Figure 9–7. Change isn't always an improvement, but it is inevitable and must be approached openly.

❑ *Ability to be creative.* Innovators take risks. They are optimistic, though not imprudent. Someone pioneered the suite-only concept, inaugurated frequent flyer programs, introduced unlimited mileage. Front runners continually devise ways to stay ahead of the pack.

With all of the communication tools available, permitting everything from the transmitting of news stories directly to publications to the instant retrieval of rooming lists or airline manifests, the human factor can't be ignored. You still need intelligent input at some stage. Content shouldn't be eclipsed by gadgetry. True, the ordinary business letter can now be assembled more quickly, look more uniform, be filed instantly, even transmitted electronically, but someone still has to compose an intelligent, accurate, and compelling message.

CHAPTER HIGHLIGHTS

❑ Since the telephone is an essential tool in all areas of the travel industry, its use and misuse must be considered, and techniques of good phone etiquette mastered.

❑ Intelligent composition of recorded messages, efficient use of long-distance lines, and the more frequent use of mobile phones are industry musts.

❑ FAX machines, teleconferencing, and the integration of telephones and computers are modern advances.

❑ As telephone sales pitches proliferate, and as travel firms increase their reliance on this medium, telemarketing skills need to be better than ever.

❑ Consultants, who should be hired when you need and can afford expert outside counsel, should be screened in advance, given specific direction, and assisted with backup research.

❑ Among the concrete aids to the travel professional are travel schools, seminars, books, trade journals, and the assistance provided by professional organizations.

❑ Those in the travel field should make it a practice to read and save useful materials, from appropriate speech content to the reports of familiarization tours.

❑ While advertising and public relations firms may not be practical for the small travel agency, they are likely to be affiliated with airlines, cruise lines, tour companies, tourism bureaus, and large travel firms. Experts in communication, they can greatly enhance any company's image and effectiveness.

❑ The new technology has revolutionized the travel field, with computers tackling chores ranging from bookings and bookkeeping to printing and publishing.

❑ Computer needs should be carefully analyzed and both hardware and software should be selected on the basis of their applicability to the needs of the specific travel office.

❑ There will always be problems with communication tools, from electrical blackouts to high tech vandalism. Repeated use of VDTs also seems to be causing health problems.

❑ Whether automation is viewed as hero or villain, it is a fact of travel industry life and the progressive firms and individuals must adapt to its demands and potential.

■   ■   ■

❏ *EXERCISES*

1. Locate and report on in class, three trade journal articles you feel will have impact on the travel industry, or that discuss events or trends that will impact on the industry.
2. Strictly from a human relations viewpoint, what do you see as some of the potential negative aspects of travel industry automation?
3. Your travel agency is open 9–5 on weekdays and until noon on Saturday. During the hours you are not open, calls still come in. Devise a message for your phone answering machine that combines information with promotion. Keep it under thirty-five words.

❏ *CASE PROBLEMS*

1. As local manager of a national airline, with full authority to hire and fire, you are informed that one of your reservations agents is rude and curt over the telephone, and that this behavior projects a negative image for the airline. Do you fire this person on the spot? If not, what actions do you take? Assuming the report proves to be true, what further actions can you take? In deciding, consider this person's legal rights, personal dignity, potential for reform, and the impact on other employees.

1. Assume you had the money and wanted to buy your own travel agency. What sort of information would you want to know about this agency? Would you hire a consultant to help you check out this firm? If so, on what basis would you select this consultant? What sort of things would you expect the consultant to find out? Besides buying space and equipment, what else would you hope went along with the purchase of this travel agency?

10

COMMUNICATION CAREERS AND CONSIDERATIONS

JOB OPPORTUNITIES

While there are ample opportunities to employ one's communication skills within the travel industry, not every situation satisfies individual preferences and talents. Eventually, a person should try to get into the branch of the industry and size of office that seems to fit, Figure 10–1.

At the outset, however, it's wise to take a look at any opportunity that arises, especially if the salary is adequate and the opportunities apparent. In his sixth-edition paperback titled *Your Career in Travel, Tourism, & Hospitality* (Delmar), Laurence Stevens details

Figure 10–1.   The travel agency is still one of the major employers in the travel industry. (Courtesy Travel and Transport)

responsibilities in this wide-ranging profession and also provides tips for the job search. Communication jobs are a small segment of an industry that attracts everyone from pilots to desk clerks to master chefs, but every major unit employs this specialty and even some of the smaller firms may tap into communication expertise via agency or consultant help.

Breaking In

Travel and hospitality posts are different from other jobs only in the nature of the duties. Looking for these jobs is pretty much the same as searching for any communication position.

Background

Individuals used to enter this field from a variety of backgrounds, including a multiplicity of college degrees or no degree at all. Today, with competition more intense, employers expect a little more. Ideally, those hiring for communication slots would like to find someone with at least a bachelor's degree in communication/journalism, with some additional courses in travel, plus a bit of practical experience in the industry, perhaps as an intern or as part of a summer job. They'd also look for writing and speaking skills, personality, and all of the other traits that characterize a desirable employee, Figure 10–2. And that's for an entry-level post!

The good news for applicants is that the employer probably won't find this ideal individual, partly because salaries aren't overly generous in the travel/hospitality industry and the best people may be tempted by other offers. So employers eventually hire those people they feel come closest to the ideal and who seem to have the most potential.

What this suggests is that students interested in working in travel or hospitality, within the framework of communication, should prepare themselves by taking the requisite curriculum, along with seeking part-time employment that adds to their experience level, Figure 10–3. The person with some real-world work record nearly always has an edge over the individual whose background is solely classroom oriented. Most colleges and universities assist students in finding part-time employment or internships. If the institution doesn't offer these services, the student may still seek out opportunities on his/her own. This search may well include convincing the prospective employer that you really have something to contribute to the organization and that you won't merely be in the way.

Figure 10–2. Regardless of a person's role within the travel industry, good interpersonal communication skills are essential. (Courtesy Travel Careers Institute)

Figure 10–3. Entry into the travel field, and advancement in this profession, demand both study and demonstrated proficiency. (Courtesy Travel Careers Institute)

Besides taking appropriate courses (in subject areas like journalism, public relations, English, business, and travel, to name a few), the communication aspirant should try to get some work published, even if it's only in the campus newspaper. Compared to an article in *Travel/Holiday,* a column in the university weekly may not seem like much, but the employer is likely to ask for samples of your writing, and a piece set in type is far more impressive than a collection of your graded papers from a literature course. Besides campus publications, there are inevitably local papers and magazines that may accept free-lance work and there are national periodicals that also feature student efforts.

Many of today's students also travel on their own, taking in places like Europe on the hostel or B & B plan. Having this in a resume also makes points. So does the knowledge of a second or third language, even if that language is not employed daily in the travel post. These things say something about your interest and commitment. Reading widely does, too. Travel books, guides, and trade journals enable an applicant to contribute intelligently during a job interview.

Where Do I Find Out About Job Opportunities?

One tricky aspect of the communication job search is that so many of the opportunities are circulated by word of mouth before any public notice is given. That means the aggressive applicant must find a way to get into the rumor pipeline. Organizational memberships help, especially those with some relationship to travel or communication. Remaining in touch with former professors is wise, and so is the practice of calling periodically on members of the travel industry. Even if they have no openings, they may know of some elsewhere, Figures 10–4 and 10–5.

You may want to use the services of an employment agency, either the free governmental kind or the ones that charge a fee. In some areas, these agencies do have listings of travel-related positions, but the opportunities may be limited, especially in the communication field. In other areas, the postings will be nonexistent.

You can, of course, initiate your own job search, using the Yellow Pages and City Directory or other available directories. If you do this, be thorough and realistic. Try to match the job to your background and try to concentrate on travel units that have potential. There is not much sense in applying to a three-person travel agency about their openings in public relations. Learn what you can about the firm, so that you arrive with some concept of what they do, what

Figure 10–4. Airlines employ a variety of personnel, from pilots and ground crew to passenger agents and flight attendants.

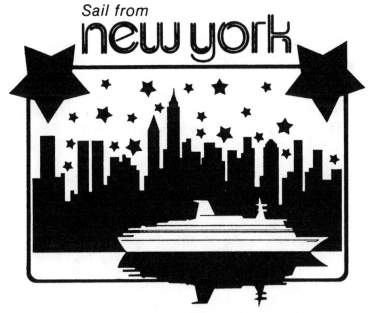

Figure 10–5. Opportunities on cruise lines have increased in recent years with the rediscovery of the pleasure ship.

they may need, and what you can say to create an impression. This sort of search takes time, and you'll experience a great deal of rejection, but persistence often pays off. Timing always plays a major role in securing entry-level jobs, so you need to keep reminding prospective employers of your interest and qualifications. It isn't easy to keep knocking on doors, but it's necessary.

The daily newspaper may occasionally list communication positions in the travel industry, but that's fairly rare. Trade journals also provide job listings, but you have to be willing to consider a change of location. A glance at a succession of *Travel Weekly* want ads reveals agencies for sale, and both services and equipment for sale, along with a lot of sales job. Firms advertise for executive-level openings, for tour managers, reservations managers. Here's one for a travel writer to "write and edit travel brochures for 55-plus age market for major travel co. in Kansas City. Minimum five years proven writing experience. Must have worked with deadline. Salary based on proven ability. Send writing samples and resume with travel you've done to . . ."

Travel Weekly is merely one journal. There are others in the travel agency business, plus trade publications in the hotel, restaurant, and carrier fields, and newsletters that cover tourism department openings. Even reading these "classifieds" is a good exercise, providing tips on what's available and what they are looking for.

HOW TO MAKE CONTACT

The best advice is to use whatever means are available to you and promise the most positive results. After all, if you have a relative or friend in the business, it would be foolish to ignore that door-opening prospect. Without that plus feature, there are the telephone, the mails, and personal visits . . . and any other form of contact ingenuity can devise. Job seekers have tried thousands of different ways to attract an employer's attention, from skywriting to notes enclosed in fast-food deliveries. These ruses have to be employed prudently because they appeal to some executives and turn others off.

Making personal calls on prospective employers is the most effective method, but it takes time and involves its own set of frustrations. While you may sometimes get to see the person in charge, chances are you'll be redirected to the personnel office or just requested to leave your resume. Still, you could get lucky and, even if not, you have an opportunity to see the premises and gather a little information.

If you do make a cold call, you should be prepared to present your case quickly and with as much impact as possible. What you're after is an appointment, an opportunity to state your case. Everything that is done in the job search comes down to securing an appointment.

If distance or company policy prevents you from making a personal visit, the telephone may be used to get you an audience. The applicant should practice the opening comments and should attempt to speak with the personnel department, the supervisor of the department in question, or the travel agency manager. You shouldn't settle for being turned away by a secretary. Find out who you can contact and where you can mail or deliver a resume.

Placement experts regard a mail approach as the least effective and the easiest to ignore. They also stress that it's better to do a thorough job of researching the market and sending out fewer resumes, than it is to blanket the field with your appeals, hoping one will find a home. Again, the purpose of the letter and resume remains the opportunity to secure an interview, Figure 10–6.

Some applicants combine these methods, sending a resume and then calling for an appointment. A person interested in locating in a certain area may write ahead to several firms, indicating dates he or

Figure 10–6. The main purpose of a resume is to secure an interview. (Courtesy Tim Fitzgerald)

she will be in town, and mentioning that a call for an appointment can be expected.

Whatever means are used to establish the contact, it shouldn't end there. Follow-up is important. That's why it's good to get the name and phone number of someone to ring back. There's also a difference between being persistent and being a pest and the applicant must learn to sense when to retrench a bit and when to press ahead. Until the door is definitely closed, the job hunter should leave each contact with a promise to check back within a specified period of time. Keep a list of these prospects and make the calls as promised. Be reluctant to drop a potential job until all hope is gone. Even then, you could say you'll check back again at some future date.

And always remember to thank people!

THE RESUME

Resume writing has become a business and you can hire people to write and package your biographical data. As with everything else, eventually these begin to look canned and employers may react against them. Still, if you are unable to draft an acceptable resume yourself, it may be worth the money.

Some larger organizations also provide their own preferred application forms, so you may have to merely fill in the appropriate spaces. Still, for the job search itself, you'll need your own resume.

Today, there are three general types of resume:

❑ The *chronological* resume, which outlines your educational and work background, together with other pertinent data, all organized chronologically. This is the traditional resume and is still the most common form.

❑ The *functional* resume, which also gives information on employment and education, but which focuses on the skills you possess rather than on titles and dates. For individuals who have developed certain talents, like photography, as hobbies or in volunteer work, this sort of resume has merit. Perhaps you have no impressive employers to list, but you could cite skill with computers, television cameras, or management of special events.

❑ The *targeted* resume, which is prepared for a specific job opportunity. The entries in this type of resume are organized and emphasized in such a way as to fit the limited job specifications.

Resumes should be neatly typed or printed, with adequate spacing and with all relevant detail. While the resume shouldn't be effusive, it should be comprehensive enough to include all pertinent facts.

In general, the chronological resume starts with personal data, like name and address and phone, followed by educational acheve-ments, and then by an outline of jobs held, from the most current to the earliest. Both of these categories can be expanded — to include a student's Grade Point Average, for example, or some graduation distinction, like "cum laude." The work record, too, may contain titles and duties.

Honors and awards may be listed, along with hobbies, any pub-lications, fluency in languages, and other items that could attract attention. References may be included or a line, "References Avail-able on Request," could be appended. For jobs demanding writing skills, the applicant may also be expected to include writing sam-ples.

THE INTERVIEW

A little common sense is advisable here. Appropriate dress is a must and so is being on time. Prior to the interview, it's wise to bone up on the firm and industry, because the bottom line will be what you can accomplish for them.

The interview is the moment of truth, so you should prepare for these few important minutes. While in college, it pays to sign up for a number of interviews, even when that job may not be one you want. The experience of interviewing helps you relax when the seri-ous opportunity arrives. The interviewer may wish to have you expand on resume items, may test your knowledge of the travel industry, may toss out queries to see how you react, and will be noting things about the way you present yourself, physically and verbally. Applicants should normally refrain from smoking during the interview, should minimize their nervous habits, and should continually maintain interest.

Following the interview, whether you got the job or not, you should send along a note of thanks.

TYPES OF JOB OPENINGS IN TRAVEL

One nice thing about the travel/hospitality field is that there are so many different courses to pursue. Some people gravitate toward the flight attendant role, while others opt for restaurant management.

Even within the narrower confines of communication, there are a multitude of challenges.

Airlines and cruise ships employ people to edit their in-flight magazines; write and circulate news releases; manage special events (like parties for travel agents); help produce brochures; supervise the advertising campaigns which are likely to be created by advertising agencies; take file photos; put together annual reports; communicate with a number of publics, from travel writers to financial analysts; and handle media relations in times of emergencies. Railroads, car rental agencies, and bus companies handle many of these same functions although, except for the freight side of the railroads, the staffs are likely to be smaller and the reliance on outside help more common. In short, these carriers and suppliers have a great many of the tasks any corporation would experience. They could range from a mundane chore like overseeing the printing of schedules to the highly visible responsibilities inherent in a fatal accident.

Hotels and resorts also produce a lot of printed material, from wine lists and brochures to floor plans and convention appeals. Major units and chains advertise heavily — in consumer travel magazines, or to the travel agency trade, or, less frequently, on television. Often, the communication specialist will be involved in correspondence, answering complaints, perhaps, or wooing a convention group. Hotels occasionally create news or change logos or add to their facilities. Resorts may commission films or videocassettes, design and staff booths at conferences, dispatch a team of speakers.

Only the more exclusive restaurants or restaurant chains do much advertising. You see plenty of fast-food pitches on television, plus campaigns for places like Red Lobster and Village Inn, but the unique restaurants are likely to be found in travel and in-flight magazines, city magazines, publications like *The New Yorker* and *The Atlantic,* directories, and the local papers. Much of this work would be done by advertising and public relations agencies.

There are tourism bureaus at the national, state, and local levels. Their principal responsibility is communication — attracting visitors and conventions via advertising, correspondence, phone calls, and personal visits; informing local citizens of attractions and opportunities; encouraging regional hotels, restaurants, and attractions to be more competitive. The work of those in this area could cover everything from conducting a training session for cab drivers to lobbying for funds before the state legislature.

Every major element of the travel industry has its own association and some have several competing associations. All of these groups maintain their own promotional staffs whose duties might include membership campaigns, printed materials, seminars and conferences, publicity, speech writing, lobbying, and related tasks.

Each of the many travel publications has an editorial staff. Some of these magazines and newsletters are familiar, like *Travel-Holiday* and *Travel and Leisure,* but there are dozens of others: *Odyssey;* AAA's *Home & Away;* Diners Club's *Adventure Road;* Eastern Airline's *Review Magazine* and those of two dozen other airlines; *Restaurant Hospitality* and others of that genre; the various travel agency periodicals; trade journals in all travel and hospitality areas; magazines like *Modern Maturity* and hundreds of others that feature travel — the roster is long.

Besides magazines, there are travel books — guides, texts, humor, commentary, picture formats, directories, and other variations. Some are staff written; most are the products of free-lancers.

Within advertising and public relations firms there may be individuals who make a specialty of travel accounts and here, too, the types of duties performed will depend on the nature and needs of the client firm. Large travel agency chains, like Ask Mr. Foster, will have some in-house staff plus outside expertise. Individual travel agencies are unlikely to have people assigned solely to communication responsibilities.

With the growing interest in the educational aspects of travel, more jobs are opening up in the teaching of travel courses and, in a few instances, the promotion of schools that specialize in such courses.

Overall, there are thousands of annual openings for good people—those who have strong communication skills, some travel experience, and the personalities to succeed in a competitive world.

LEGAL ASPECTS OF COMMUNICATION

Anytime you circulate information to a general audience, you run the risk of doing something that could be considered illegal. The travel industry has some built-in hazards because of the uncertain nature of its work and because of the reliance on a variety of service vendors. Most tour brochures, for example, contain a section on "Conditions" which carefully spells out the tour company or travel agency responsibilities, so that tour members may not later sue the sponsoring firm over some undelivered portion of the trip, assuming that omission was beyond the tour company's control.

For starters, the communicator must avoid issuing any exaggerated claims, incorrect prices, misleading statements, or other deceptive wording. Since 1914, with the creation of the Federal

Trade Commission, "unfair methods of competition" were declared illegal and this stricture included "deceptive advertising," which was defined as anything that was made to appear different from the reality and anything that affects buying behavior to the detriment of the consumer. A hotel brochure showing an ornate lobby that doesn't actually exist is an obvious falsehood, but copy is also sometimes worded so that one assumes a benefit that really isn't there. That could also be deceptive. Let's say a resort mentions a pair of eighteen-hole golf courses you think must be on their property but which are really local public courses in the vicinity. This could be actionable.

Other factors are usually considered in these disputes. The resultant damage might be weighed, and the entire advertisement is normally judged rather than a single word or sentence. Obvious puffery, the sort of claims no person could take seriously, is also generally excluded, as are cases that are patently silly. If a theme park says its Fourth of July fireworks display will have you humming "Yankee Doodle Dandy," it's unlikely any judge would tolerate a litigant who said they watched the display but didn't hum the tune. Similarly, if a rodeo billed itself as being "As Big as All Outdoors," the courts or the FTC aren't going to hold the sponsors to this impossible measurement.

But while common sense is invoked on occasion, there are other times when misleading writing is ordered stricken and a correction made. Damages may also be assessed. A tour can't advertise a private audience with the Pope unless it can deliver that personal touch. A rental car company can't offer unlimited mileage and then impose a per mile charge.

There are many other laws copywriters must be aware of. Restaurants should not advertise two-for-one specials unless you actually get two meals for the same price you pay for one, and not some price in between. Airlines advertising special fares have to word the offers carefully. Hotel chains can't discriminate against individual units when handing out perks. Survey claims—like saying your bus tour is the cheapest—have to be substantiated. Counter-advertising that contains negative statements about a competitor must be proven and, even then, they could be legislated against. The use of obscenity, which is a bad advertising idea anyway, could get the writer into trouble.

Besides concerns about advertising lapses, the travel communicator must be wary of promoting a lottery, falsifying documents, omitting taxable items from the books, and performing any other act that would get any business person into trouble. If, for example, a travel agency promoted a certain tour in the media, but when prospects came to the agency, they told these individuals that tour was filled but that there was room on another, more expensive, trip, that could be viewed as "bait-and-switch" tactics which are illegal.

Among the areas that have to worry writers the most are: defamation, privacy, and copyright.

Defamation

Defined as the damaging of another's reputation, defamation embraces everything from a loss of respect to outright hostility. The harmful statements must be made in the presence of a third party, meaning that a heated exchange between two individuals would not normally be actionable. Once others are involved in the defamatory comments, that becomes another matter altogether.

Defamation is usually divided into *slander* and *libel*. Years ago this separation was neater; slander referred to oral defamation and libel covered written defamation. With the advent of radio and television, however, the distinction was clouded. Did the accused read the remarks from a script (libel) or was the commentary ad libbed (slander)? Today, the trend is toward classifying all media utterances as libel. Both libel and slander are cause for concern, but, of the two, libel is generally considered the more serious.

If, for example, one travel agent accused another of overpricing all of her tours, either in conversation or in print, this could be the subject of a law suit. If a hotel accused a guest of departing with towels and other property, the guest might decide to sue. If an inflight magazine editor printed a statement that impugned the character of some private person, that, too, could be actionable. And, if a speechwriter inserted into his CEO's speech a comment to which another person might take offense, the corporate lawyers could be called in.

Besides the stipulation that the alleged defamation must be communicated to at least a third person, there are other generally accepted conditions:

❑ *The accuser must be able to prove that the remarks were directed at him or her.* Saying that people who frequent a certain resort are unscrupulous and untrustworthy is a bit too broad for action. However, the individual does not have to be named. Slanderous statements about "that young, blond desk clerk from Sioux City who works in a motel on 60th Street" would be enough to identify the person.

❑ *Public figures have far less protection than private citizens.* In order to enhance the First Amendment freedom of speech, courts have found that individuals who have "thrust themselves into the public light" are entitled to less protection than a private citizen. Recent law cases have weakened the definition of a "public figure," however, so the communicator still has to be wary. An elected official is generally thought of as a public figure, even an elected official of a travel association, and so are rock stars, sports heroes, television hosts, and others who seek the public eye. In order for these individuals to prevail in a libel suit, they must prove "actual malice," meaning they must show the speaker or writer deliberately circulated the information, knowing it was false, with the intent of injuring them. There are other considerations, as well, such as whether the statement was made in the context of the public figure's private or public life. Public figures themselves are sometimes divided into "limited-purpose" public figures who may be temporarily involved in a public controversy, like the leader of a consumer action group, and "all-purpose" public figures whose positions automatically bring notoriety.

Public figures aside, it's certainly possible to innocently libel an individual, through careless writing or off-hand commentary. Despite the lack of intent, these errors could bring you to court.

If you are accused of libel, there are some generally accepted defenses—none of which, except perhaps for the statute of limitations, is absolute:

- ❏ *Consent.* The individual gave you permission—hopefully in writing—to write what you did, or he or she approved the material after it was committed to paper.
- ❏ *Self defense.* Assume, for example, that one airline executive questioned the ability of the president of a rival airline to manage that company. The second CEO might retaliate by debunking the first person's own qualifications and his authority to make such a claim.
- ❏ *Privilege.* A rare defense for travel communicators, this provides protection to those—like legislators and judges—who take part in official proceedings.
- ❏ *Statute of limitations.* After one, two, or three years, claims for libel may not be heard, but these restrictions differ among states and the communicator had better be certain of the local regulations.
- ❏ *Truth.* What you said was accurate—but you must be able to prove it.
- ❏ *Privilege of reporting.* Journalists have a right to pass along to readers and listeners what was said at public meetings, even if

these comments themselves may contain potentially libelous material.

❏ *Fair comment.* In their role as reviewers, critics have a right to make negative remarks. A restaurant critic, for example, writing in a travel magazine, might say the food is lousy at a certain bistro, and might also pan the service, prices, and decor.

❏ *Actual malice rule.* Described previously.

Privacy

Like libel, the violations of privacy are also vague, ranging from stars suing celebrity lookalikes to complaints from individuals whose names or pictures were used without their permission.

Privacy generally centers on these four areas:

❏ *Intrusion*—where you actually invade another person's office or home, or intrude on their solitude or private affairs. If a house detective erroneously breaks into a hotel room because of suspicion of a drug deal going down, you can bet a lawsuit will result. And, as an airline PR person, you can't abet the actions of a television camera crew that wants to film a passenger who has requested anonymity. Nor do you release passenger manifests to anyone who requests them.

❏ *Disclosure*—where you reveal embarrassing private information about an individual. Editors of company newsletters have occasionally faltered here, printing something they thought was funny but which the subject felt was embarrassing. Disclosure may also occur innocently, via typographical error, miscaptioning photos, or, perhaps, listing in the birth announcements the name of a female employee who is unmarried and who has no children. Editorial care should always be exercised.

❏ *False light*—has to do with misleading juxtapositions or captions or with the use of outdated materials and the like. Showing a vacationing couple in a file photo and using it to warn travelers to be careful about losing their cash may be an infringement of privacy.

❏ *Appropriation*—involves the use of a person's name or likeness without the individual's permission. You can't take a group snapshot of people boarding your cruise ship and later use it in an ad—unless you get releases from those pictured. You can't list a person as a veteran hotel guest, even if he or she is, unless that person allows you to do so.

Remember that privacy has often been used as a catchall complaint, so a brief list doesn't begin to cover the cases that could be filed.

Copyright

The original copyright law of 1909 was substantially amended in 1976 and some clarifications have been appended since. The intent of copyright is to protect original work from appropriation by another. The best safeguard against breaking the copyright law is to always secure permission before using copy or graphics from another source. There are exceptions, of course.

Once a work is in "public domain," 50 years after the death of the author or 75–100 years after the publication or creation of a "made-for-hire" work, you may feel free to use the material. ("Made-for-hire" means that the work was done while in the employ of someone else, like an AAA staffer putting together a training manual at the behest of her boss.) Still, caution is the watchword. Sometimes, even though the author is deceased for 50 years, some rights may remain with surviving relatives.

A book reviewer can normally feel free to cite a limited number of words from a book being critiqued. A textbook writer might want to use a few words from an article, crediting the original author and publication. To be safe, even in the last situation, it's wise to get permission. There is no magic number of words you are allowed to quote. The test will be "fair use," meaning that your use of the copyrighted material shoud not in any way infringe upon the value of that copy to the creator. Cutting into an author's future sales, for example, would be a clear violation.

Plagiarism is always wrong, passing off the work of others as your own. However, there is sometimes a thin line between plagiarizing and using the work of another to stimulate your own thinking. You obviously can't lift brochure copy or speech material as is and then employ it for your own purposes, neglecting to obtain permission or to even reveal that this work is not your own. Someone may steal the layout of another agency's ad, for example, or copy verbatim the words of a direct-mail piece. There have been instances where entire travel articles have been stolen, rewritten slightly, and then submitted elsewhere as original work. These practices are both unethical and illegal. But you may still keep a file of things you admire and employ them as inspiration when you start your own project. But you must be certain of what is merely guidance and what is appropriation. If you're not, the law may decide for you.

Current laws are more precise than in the past and should be reviewed. Travel courses, for example, can't multicopy workbooks or feel as free to copy and circulate articles to students. Travel agencies can't decide to make copies of TV programs or travel cassettes for their own use. The situations themselves may get complicated, and there can be arguments over what is being used for research, or teaching, and what has an obvious commercial purpose. The major consideration remains the question of fairness to the author of the work.

Those in the travel industry must remain cognizant of other laws, from postal regulations to the binding nature of contract provisions. Travel agencies may run afoul of antitrust laws in their attempts to be more competitive. Hotels might violate state laws in distinguishing among types of guests or failing to include certain safety features. Ultimately, all of these lapses involve the communicator, since they must be explained to a variety of publics.

ETHICS IN COMMUNICATION

Even when something may be legal, it could still be unethical. Taking uncopyrighted material without attribution may not result in a suit, but it's still a shoddy practice.

There are some businesspeople, thankfully a minority, who continually skirt the edges of illegality. They conjure up unfair competitive practices, bad-mouth their opposition, lie to the media, fail to report profits, badger suppliers, and engage in other questionable maneuvers. Frequently, though not always, these offenders are caught and their businesses suffer.

The potential for unethical behavior is vast. Two travel agencies vying for a lucrative corporate account may promise the prospective client certain perks that are not within the confines of the contract. There are sometimes payoffs in travel expenses for people delivering incentive groups. Salespersons may pad their expense accounts. Items like towels and robes and ashtrays disappear from hotels. The infractions may involve a few dollars or millions, but the principle remains the same. Once you succumb to temptation, it's that much easier to succumb again.

The question of ethical behavior is currently big news. Various political leaders make headlines via charges of their accepting gifts, circumventing proper authority, peddling influence, or exceeding limits set by governing bodies. In business, leaders are accused of seeing only the bottom line and not worrying how profitable results are achieved.

As a result of all this, many major firms have employed ethicists to guide their thinking and planning. Is it okay to read what's on another person's desk? Should you lie about who you are in order to gain access to another individual? The ethicist helps management put these topics in perspective, helps the CEO distinguish right from wrong in shaky situations. Business schools are introducing courses in business ethics to help students better understand this aspect of their careers, and many firms conduct workshops on the topic to remind employees of ethical expectations. But the bottom line may be a simple grasp of moral responsibility.

You're either an honest person or you're not. There isn't much room for maneuvering. And communicators can be as dishonest as anyone else. There are opportunities to lie, to exaggerate, or to hide information. Chances to run down the competition abound. And there are even some instances of bribery, threats, a lot of hustling prose and other sins.

One observer suggested that the way to always be ethical was to assume your actions would be reported in that evening's paper. If you knew that, would you still behave the same way? If so, forge ahead. If not, forget about pursuing that line of conduct.

The Public Relations Society of America issues its own "Declaration of Principles," last revised a dozen years ago. It's a handy list for communicators to check. Among its features are these:

- ❏ A member shall adhere to truth and accuracy and to generally accepted standards of good taste. (Some ads for the swinging singles resorts might be considered borderline.)
- ❏ A member shall deal fairly with clients or employers, past or present, with fellow practitioners and the general public. (No padded expense sheets, no false statements about competitors, no manipulated charges.)
- ❏ A member shall conduct his or her professional life in accord with the public interest. (Airline safety, for example, takes precedence over any profit motive, and even things like airport noise must be weighed with the public good in mind.)
- ❏ A member shall not represent conflicting or competing interests without the express consent of those involved, given after a full disclosure of the facts . . . (Can an ad agency successfully handle a pair of competing travel agencies? Can a salesperson combine representation of two car rental companies? Should an employee of a tourism bureau be moonlighting at a travel agency?)

❏ A member shall safeguard the confidence of both present and former clients or employers and shall not accept retainers or employment that may involve the disclosure or use of these confidences to the disadvantage or prejudice of such clients or employers. (You have been hired away from one restaurant chain to another, and the new employer begins to pump you for the secrets of the previous job. You should not cooperate.)

❏ A member shall not engage in any practice that tends to corrupt the integrity of channels of communication or the processes of government. (You don't bribe legislators and you don't offer elaborate enticements to travel writers in exchange for a favorable report on your establishment.)

❏ A member shall not intentionally communicate false or misleading information and is obligated to use care to avoid communication of false or misleading information. (You shouldn't write things about a tour, for example, that simply aren't true, nor should you circulate such falsehoods, even if someone else writes them.)

❏ A member shall not intentionally injure the professional reputation or practice of another practitioner.

❏ A member shall not guarantee the achievement of specified results beyond the member's direct control. (You can't assure your boss you'll get a story published in a certain magazine unless the editor promises that in writing. You can't warrant that you'll achieve an increase in a corporation's stock value through dint of your publicity.)

This code also covers prohibitions about accepting fees for reselling the results of services for one client to another client without the consent of all involved. If you surveyed tourism prospects for the state, you can't peddle these to a local hotel unless the state agrees. And the code warns practitioners that they should sever relations, as soon as possible, with any firm or organization that fails to subscribe to the principles set down for the fair practice of public relations.

The philosopher Immanuel Kant cautioned citizens to always behave so that their action could become a universal. Good advice. If your own code was predicated on everyone behaving in this manner, far fewer ethical lapses would occur.

THE COMMUNICATION PLAN

One of the tasks many travel communicators face is convincing the administration of the need for and value of good communication.

This is especially true when some commitment of dollars is involved. Many in the travel industry are so caught up in other aspects of the work, they fail to realize how much a promotional plan might accomplish. So the communicator has to sell this idea.

Every well-run travel firm, from the small agency to the large cruise line, initiates its own agenda, some sort of plan to carry it through the current year and succeeding years. This plan anticipates income and expenses, expansion, employee requirements, account development, and other variables.

It should also include a communication plan.

Any plan starts with objectives, so a communication plan must identify the goals it wishes to reach and the time periods it feels will be necessary to accomplish these ends. These objectives must coincide with the overall objectives of the company. If the firm's aim is to establish itself as the top travel agency in terms of corporate travel in this market, how can the communication arm support this prospect? If an airline wants to expand its routes over the next three years, how can promotional efforts help? If a department of tourism hopes to increase the number of visitors by twenty-five percent within two years, how will the communication plan abet this program?

To assist in planning, the communicator must be able to isolate the publics that need to be educated or persuaded. Once these are determined, programs directed at each target audience must be discussed, along with individual goals for these programs. Eventually, the plan works itself down to specifics, like a realistic goal for articles appearing in national magazines, or the convening of a number of meetings, or the development of a new corporate image and logo, or the upgrading of internal employee publications, or the renewed efforts to better communicate with security analysts.

The top of the planning chart will find overall corporate goals, followed by overall communication goals, followed by goals for each target audience, eventually working its way down to separate items like the company picnic or expansion of the in-flight magazine or more dollar commitment to advertising. Discuss each step, secure agreement, then implement the actions, pausing periodically to evaluate them and their application to the company goals.

Communication is always a key element in success. It encompasses small matters, like the issuance of a professional news release, and large matters, like the ability to advise senior management on relationships with a variety of publics. It can be terribly pragmatic, like explaining to a ship's crew the rules for fraternization with passengers, or very ephemeral, like a travel consultant conjuring up images of Spain for a prospective tourist.

But even when it doesn't show up in the balance statement, communication is always part of the bottom line.

CHAPTER HIGHLIGHTS

☐ Education and experience make a winning combination in seeking entry-level jobs in travel communication.
☐ Personal contacts, employment agencies, classified ads, directories, trade journals—and persistence—all help locate opportunities.
☐ There are three forms of resumes—chronological, functional, and targeted—and the goal of each is to secure an interview.
☐ Job applicants should research the prospect firm, dress properly, anticipate questions, and focus on how they can be of help to the employer.
☐ Each element of the travel/hospitality industry offers different communication challenges, with jobs ranging from posts on the corporate magazine staff to ones focusing on investor relations.
☐ Legal aspects of travel communication embrace false and misleading advertising, libel and slander, privacy, copyright, and a number of other concerns.
☐ While the best ethical stance is to always be honest and forthright, there are professional codes of conduct to guide the individual.
☐ Just as a travel firm has a sales plan or overall growth plan, so, too, it should compile a communication plan.

■   ■   ■

☐ *EXERCISES*

1. Prepare your own resume, using the chronological method.
2. Write a letter to accompany your resume, directed to any major company in the travel industry, convincing the reader why they should interview you for a communication post in their firm.
3. Read through several issues of trade journals in the travel and/or hospitality industries and find an article that deals with a legal problem and one that deals with an ethical problem. Summarize the major points and bring to class for discussion.

❏ CASE PROBLEMS

1. A television program on Hawaii is scheduled to preview on PBS and a geography teacher who plans to discuss Hawaii in class feels this would be an excellent visual aid to the lecture. It would also be a good program to show to prospects for a tour he plans to lead to Hawaii during the Christmas break. So he tapes the show.

Will he have any legal problems if he uses this videotape for his own research on Hawaii, in putting together the itinerary?

Can he show it in class to his students?

Can he show it to the tour prospects?

2. You've just assumed a new public relations post with a major airline, after serving nine years with a competing airline. Just before you left the other airline, you completed a survey revolving around a bid for a new route to Washington and Baltimore. You now discover your new employer is also bidding for this same route. Obviously, you can't give the results of the survey to your new employer, but you are familiar with the details. What can you do? What should you do?

INDEX